The Cuisine of Peru
Copyright © Olenka Cooks by Olenka Brandon, 2024

Front cover image: Erik Castro
Photographs: Archive Olenka Cooks
Design: Susana Tejada Lopez

All rights reserved

First printing edition: 2024

No part of this publication may be reproduced, distributed, or transmitted in any form or by any means, including photocopying, recording, or other electronic or mechanical methods, without the prior written permission of the publisher, except as permitted by U.S. copyright law. For permission requests, contact olenka@olenkacooks.com.

Hardcover ISBN: 979-8-218-96811-3
Paperback ISBN: 979-8-8229-3859-5
eBook ISBN: 979-8-8229-3860-1

Printed in the USA

CONTENT

APPETIZERS, SOUPS & SALADS

Ceviche / Ceviche	12
Chicken Brochettes with Anticuchera marinade / Anticuchos de Pollo	14
Chicken Zucchini Poppers / Croquetas de Pollo y Zucchini	16
Crispy Quinoa Patties / Torrejas de Quinua	18
Crispy Rice Patties / Torrejas de Arroz	20
Fried Yuccas with Huancaina Sauce / Yucas Fritas con Salsa Huancaína	22
Huacho Sausage / Salchicha de Huacho	24
Huancaina Deviled Eggs / Huevos Rellenos con Salsa Huancaína	26
Mussels Chalaca Style / Choritos a la Chalaca	28
Parmesan Scallops / Conchitas a la Parmesana	30
Pop Corn / Canchita	32
Potatoes with Huancaina Sauce / Papa a la Huancaína	34
Scallop Croquettes / Croquetas de Conchas	36
Shrimp Cocktail / Cóctel de Camarones	38
Stuffed Corn Pie / Pastel de Choclo	40
Tuna Salad Stuffed Tomatoes / Tomates Rellenos	42
Tiger's Milk / Leche de Tigre	44
Tuna Nikkei / Tiradito Nikkei	46
Tuna Patties / Torrejas de Atún	48
Wonton Pockets Stuffed with Cheese / Tequeños Rellenos con Queso	50
A la Minute Soup / Sopa a la Minuta	52
Asparagus Soup / Crema de Espárragos	54
Butternut Squash Soup / Crema de Zapallo	56
Celery Soup / Crema de Apio	58
Chicken Cilantro Soup / Aguadito de Pollo	60
Bean Salad / Ensalada de Frejoles	62
Beet and Potato Salad / Ensalada Rusa	64
Chicken Potato Salad / Causa Rellena con Pollo	66
Crab Potato Salad / Causa Rellena con Cangrejo	68
Fava Bean Salad / Solterito de Habas	70
Shrimp Stuffed Avocado / Palta Rellena con Camarones	72

SIDES & SAUCES

Apple Sauce / Puré de Manzana	76
Arabic Rice / Arroz Árabe	78
Canary Beans with Bacon / Frejol Canario con Tocino	80
Creamy Polenta / Polenta a la Crema	82
Garden Rice / Arroz a la Jardinera	84
Lentils / Lentejas	86
Mashed Potatoeswith Spinach / Puré de Papas con Espinacas	88
Mashed Sweet Potatoes / Puré de Camote	90
Orange Glazed Sweet Potatoes / Camotes Glaseados con Naranja	92
Pecan Rice Crown / Corona de Arroz con Pecanas	94
Purple Corn Rice / Arroz Morado	96
Turmeric Rice / Arroz Amarillo (con Palillo)	98
Whipped Mashed Potatoes / Puré de Papas Batido	100
White Garlicky Rice / Arroz Blanco	102
Anticuchera Sauce / Salsa Anticuchera	104
Black Mint Sauce / Salsa de Huacatay	106
Garlic Paste / Pasta de Ajo	108
Golf Sauce / Salsa Golf	110
Old Fashioned Huancaina Sauce / Salsa a la Huancaína de Antaño	112
Onion Relish / Sarza Criolla	114
Quick Huancaina / Salsa Huancaína	116
Rocoto Sauce / Salsa de Rocoto	118
Street Hot Pepper Sauce / Ají Carretillero	120
Tartar Sauce / Salsa Tártara	122
Yellow Hot Pepper Paste / Pasta de Ají Amarillo	124

MAIN COURSES

Adobo Pork Stew / Adobo de Cerdo	128
Beef Cilantro Stew / Seco de Carne	130
Beef Milanese / Bistec Apanado	132
Beef Stir-Fried / Lomo Saltado	134
Butternut Squash Medley / Locro de Zapallo	136
Chicken Cau-Cau / Cau-Cau de Pollo	138
Chicken Cilantro Rice / Arroz con Pollo	140
Chicken Fricasé / Fricasé de Pollo	142
Chicken Quinoa Medley / Guiso de Quinua con Pollo	144
Chickpeas with Swiss Chard and Sausages / Garbanzos con Acelgas y Chorizos	146
Creamy Pesto Pasta / Tallarines Verdes	148
Crispy Pork Belly / Panceta Crocante	150
Fish a lo Macho / Pescado a lo Macho	152
Freeze-Dried Potato Medley / Carapulcra	154
Fried Rice / Arroz Chaufa	156

Green Risotto with Seafood / Risotto Verde con Mariscos	158
Huancaina Risotto / Risotto a la Huancaína	160
Mamama's Poom Chicken / Pollo Pum de mi Mamama	162
Mamama's Spanish Eggs / Huevos a la Española de mi Mamama	164
Marinated Fish Escabeche / Escabeche de Pescado	166
Olluco Medley / Ajiaco de Ollucos	168
Picadillo Stuffed Potatoes / Papas Rellenas	170
Picadillo Stuffed Rice / Arroz Tapado	172
Pork and Peanut Quinoa Medley / Guiso de Quinua con Cerdo y Maní	174
Roasted Turkey / Pavo al Horno	176
Seafood Cau-Cau / Cau-Cau con Mariscos	178
Seafood Rice / Arroz con Mariscos	180
Steamed Fish / Sudado de Pescado	182
Shrimp Fried Rice / Arroz Chaufa con Camarones	184
Spicy Beef Stew / Picante de Carne	186
Spicy Creamy Chicken Medley / Ají de Gallina	188
Spicy Creamy Tuna Medley / Ají de Atún	190
Spicy Seafood Stew / Picante de Mariscos	192
Spicy Shrimp Stew / Picante de Camarones	194
Top-Round Beef / Asado	196

DESSERTS

Apple Fritters with Chancaca Syrup / Torrejas de Manzana con Miel de Chancaca	200
Apple Oatmeal Bread / Queque de Manzana y Avena	202
Apple Pie / Pie de Manzana	204
Baked CreamCaramel Custard / Crema Volteada	208
Banana Bread / Queque de Plátano	210
Bavarois / Bavarois de Durazno	212
Butter Cookies / Galletitas de Mantequilla	214
Caramel Cookies / Alfajores	216
Chancaca Syrup / Miel de Chancaca	218
Chocolate Cake with Strawberries and Cream / Torta de Chocolate con Fresas y Crema	220
Cinnamon Layered Cake / Encanelado	222
Coconut Flan / Flan de Coco	224
Crepes / Crepes	226
Fluffy Banana-Oatmeal Pancakes / Panqueques de Plátano y Avena	228
Glorious Go-To Brownies / Gloriosos Brownies	230
Homemade Caramel Manjarblanco / Manjarblanco Casero	232
Key Lime Pie / Pie de Limón	234
Lime Blueberry Bundt Cake / Queque de Limón y Arándanos	236
Lime Charlotte / Carlota de Limón	238

Lucuma Mousse with Brownies / Mousse de Lúcuma con Brownies	240
Mamama's Rice Pudding / Arroz con Leche de mi Mamama	242
Marbled Cake / Queque Mármol	244
Old FashionedPudding / Mazamorra de Cochino	246
Orange Bundt Cake / Queque de Naranja	248
Passion Fruit Cake / Queque de Maracuyá	250
Passion Fruit Mouss / Mousse de Maracuyá	252
Pisco-Amaretto Affogato / Affogato de Pisco con Amaretto	254
Roasted Milk / Leche Asada	256
Soursop Mousse / Mousse de Guanábana	258
Sweet Potato Bars / Camotillo	260
Sweet Potato Bread / Queque de Camote	262
Sweet Walnut Balls / Bolitas de Nuez	264
Volador / Volador	266

COCKTAILS & DRINKS

Carob Syrup Cocktail / Cóctel de Algarrobina	270
Coconut Sour / Pisco Sour de Coco	272
Coffee Piscotini / Piscotini de Café	274
Chilcano de Pisco / Chilcano de Pisco	276
Cholopolitan / Cholopólitan	278
Cinnamon Sour / Pisco Sour de Canela	280
Hot Chocolate / Chocolate Caliente	282
Orange Piscotini / Piscotini de Naranja	284
Passion Fruit Sour / Maracuyá Sour	286
PiscNog / Ponche de Huevo con Pisco	288
Pisco Punch / Pisco Punch	290
Pisco Sour / Pisco Sour	292
Purple Corn Drink / Chicha Morada	294
Rosé Sangria / Sangría de Vino Rosé	296
The Captain / El Capitán	298

GLOSSARY 301

ACKNOWLEDGMENTS 307

Before we get cooking together, I'd like to introduce myself with a few stories of my childhood experiences growing up in Lima, Peru. My family immigrated to Peru, originally from Italy and Ireland. Now, generations later, here I am, living in Oregon's beautiful Wine Country with my husband and young twins. I hope you'll allow me to share these little slices of my life —as well as my recipes— with you.

Ever since I was a child, I've thought how wonderful it would be to become a chef. It was not because of the title (or the *toque*!), but it was fascinating to observe my Mamama's (grandmother's) creations in the kitchen. She could make food in no time at all, with barely anything! She would open the refrigerator, and take out the homemade garlic paste, which was a must. Then she would bring the kettle to a boil, another must! Next, she grabbed some veggies and some protein. And there I was, in the middle of the show, while at the same time being her audience. And most importantly, asking many questions. Mamama had lots of patience and would explain why she was doing things a certain way. She was just awesome! But at times, when she was really in a hurry, she had a phrase that even now makes me laugh: "Quita hijita, que te me enredas en las piernas!" This means, "Move away my little daughter, you are getting entangled in my legs!" Now that I'm a mom myself, I totally get it!

Looking back at my childhood makes me feel so blessed, not only because of my grandparents Tata (grandfather) and Mamama (grandmother), who taught me—by example— the real meaning of what it is to be a couple, showing me the love, respect and consideration, they had for each other. I was fortunate also because of the place and environment I grew up in, and I have many cherished memories of the times I got to spend there. They are still so in my everyday life and deep in my heart. That love also lives on in my food, which I'm so happy to share with you!

I was born in Lima, Peru, on a small peninsula named La Punta. My family immigrated to the area, where the fish and seafood were the freshest. So fresh that fishermen would knock at the neighbourhood's doors, offering the day's latest catch. I remember Papelito coming to the back porch of the house with a big sack of fresh scallops. Oh boy—cleaning an entire sack of scallops was an ordeal, but then it was the time to prepare some deliciousness for lunch or dinner. We would call our nearest friends to invite them over the same day. It was so much fun… friends and family always coming and going and enjoying a good meal!

When I was 17 years old, I began working in Lima and continued until I was 35, when I left my position in banking. That was the beginning of my journey to pursue my passion— when it developed wings to allow me to fly as high as my dreams— thanks to the support and love of my husband, who has always believed in me, and who loves my cooking, too!

After meeting my husband-to-be in 2010 at a wedding in Lima, he invited me to come and visit him in Sonoma County, California, where he lived and worked. Our meeting eventually led me to establish myself in the US in 2012. When my life and belongings were all organized (incidentally, some of my clothing got shrunk in the washing machine!), I was ready to get back to work. So, I told my husband: "I'm going to start looking for a job at a bank." With surprise, he replied, "Why at a bank?" I didn't understand his reaction, and answered, "Well, banking was my career when I first met you in Lima." He looked at me with his beautiful blue eyes, and in his serene voice said the following inspiring words: "Amor, listen to me: this is the land of opportunity, you get to do whatever you love the most, whatever you are passionate about." I was literally speechless (very unusual for me!). He continued, asking me what I love to do the most. And my immediate answer was: "I love to cook!" So he said, "Well then, cook!" And that's how, in 2013, I began my journey at the Culinary Arts Program, one step closer to achieving my goal. It wasn't always easy, but I worked very hard, and I am so happy I pursued my wish. I was soooo excited… my forever dream was becoming true!

I quickly embraced my new life in California, getting used to a new location, a new language, new cooking lingo, and softening my accent to make myself better understood. I had to learn new concepts: "Yes, chef!" And the fast pace and importance of timing when working in a professional kitchen. And no hugging people! (I admit: I'm a big hugger!) There would be no more days and evenings in Lima, sharing coffees with my cousins, joining friends at night after work, or cooking and entertaining myself on the weekends. I had to exchange my high heels for more practical shoes, but I was happy to take on all the changes and challenges.

However, this transitional chapter of my life was filled with more than a few comic hiccups, mostly due to language differences and cultural misunderstandings. I'm sure you'll laugh at some of these stories I'm sharing because I certainly laughed at myself!

"Punish the Meat". My husband's birthday was coming up (we were not yet married at the time), and I wanted to cook his favorite food. He said it was "Bistec Apanado", which I now know translates to pounded beef—or beef Milanese– with Peruvian Pesto Spaghetti. Perfect, I thought. I went to the market but couldn't recognize the names of the different cuts of meat; they were all in English, of course, and I wasn't yet familiar with the different US beef cuts. It was time to look for the butcher and ask for help.

"Hello, sir. How are you? Could you please help me find the right cut of meat? It's for my boyfriend's birthday and I want to make it special." He asked me what I was planning to cook, and I told him, "My boyfriend likes his meat "punish, punish, punish" (instead of "pound") so you make it flat." The butcher looked astonished, and I don't know if he wanted to laugh or cry, but he gave me exactly the cut of meat I wanted, and then said, "I'm sure your boyfriend is a very lucky man." And, making things even more awkward, I candidly replied, "Oh yes, and me too!"

"The Phantom Eggs". One of the first dishes I prepared when I came to live in the US was Arroz Tapado (a delicious—and very adaptable— entrée of seasoned beef, tomatoes and hard-boiled eggs, sandwiched in a mold between two layers of luscious rice). I was very happy, and in the middle of the preparation, when my timer rang, it was time to take the hard-boiled eggs off the stove. I drained the boiling water, put the pot aside, and left the eggs sitting in the sink.

I kept cooking and dancing among my pots and pans. Then, I started working on the parsley. When I was done, I went to look for the eggs. Imagine my surprise when there were none! What? I couldn't believe it. Where were my eggs? They were not in the sink.

My husband came in the kitchen and saw me looking confused while searching everywhere for the eggs. He asked what I was looking for, and I explained the mysterious situation. Very calmly, he went straight to the sink, plunged his hand in a black hole at the bottom, and guess what? He started pulling out eggs, one by one, like a magician. My eggs had decided to spelunk into the garbage disposal! Who knew? I certainly didn't!

In this book, I share some history and heartfelt personal stories associated with each recipe, to bring them to life for you.

Even if you're confident in the kitchen when cooking at home and are good at it, when studying to become a professional chef it can be intense, and precise planning, timing and focus are very important. But so is curiosity. You can't be afraid to ask questions, even if people get impatient (and sometimes, maybe even a bit annoyed!). I believe it's the best way to quickly educate yourself, clarify misunderstandings and dispel confusion in the kitchen. So, the best advice I can share with any cook is to be curious and enjoy the process!

Years later, I'm still loving what I do, and I am passionate about the next steps in my life. The thing is, when you cook with all your love, you can taste it. Passion, intention, and sincere feelings impart flavor, and each of my dishes is infused with those flavors. You'll bring your own unique essence to your cooking, so make these recipes your very own! The kitchen is my happy place, and I hope yours is for you!

Appetizers, Soups & Salads

CEVICHE
Ceviche

Ceviche makes me salivate...
    When I was little, my Mamama used to take me to the market during summers to do the grocery shopping with her. When I was 6 years old, we were in the market when I saw Garretón, one of the garbage men of the district. He was enjoying lunch when I asked my Mamama if I could please have a Ceviche. She answered: "I'm in a rush, and I have nobody to leave you with while you eat your Ceviche." Garretón, sweet and kind as usual, told my Mamama, "Ma'am, I can keep an eye on the girl, don't worry." My Mamama gratefully agreed. And that was an incredible moment. But when we were walking home, she asked me please to keep it our secret, and I agreed. However, La Punta, the peninsula where I was born and where my Tata was the Mayor, is such a small town that everybody knows everybody's business. So, surprise! When my Tata came home that night from the City Hall, he said to my Mamama: "You know something? Today I saw Garretón, and he could not stop talking about how amazed he was watching Olenka while she enjoyed her Ceviche at his table at the market..." Plop!

Ingredients

<u>For the corn</u>
1 ½ cups frozen corn kernels
1 tablespoon white sugar
½ teaspoon anise seeds
½ fresh lime

<u>For the Ceviche</u>
1 pound rock cod fish fillets
½ cup fresh key lime juice (use regular limes if key limes not available)
1 yellow hot pepper, rib and seeds removed and diced small
1 Limo hot pepper, diced small
1 teaspoon celery finely chopped
½ teaspoon fresh ginger finely grated or minced
2 garlic cloves, minced
2 teaspoons cilantro leaves finely chopped
Salt and pepper
2–3 small ice cubes
1 red onion, cut in half lengthwise and sliced thin (julianne)
1 sweet potato, boiled, cooled and sliced into ¼-inch rounds

Preparation

<u>Corn</u>
1. Place the frozen corn kernels, the sugar, and the anise seeds in a medium saucepan with enough water to cover the corn. Cook over medium-high heat for about 20 minutes.
2. When done, turn off the heat and squeeze in the lime juice; stir and keep the corn in the water until ready to use.

<u>Ceviche</u>
1. Cut the fish into ¾-inch to 1-inch cubes, place in a cold bowl and season with sea salt.
2. In a separate bowl, combine the key lime juice, yellow hot pepper, Limo hot pepper, ginger, garlic, celery and cilantro. Season with salt and pepper to taste. Add the fish. Stir in the ice cubes to thoroughly cool the Ceviche, then remove any partially melted chunks of ice.
3. Briefly soak the sliced onion in cold salted water. Rinse thoroughly and strain;

   add the onion to the Ceviche. Briefly combine and serve immediately.

Note: This dish is traditionally served in shallow bowls with the corn kernels, boiled sweet potatoes, and pop-corn (see page 32, Appetizers).

CHICKEN BROCHETTES WITH ANTICUCHERA MARINADE

Anticuchos de Pollo

Many countries around the world have some version of "meat on a stick" in their food culture. But Peru might be able to claim theirs—which originated in the Andes mountains—as one of the oldest skewered meat traditions. Originally, Anticuchos were made with llama meat, but nowadays the most popular version is made with beef heart.
The Anticuchera marinade helps break down the meat fibers, making it tender and flavorful, thanks to the unique taste of Panca hot pepper paste, red wine vinegar, garlic, cumin and other spices. This dish is a staple of Creole cuisine, evolving from humble street fare food to a fine-dining favorite. It is served at the best Peruvian restaurants, offered in many different versions, all of them tasty.

Ingredients

1 pound chicken thighs or breasts, boneless and skinless

For the marinade
½ cup vegetable oil
½ cup Panca hot pepper paste (available in some Latin markets or online retailers)
4 tablespoons red wine vinegar
2 tablespoons garlic paste, or minced mashed garlic
1 tablespoon soy sauce (regular or low sodium)
1 tablespoon dried oregano
½ tablespoon ground cumin
Salt and pepper to taste

Preparation

1. The day before, mix all the marinade ingredients in a bowl, large enough to hold the chicken.
2. Cut the chicken into 2-inch cubes.
3. Add the chicken to the marinade ingredients and marinate overnight.

Next day
1. Preheat your grill to medium-high.
2. While the grill is heating, place three pieces of chicken on metal or soaked wooden skewers.
3. Cook the chicken Anticuchos for about 10–14 minutes. Turn once halfway through. Cook until the chicken in golden brown and cooked.
4. Transfer Anticuchos to a clean plate, and loosely tent with aluminum foil for about 5 minutes. Then, serve while they're still nice and warm and juicy, accompanied by any of your favorite dipping sauces such as, Ají Carretillero (see page 120, Sides & Sauces).

CHICKEN ZUCCHINI POPPERS

Croquetas de Pollo y Zucchini

When my kids started to eat solid foods, I wanted them to try everything. Learning that little kids need to experiment with their little hands, I remembered a dish that was a tradition when I was growing up: Poppers or Croquetas. So, I grabbed my ingredients, seasoned, mixed, shaped, and *voilà*! Chicken Zucchini Poppers! They still love it! And it makes me very happy, because, even if it's the only thing they are eating, it has a little bit of everything and, most importantly, my secret ingredient: LOVE!

Ingredients

1 ½ pounds ground chicken breast
2 ½ cups shredded zucchini, excess moisture squeezed out
2 eggs
½ cup grated Parmesan cheese
1 tablespoon Worcestershire sauce
1 teaspoon dried oregano
¼ teaspoon black pepper
¼ teaspoon ground cumin
Salt to taste
½ to 1 cup vegetable oil for frying (olive or avocado oil)

Preparation

1. In a large bowl, lightly mix together all the ingredients except the oil. The mixture will be quite wet.
2. Measure out the mixture using a small scoop or a heaped tablespoon, then gently smooth into balls or oblongs using your hands, and place them separately in a large dish or tray. Depending on the size of your scoops, you should have about 20–24 poppers.
3. If frying, preheat oven to warm, 175 °F. In the meantime, heat the oil in a medium pan over medium-low heat. Cook the poppers in batches, 4–5 at a time, for about 5–6 minutes on the first side. Flip and cook an additional 4–5 minutes, or until golden brown and the centers are cooked through. Place in the oven over a wire rack to keep warm while you cook the remaining poppers.
4. If baking, turn oven to 400 °F.
5. Line a baking sheet with aluminum foil and coat with a drizzle of olive or avocado oil.
6. Bake poppers 15 to 20 minutes or until cooked through. If desired, place under the broiler for an additional 2–3 minutes or until nicely browned on top.

Note: Serve the Chicken Zucchini Poppers with your favorite dipping sauce.

CRISPY QUINOA PATTIES

Torrejas de Quinua

When I became a Mom, my mission was to nourish my kids not only with my love, but with my food. When they started eating solid food, I had to create a variety of things for them to eat with their little hands. There's something about little patties, or pieces of food that the kids love. One way that I try to repurpose leftovers is by making patties, very popular in my Mamama's repertoire, and in many households in Peru. So, here I share with you a great way to present something tasty and nutritious with the ones you love the most.

Ingredients

1 cup cooked black quinoa
2 large eggs, beaten
½ teaspoon fine-grain sea salt
½ teaspoon fresh black pepper
2 medium size Portobello mushrooms stems included, finely chopped
3 garlic cloves finely chopped
1 small shallot finely chopped
⅓ cup celery finely chopped
⅓ cup leeks finely chopped
⅓ cup tomato finely chopped
½ cup Parmesan cheese
½ cup panko bread crumbs, or rolled oats
¼–½ cup olive oil

Preparation

1. In a medium bowl, combine the cooked quinoa, eggs, salt and pepper. Stir in the mushrooms, garlic, shallots, celery, leeks, tomato and Parmesan. Add the panko or oatmeal; stir and let stand for a few minutes.
2. Heat the oil in a large heavy skillet, over medium heat. Meanwhile, form the quinoa mixture into approximately 2 ½ inch diameter patties. Working in batches to avoid crowding the pan, add patties and cook until bottoms are deeply browned, about 6 to 8 minutes. Flip patties with a spatula and cook for another 7 minutes, or until golden.
3. When patties are cooked, remove from skillet and cool on a wire rack. Repeat with remaining patties.

Note: Enjoy the Crispy Quinoa Patties with your favorite dipping sauce!

CRISPY RICE PATTIES

Torrejas de Arroz

Growing up, whenever we had leftover rice in our home, we were all very happy because my Mamama would make Torrejas de Arroz. Yay! A kiss of fresh parsley and fresh yellow hot pepper were her signature embellishments.

These patties are crunchy and savory, and can be made in no time. They can be eaten immediately, or you can freeze them and re-heat them in a toaster oven. Eaten as-is or served with a dipping sauce, these patties are a great way to repurpose your leftover rice, whether it's homemade and garlicky, white or brown steamed rice from last night's Chinese takeout, or any other type of rice. Easy to make, they can be enjoyed as a snack, appetizer or side dish.

Ingredients

2 ½ cups cooked rice (any type of leftover rice)
2 eggs, beaten
4 tablespoons all-purpose flour
½ teaspoon baking powder
1 yellow hot pepper, seeded and deveined, finely diced
¼ cup fresh parsley finely chopped
1 tablespoon minced garlic
Salt and pepper to taste
1 cup vegetable oil (for frying)

Preparation

1. In a bowl, combine all the ingredients except the oil, and season with salt and pepper.
2. Heat the oil in a large skillet over medium-high heat. Working in batches, drop in heaping tablespoons of the rice mixture, as many as will fit into the pan without crowding.
3. Flatten each fritter with the back of a spoon and fry until golden brown on both sides. Repeat until all the batter is used.
4. When done, remove the cooked patties from the oil and drain on a wire rack or paper towels.

Note: Serve the Crispy Rice Patties warm with your favorite dipping sauces.

FRIED YUCCAS WITH HUANCAINA SAUCE

Yucas Fritas con Salsa Huancaína

Pronounced /yoo-ka/, the Yucca is also known as cassava or tapioca root. It looks a little like a small bark-covered baseball bat, with deep white flesh inside. It's easy to find year-round, fresh or peeled and frozen. It's the star of what is probably the most popular Peruvian appetizer I know of. There's something unique about warm, fried yucas; with their crispy exterior, creamy interior texture, nutty flavor and the crunchy dusting of salt. These bite sized treats are perfect complemented with Huancaina dipping sauce.

Give these a try and you'll get hooked on them, whether served as a side dish, or as tasty appetizers—the perfect pairing for refreshing cocktails and aperitifs.

Ingredients

For the Huancaina Sauce
3–5 yellow hot peppers, stems removed, cut in chunks
10 ounces Queso Fresco (Casero or Cotija) cut in cubes
¼ cup evaporated milk (unsweetened)
¼ cup vegetable oil
Pinch of salt

For the Fried Yuccas
1 pound frozen Yuccas
1 cup rice starch
Pinch of salt and white pepper
4 cups vegetable oil

Preparation

Huancaina Sauce
1. Mix in a blender the yellow hot pepper chunks with the cubed Queso Fresco, evaporated milk, oil and salt. Verify salt and consistency.
2. If the sauce it is not thick enough, add 4 soda crackers, one by one, and blend until you get the appropriate consistency.

Fried Yuccas
1. In a large pot with water and salt, cook the Yuccas until they feel tender and soft. Drain in a colander and let them dry for some minutes over a cookie sheet or platter.
2. Remove the veins and cut Yuccas in pieces 2 x 1 inches.
3. In a bowl or a bag, mix the rice starch salt and white pepper; add the boiled Yuccas, and shake it baby!
4. Preheat the oil, and fry the Yuccas in batches. When they look kind of gold, place them in a paper towel or on a wire rack to drain the excess oil.
5. To finish, a little sprinkle of salt.
6. Serve Fried Yuccas with the Huancaina Sauce on the side.

HUACHO SAUSAGE

Salchicha de Huacho

Huacho is a city 76 miles north of Lima, Peru's capital city. Huacho is famous for its traditional spicy Huacho Sausage or Salchicha Huachana. The unique spices, which include annatto, give it its almost red-orange, radioactive color. Here, cooked with scrambled eggs, and served in a crunchy bread roll, it makes a delicious and satisfying Peruvian breakfast.

Ingredients

5 eggs
½ teaspoon salt
¼ teaspoon ground black pepper
1 teaspoon chili flakes
1 pound Huacho Sausage (available in the frozen foods section of Latin markets)
2 tablespoons whipping cream, or whole milk
Crusty baguette or ciabatta bread

Preparation

1. In a medium bowl, mix the eggs with salt, pepper and chili flakes.
2. Pour half a cup of water into a large sauté pan over medium-high heat. Remove and discard the sausage casings, then add the sausage meat to the pan.
3. Break up the sausage meat with a spoon or spatula and let the sausage cook until the water evaporates completely.
4. Add the beaten eggs to the pan with the cooked sausage and mix until the eggs reach your preferred consistency. Immediately remove the pan from the heat and stir in the cream.
5. Serve the scrambled sausage and eggs with crunchy bread and a good cup of coffee!

HUANCAINA DEVILED EGGS

Huevos Rellenos con Salsa Huancaína

Inspired by traditional American deviled eggs, I decided to try a twist on the classic recipe. A popular Peruvian pepper —and one we use most often in our cooking— is yellow hot pepper, which is the number one star of most well-loved and delicious sauces: Huancaina.

Yellow hot pepper may not be something you customarily keep in your pantry or fridge, but you can find the peppers frozen or as a paste in jars at some Latin markets, or online. At Easter, summer barbecues, or as anytime hors d'oeuvres, try yellow hot pepper in this twist on deviled eggs and add it to your repertoire. You won't regret it!

Ingredients

For the Huancaina Sauce
3–5 yellow hot peppers (fresh or frozen)
10 ounces Queso Fresco (Casero or Cotija) cut into large chunks
½ cup evaporated milk (unsweetened)
¼ cup vegetable oil
Pinch of salt
4 saltine crackers (optional)

For the Deviled Eggs
12 large eggs
⅓–½ cup Huancaina sauce
Salt and pepper to taste
Freshly chopped chives, to garnish

Preparation

Huancaina Sauce
1. Remove the stems of the yellow peppers, and cut in chunks.
2. Mix the yellow pepper chunks in blender with Queso Fresco chunks, evaporated milk and oil. Verify salt and pepper consistency. If the Huancaina Sauce is not thick enough, add about 4 saltine crackers to the blender, until you get the appropriate consistency. Set aside while the eggs cook.

Deviled Eggs
1. Place the eggs in a single layer in large pot and fill with enough cold water to cover them by one inch. Cover the pot with a lid and cook over high heat for 13 minutes. Remove from heat and shock the eggs with cold water before peeling.
2. Using a sharp knife, slice the cooled eggs in half lengthwise. Arrange the egg white halves on a serving platter.
3. Gently remove the yolk halves and place them in a food processor. Add ¼ cup of Huancaina, and process until thick and smooth.

<u>Assemble</u>
Using a piping bag fitted with a star tip, pipe the yolk and Huancaina mixture into the egg whites halves. Alternatively, you can use a teaspoon to scoop the mixture into the egg whites. Top with a sprinkle of chives before serving.

MUSSELS CHALACA STYLE

Choritos a la Chalaca

Being a Chalaca is quite a statement in Peru. It means Callao-style, which in my book reflects the character of the people who live or come from this province. They are brave people—fun, very in tune with music and dancing; seafood eaters and lovers of the ocean.

This mussel dish originated in the port city of Callao, just west of Lima, Peru's capital. The best mussels are served in some traditional restaurants in Callao. It is made with tender, steamed mussels topped with Chalaca sauce, a spicy, fresh vegetable medley made with tomatoes, corn, Rocoto hot pepper, red onions, lime juice, and fresh herbs.

This fresh and light appetizer is sweet, lemony, and spicy, and is enjoyed any time of the day with a super-chilled beer or a good Pisco Sour!

Ingredients

For the corn
1 cup corn kernels
1 tablespoon white sugar
½ teaspoon anise seeds
½ fresh lime

For the mussels reduction
2 pounds cleaned mussels (shelled)
1 small yellow or white onion, julienned
1 celery stalk
1 cup water
½ cup Pisco
4 large garlic cloves, peeled and mashed

For the corn and onion salsa
1 cup red onion, diced and well rinsed
1 large firm Roma tomato, seeded and diced small
1 tablespoon Limo hot pepper, finely diced or minced
1 or 2 tablespoons Rocoto hot pepper, finely diced
3 tablespoons cilantro, finely chopped
1 cup cooked corn kernels
¼ cup freshly squeezed lime juice
2 tablespoons mussel reduction
Salt and pepper to taste

Preparation

Corn
1. Place corn kernels, sugar, and anise in a pot with water to cover. Cook for about 20 minutes medium-high heat. When done, turn off stove. Squeeze the lime into the water, stir and allow the corn to sit in the water. Drain the corn when ready to use.

Mussels
1. In a large pot add julienned onion, celery, water, Pisco, and smashed garlic cloves. Cover and bring to a simmer over medium heat. Add clean mussels (shelled); cover and cook for 5 minutes.
2. After the mussels have cooked for 5 minutes, uncover the saucepan and remove the mussels that have opened, transferring them to a sheet pan. Continue simmering and removing remaining mussels as they open, until you have transferred all to the sheet pan. Set the cooked mussels aside.
3. Turn the burner to high and reduce the mussels cooking liquid by half. Reserve 2 tablespoons of the cooking liquid and set aside (remaining mussels reduction may be frozen and saved for another use).

Corn and onion salsa
1. In a separate bowl, combine the diced red onion, tomato, Limo hot pepper, Rocoto hot pepper, cilantro, the cup of cooked corn kernels, lime juice, and the 2 tablespoons of the mussels cooking liquid reduction set aside.
2. Season with salt and pepper to taste. Adjust the acidity and spiciness by adding more lime juice and Limo hot pepper to your taste.

Assemble
1. Separate the mussels shells, discarding the empty half, and on a serving platter, arrange each mussel on their half shell and top each with a generous amount of the corn and onion salsa.
2. Serve the Mussels Chalaca Style cold.

PARMESAN SCALLOPS
Conchitas a la Parmesana

Growing up on a peninsula, we had access to the freshest of fresh seafood, and scallops were not an exception. This dish is a traditional appetizer of bay scallops with lots of freshly grated Parmesan cheese, and other ingredients that enhance the sweet, savory, lemony, loaded with tons of umami flavors. As soon as it comes out of the oven serve immediately garnished with a lemon wedge for squeezing, and a glass of your favorite chilled white wine.

Indubitably, a seductive crowd pleaser!

Ingredients

12 bay scallops, on the half shell
Freshly grated nutmeg
1 tablespoon sea salt
2 fresh limes
12 drops Worcestershire sauce
¾ cup grated Parmesan cheese
6 tablespoons unsalted butter
Lemon wedges, for serving

Preparation

1. Preheat oven to 450 °F.
2. Clean and rinse the shells and the scallops.
3. In a shallow baking pan, place the scallops with its
   12 half shells.
4. Then season each scallop with a pinch of ground nutmeg, salt, a drop of Worcestershire sauce, and a light squeeze of lime juice. Sprinkle the top with grated Parmesan, and ½ tablespoon of butter.
5. Bake 4 minutes, or until the cheese turns into a golden-brown color. Do not overcook.
6. Serve immediately, garnished with a lemon wedge for squeezing.

Note: Enjoy with a glass of your favorite chilled white wine, a shot of Pisco, or Pisco Sour (see page 292. Cocktails & Drinks)

POP CORN
Canchita

The "shy" popcorn of Peru.

Naturally gluten free and vegan, Popcorn is an addictive snack that's very popular in Peru. Often served as a garnish along with Ceviche, it's also perfect for happy hour snacks. It's made from a special variety of corn called Chulpe. This Peruvian corn can be found online and in Latin food markets. It's easy and quick to prepare. When the Popcorn is ready, sprinkle it with salt and enjoy it warm, mmm.... Crunchy, crunchy, crunchy!

Ingredients

2 cups popcorn
(dry Chulpe corn)
2 tablespoons neutral vegetable oil
Salt

Preparation

1. Soak the corn kernels in cold water for about 10 minutes. Drain the kernels and allow them to dry a bit on paper towels (about 10 minutes).
2. Using a large, heavy-bottomed pot with a lid, preheat on medium-high and add the oil.
3. When the oil has heated, add the corn kernels; cover the pot and reduce the heat to medium, shaking the pot often. The cooking and shaking process will take about 15–20 minutes.
4. When the corn has turned golden brown, stir in salt to taste, then turn the hot kernels onto a heat-resistant (non-plastic) cooking sheet, platter or shallow bowl and allow to cool.

Note: If storing for later use, omit salt before placing in an airtight container, as it will last longer without salt.

POTATOES WITH HUANCAINA SAUCE

Papa a la Huancaína

There's a saying in Peru: "I'm as Peruvian as Papa a la Huancaína," because Peru is famous for its incredible variety of potatoes. And, for its equally incredible Potatoes with Huancaina Sauce. It's one of those first courses that will hook you and make you want to explore more of Peru's diverse gastronomy. Creamy, cheesy, spicy or mild, this is a dish that I hope you'll try, using your favorite variety of potato.

If you ever visit Peru, please try some plain potatoes and you'll notice full flavors and creaminess. Each type of potato is different in color, texture, size, and flavor, and Peru has almost 4000 varieties!

Ingredients

6 Yukon Gold potatoes, boiled in salted water

For the Huancaina Sauce
¼ cup vegetable oil, divided
3–5 yellow hot peppers, fresh or frozen
¼ cup roughly chopped red onion
2 whole garlic cloves, peeled, or 1 teaspoon minced garlic
½ cup evaporated milk (unsweetened)
10 ounces Queso Fresco (Casero or Cotija), cut into chunks
Pinch of salt
2–4 saltine crackers (if needed)
Romaine or Iceberg lettuce leaves

4 hard-boiled eggs, peeled and sliced
Black Botija or Kalamata olives
Parsley sprigs

Preparation

1. Boil the potatoes previously and let then cool out of the water.

Huancaina Sauce
1. Remove the stems from the yellow hot peppers and discard. Cut the yellow hot peppers into chunks.
2. Heat a sauté pan over medium heat and add 2 tablespoons of the oil. When the oil is hot, add the yellow hot peppers and the chopped onions and sauté until the onions are golden brown. Next, add the garlic and cook for an additional minute.
3. When cooked, transfer the sautéed vegetables to a blender; add the milk and blend until very smooth.*

*If your blender is not powerful enough, pass mixture through a fine mesh strainer.

4. Next, add the Queso Fresco chunks; when the cheese is incorporated, remove the smaller center blender cover, and with the blender still running, slowly add the remaining oil in a thin stream. Blend until the sauce is silky. Taste for salt and add if needed. If the sauce is not as thick as you'd like, blend in 2–4 saltine crackers, one a time, until the sauce reaches your desired consistency.
5. Use the Huancaina Sauce immediately or store in a glass jar with a lid and refrigerate for up to five days.

Assemble
1. Slice the cooked potatoes into ½–¾-inch slices.
2. On four plates, place one lettuce leaf in each; top with some potato slices, and pour a generous amount of the Huancaina Sauce over the potatoes.
3. Garnish with egg slices, olives and parsley.

SCALLOP CROQUETTES
Croquetas de Conchas

SEAFOOD

45'

6 FRITTERS

Time ago, I was talking with my Aunt Lili, one of my dear Aunties in Peru, and she told me that she will never forget the Scallop Fritters that she enjoyed so much in the house that I grew up in, many years ago, when I was a kid.

That comment brought the memories of the flavors and textures of these fritters, and so I put myself at work, and started trying different recipes, until this one came together. I hope you'll enjoy it as much as my Aunt Lili and I did.

Ingredients

½ pound bay scallops (whole, or if larger than ½-inch diameter, cut in half)
½ cup all-purpose flour
½ teaspoon baking powder
½ teaspoon kosher salt
¼ teaspoon ground fresh pepper
2 large eggs, lightly beaten
1 yellow pepper, finely diced
3 scallions, white and green parts, thinly sliced
¼ cup fresh parsley, minced
Vegetal oil for frying (any neutral, high smoke point oil)
Lemon wedges
Onion Relish (optional)

Preparation

1. In a medium bowl, whisk the flour, baking powder, salt and pepper.
2. In a larger bowl, combine the beaten eggs, the diced yellow pepper, scallions and parsley. Add the flour mixture and stir to create a batter. Fold in the scallops.
3. In a large saucepan, heat 1 ½ inches oil over medium-high heat. Working in batches, drop heaping tablespoons of the batter into the oil and fry, turning occasionally, until the fritters are golden brown all over, about 2 minutes per side.
4. Using a slotted spoon, transfer the fritters to a wire rack or paper towels to drain.

Enjoy them warm, with your favorite sauce!

Note: Serve with lemon wedges, or if desired, with a side of Golf Sauce (see page 110, Sides & Sauces), Onion Relish (see page 114, Sides & Sauces), or Tartar Sauce (see page 122, Sides & Sauces).

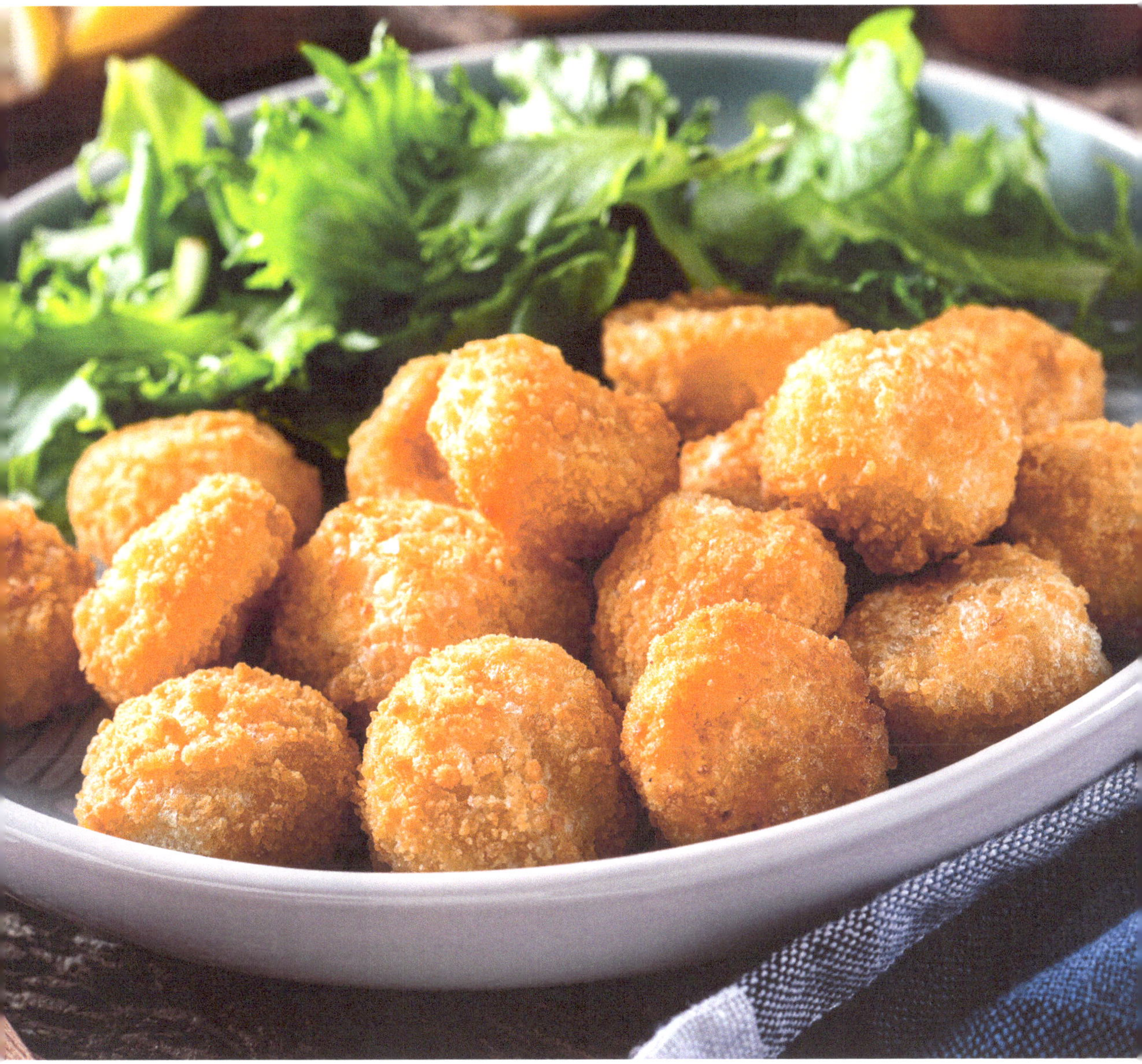

SHRIMP COCKTAIL

Cóctel de Camarones

There's a kind of sexy, glamorous elegance that seduces you to savor each and every bite of this appetizer. The combination of flavors—the briny shrimp, creamy avocado, and tangy golf sauce—makes it unique. Are you ready to have the pleasurable experience of making and enjoying this succulent classic at home? Say yes!

Ingredients

For the Golf Sauce
1 cup mayonnaise
½ cup ketchup
2 teaspoons Worcestershire sauce
1/4 cup chopped capers
1 orange zest
2 teaspoons brandy (optional)

For the Salad
1 cup romaine lettuce, chiffonade
4 hard-boiled eggs, roughly chopped
2 ripe avocados, diced
1 pound peeled, deveined, and cooked shrimps (use pre-cooked shrimps or prepare by boiling or poaching)
4–6 additional cooked whole shrimps, with heads, garnish with Parsley springs

Preparation

Golf Sauce
1. In a small bowl, prepare the sauce by combining mayonnaise and ketchup. Stir in Worcestershire sauce, capers, brandy and orange zest. Cover and refrigerate until needed.

Salad
1. Using clear, pretty cocktail glasses or dessert bowls, begin by placing a bed of the lettuce chiffonade at the bottom of each one. Next, add chopped eggs, and then a layer of diced avocado. Follow with the cooked shrimp. Add a dollop of the chilled sauce.
2. Garnish with a whole shrimp, a sprig of parsley, and serve the Shrimp Cocktail immediately.

Serving suggestion: Chill your serving glasses (martini glasses or wine glasses with a wide bowl work well or dessert bowls) in the fridge before assembling the Shrimp Cocktail.

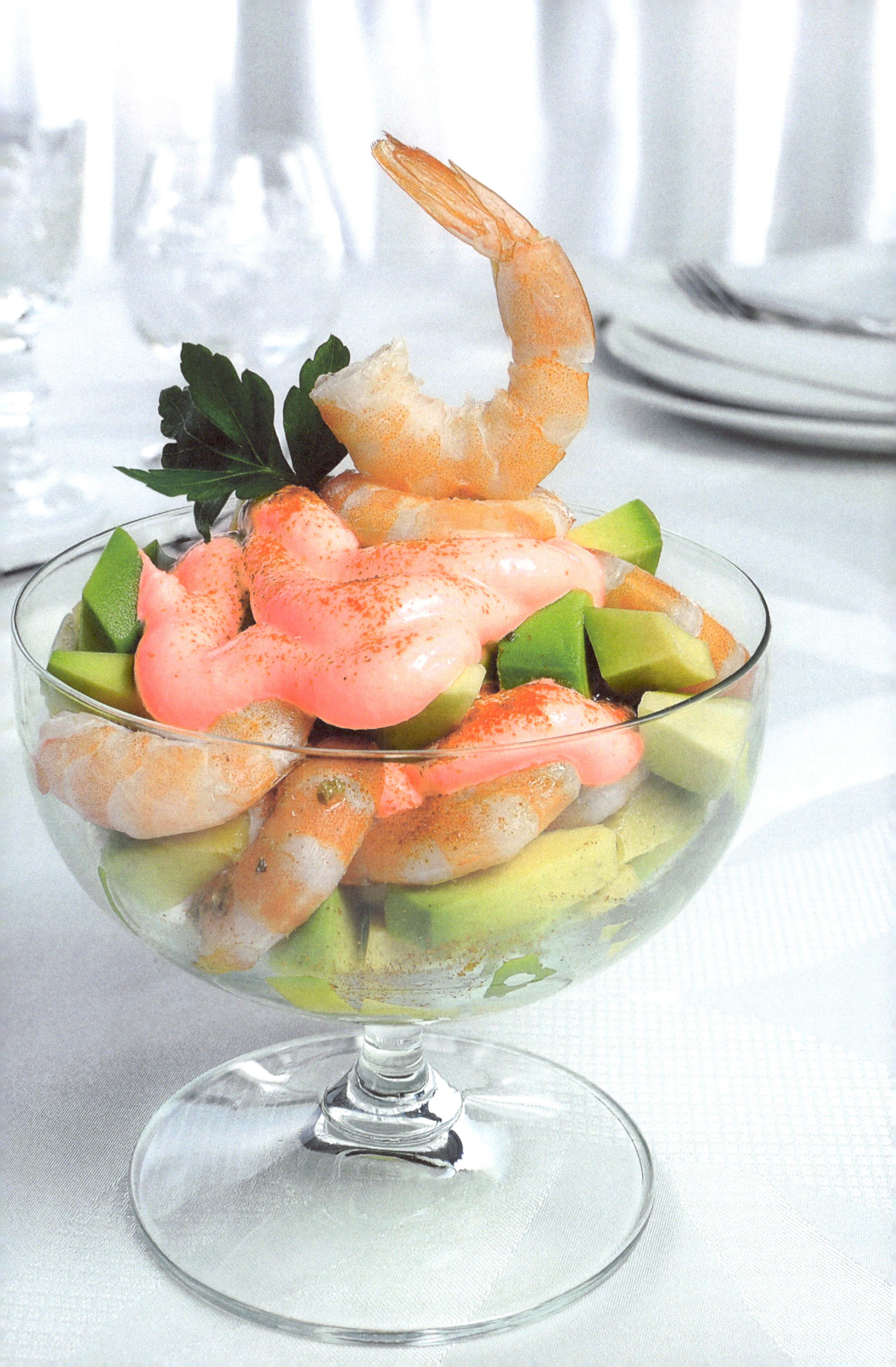

STUFFED CORN PIE
Pastel de Choclo

Gluten Free
80'
6–8 Servings

I would like to introduce a special dish—one of the most popular in Peru—to your table: savory Pastel de Choclo, or corn pie/pudding/cake. Choclo in Quechua means tender grains, and corn is the base of this main-course pie, which is somewhat similar in concept to shepherd's pie, but with more complex flavors and textures. The Stuffed Corn Pie is pudding-like, made with fresh, tender corn kernels. If you can't find fresh corn, you can also use frozen. The combination of textures, and the balance between the savory meat stuffing and the mild sweetness of the corn is absolutely glorious!

Ingredients

For the Batter
6 cups yellow or white corn kernels, fresh or defrosted frozen corn
1 red onion, diced
4 tablespoons yellow hot pepper paste
¼ cup butter (½ stick)
½ cup evaporated milk (unsweetened)

For the Stuffing
1 red onion, diced
3 tablespoons Panca hot pepper paste
3 tablespoons garlic paste, or garlic finely mashed
1 ½ pounds ground beef
¼ cup fresh parsley, chopped
½ teaspoons ground cumin
½ cup Kalamata olives, diced (optional)
½ cup raisins (optional)
½ cup diced hardboiled egg (about 3–4 large eggs)
Salt and black pepper to taste

Preparation

Batter
1. Place the corn kernels in the food processor and process briefly, until the mixture reaches a coarse consistency; set aside.
2. In a large pot, sauté the diced onion over medium-heat until translucent. Add the yellow hot pepper paste and the butter, and sauté for another two minutes.
3. Add the processed corn and the milk to the sauté pot. Continue cooking over medium-heat until the texture is creamy. Remove from heat and set aside.

Stuffing
1. Preheat oven at 375 °F.
2. In a large skillet, sauté the diced onion over medium-low heat, until caramelized, but not crispy. Increase the heat to medium and add the Panca hot pepper paste, garlic and ground beef, cook until browned.

3. Season with fresh parsley, cumin, salt and black pepper. At last minute fold in the diced eggs and olives and raisins (if using).
4. In a buttered baking pan, or 4-quart casserole, layer half of the corn batter, top with the stuffing, then layer with the remaining half of the batter.
5. In preheated oven, bake the Stuffed Corn Pie for approximately 40 minutes, until it turns golden. Cool to room temperature before serving.

TUNA SALAD STUFFED TOMATOES

Tomates Rellenos

These tomatoes are great during hot weather when you don't want to turn on the stove! The bright flavors of the tuna salad scream summer! This is a very quick meal to put together, and can be served as an appetizer or as a full lunch, depending on the size of the tomatoes you are using. The stuffing can be made ahead of time and stored in the refrigerator. When you're ready to eat, just carve the tomatoes, stuff them, and enjoy!

Ingredients

4 large firm tomatoes
2 tuna cans (6 ounces each, water- or olive-oil packed), drained and flaked
½ cup mayonnaise
2 celery ribs, finely chopped
1 tablespoon yellow hot pepper paste (homemade hot pepper paste, or finely chopped)
2 tablespoons parsley finely chopped
2 teaspoons lime juice
1 tablespoon cilantro, finely chopped
Salt and pepper to taste

Preparation

1. Cut a slice off the top of each tomato. Reserve tops for final presentation.
2. Scoop out the seeds and pulp, leaving a half-inch thick shell for each.
3. Invert tomatoes onto a strainer, baking rack, or paper towels to drain.
4. Meanwhile, combine all of the remaining ingredients in a bowl, and season the tuna salad to taste.
5. Spoon the tuna salad into tomato shells. You could use the tomato tops and some parsley or cilantro leaves to garnish.

Note: You can also stuff the tomatoes with other salads, such as chicken, veggies, shrimp, crab, cannellini beans, pasta or cooked whole grains like farro and wheat berries—whatever you choose! This is a versatile dish. Be playful and enjoy!

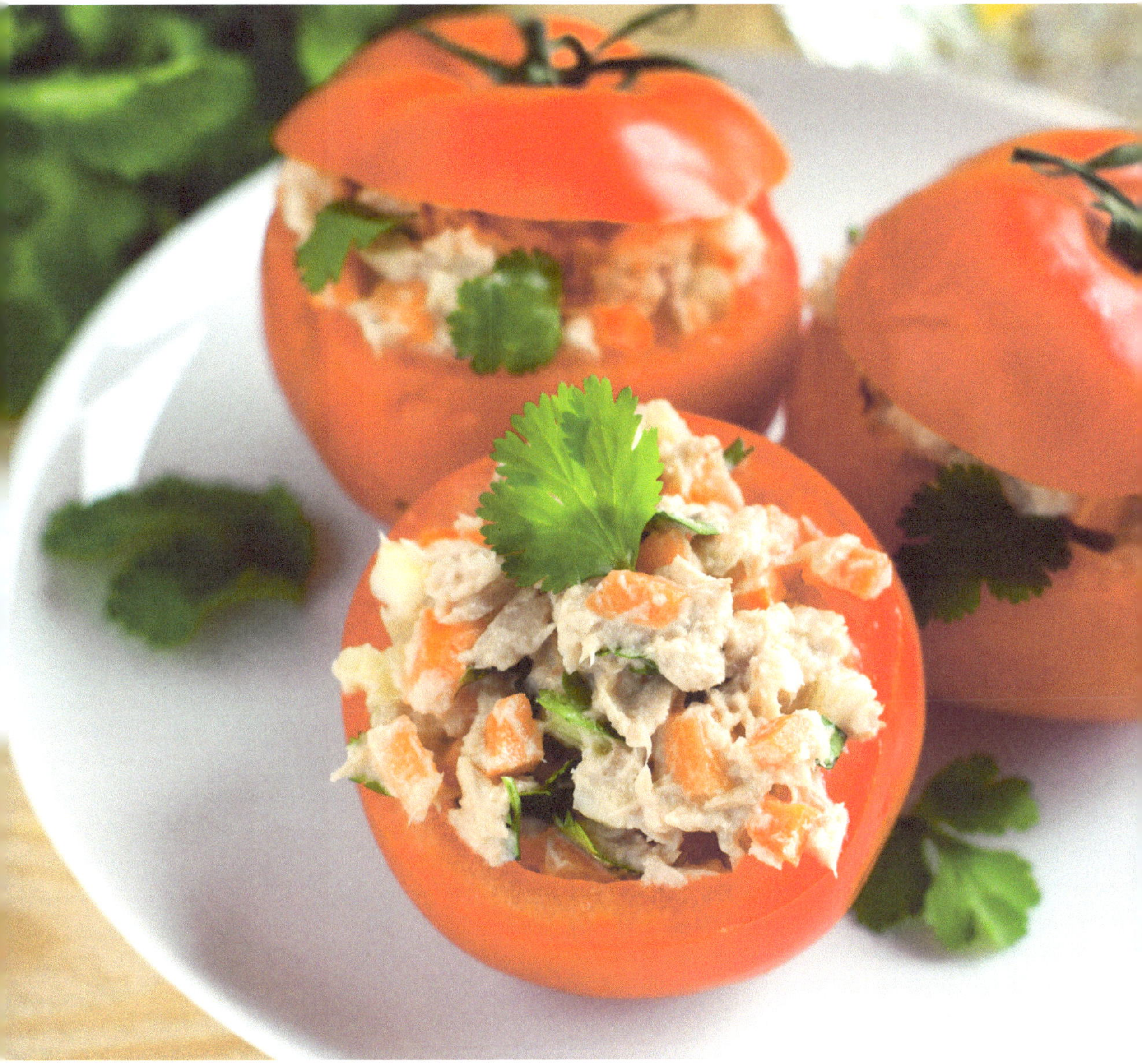

TIGER'S MILK

Leche de Tigre

SEAFOOD

70'

6 CUPS

Rumor has it this is an aphrodisiac dish and the best cure for hangovers. Maybe it's because is loaded with concentrated fish base, lime juice, and spicy peppers, which make you feel so invigorating. I'll let you be the judge after making your own tiger's milk.

    Some tips that I'd like you to consider are: It is very important for the fish to be extremely fresh for this recipe. If there are skin and bones on the fish, remove them. Let the onion soak in cold water to make it less potent. Take your time to use freshly squeezed lime juice. But most importantly use all your love and passion when you make it, you'll be able to taste it!

Ingredients

½ pound white fish
3 ½ cups fish stock
1 ¼ cup lime juice
¼ cup white onion
¼ cup celery
⅛ cup peeled and sliced ginger
2 teaspoons cilantro stems
2 garlic cloves
1 Limo hot pepper, seeded and deveined
1 ⅓ tablespoons sea salt

Preparation

1. Using a blender, mix all the ingredients together until completely smooth.
2. Using a fine mesh strainer or colander, strain the mixture into a container and refrigerate until ready to use (should be used the same day).

<u>Uses for Tiger's Milk (served in a glass)</u>
- As a base for Ceviche, using your favorite raw, firm fish, such as rock cod, sea bass, etc.
- Top with cooked panko-crusted shrimp or calamari served with Limo and yellow hot pepper and cilantro.
- Served in chilled cordial glass, as a shooter.

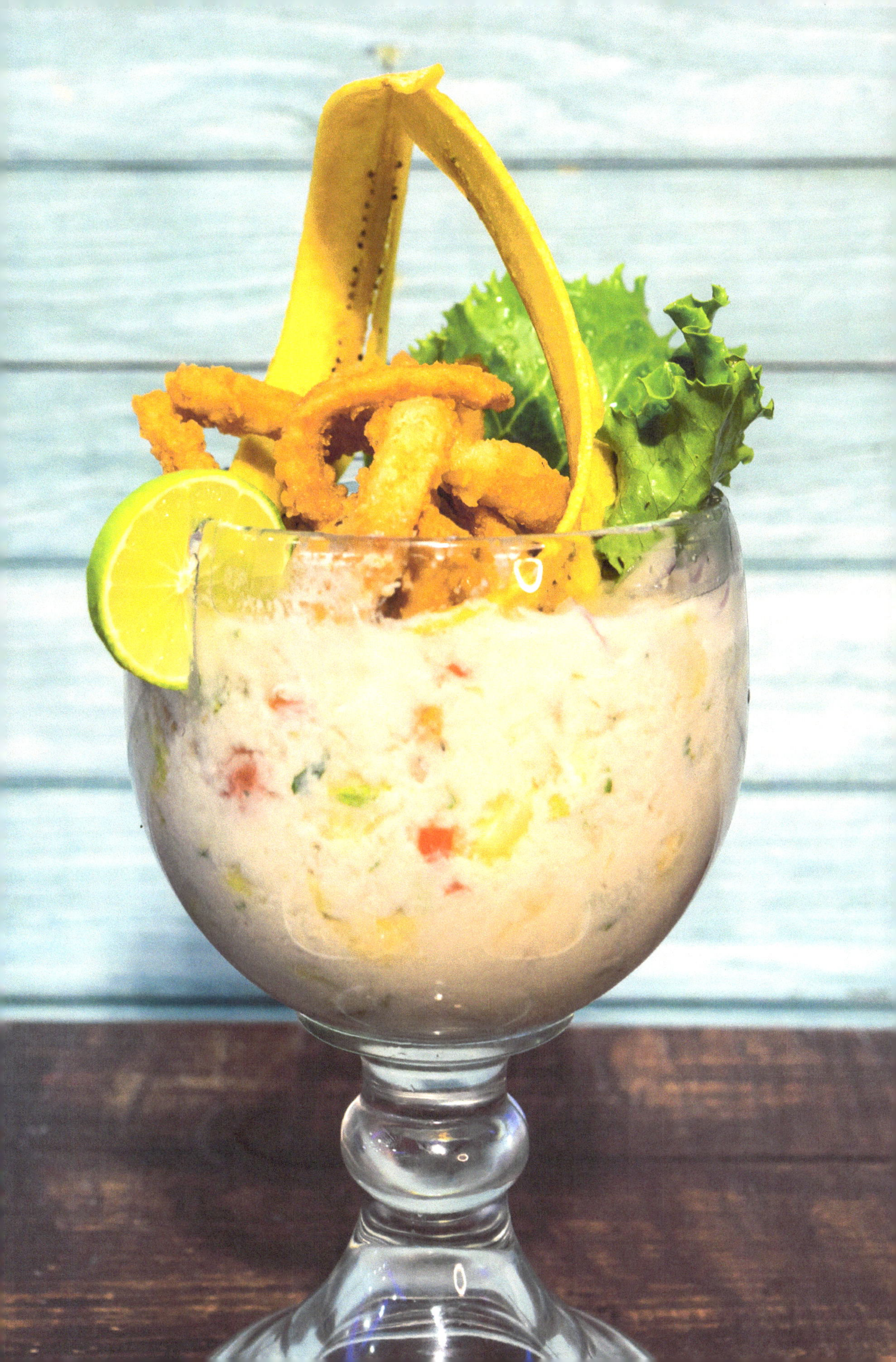

TUNA NIKKEI

Tiradito Nikkei

SEAFOOD

35'

2–4 SERVINGS

'Nikkei' is the name of the fusion between Japanese and Peruvian cuisines that started because of a large migration of Japanese people at the end of the 19th century.

This Tuna Nikkei is an incredible and easy-to-make dish, you just need good-fresh quality tuna, and once you taste the marriage of the Peruvian and Asian ingredients, you'll be wowed by the almost endless layers of flavors that will keep developing in your mouth during and after you've eaten this simple yet elegant dish.

Ingredients

½ pound fresh tuna filet
½ teaspoon salt
¼ cup oyster sauce
4 tablespoons fresh lime juice
1 tablespoon soy sauce
1 teaspoon minced ginger
1 teaspoon minced garlic
½ Limo hot pepper, finely chopped
1 teaspoon toasted sesame oil
¼ teaspoon each, black and white sesame seeds
1–2 tablespoons thinly sliced green onions (scallions)

Preparation

1. Cut the tuna into thin slices and arrange on a small platter with a high rim; season with salt, then chill for 5 minutes uncovered.
2. In the meantime, in a small bowl, whisk together the soy and the oyster sauces, lime juice, ginger, garlic, and Limo hot pepper.
3. Remove the tuna from the refrigerator and spoon the sauce on top of each piece of fish, until completely covered.
4. Sprinkle with drops of sesame oil and seeds, and garnish with green onions.
5. Enjoy immediately!

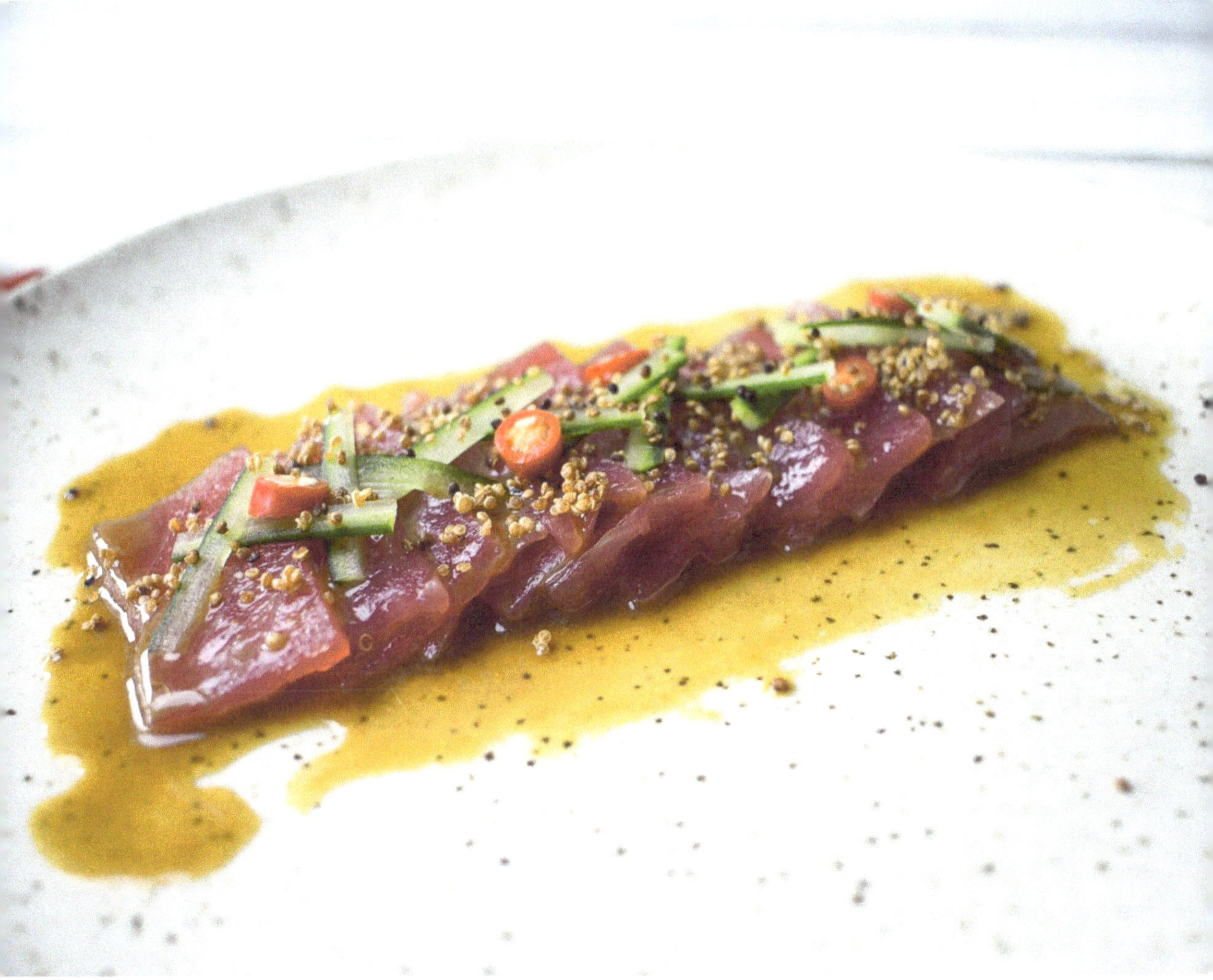

TUNA PATTIES

Torrejas de Atún

Has it ever happened to you that you taste certain foods and they leave you with a feeling that they are not what you imagined? Many years ago, it happened to me when I tried Tuna Patties. Ever since, I stopped eating them. But wait!

My sister Paula doesn't eat fish, but she loves Tuna Patties—incredible, but true—she always tells me: Today I prepared Torrejas de Atún and they were so good!

Well, once, on a Sunday, I discovered lentils and rice in the freezer, so my Monday menu was almost ready. But I was missing a little protein, so I looked in my pantry and found canned tuna … I thought about it, and I thought again, so I told my husband, and he said: "Why don't you prepare Tuna Patties?" So, I wrote to my sister and asked for her recipe. Paula is so special, she wrote it by hand, took a photo, and sent it to me. I read it and read it again … I went to the garden, harvested some ingredients, and prepared them Olenka's style, adding my own touch, of course … My husband and children ate them all, about 12 patties. What a success!

I wrote to my sister to let her know that it was a total success and to confess that I made some variations to her recipe, and she said: "Great! I knew you would, that's why I wanted you to make them long ago! Send me the new recipe please."

Ingredients

15 ounces canned tuna (water- or oil-packed), drained
3 large eggs, lightly beaten
¾ cup red or yellow onion, finely diced
½ cup tomato, finely diced
¼–½ cups flour (all-purpose or whole wheat)
¼ cup yellow hot pepper, finely diced
¼ cup fresh parsley, finely chopped
½ teaspoon garlic paste
1 teaspoon salt
Pinch ground black pepper
¼ cup vegetable oil, for frying

Preparation

1. Drain the tuna.
2. In a mixing bowl, break up the tuna, then gently mix in all the other ingredients except the oil.
3. Heat the oil in a frying pan over medium-high heat. Spoon dollops of the mixture (about 2–3 tablespoons each) into the oil and fry until golden. Flip the patties and cook for a few minutes longer.
4. When golden brown on both sides, remove the patties to a cooling rack or paper towels to drain excess oil.
5. Enjoy the Tuna Patties with your favorite dipping sauce.

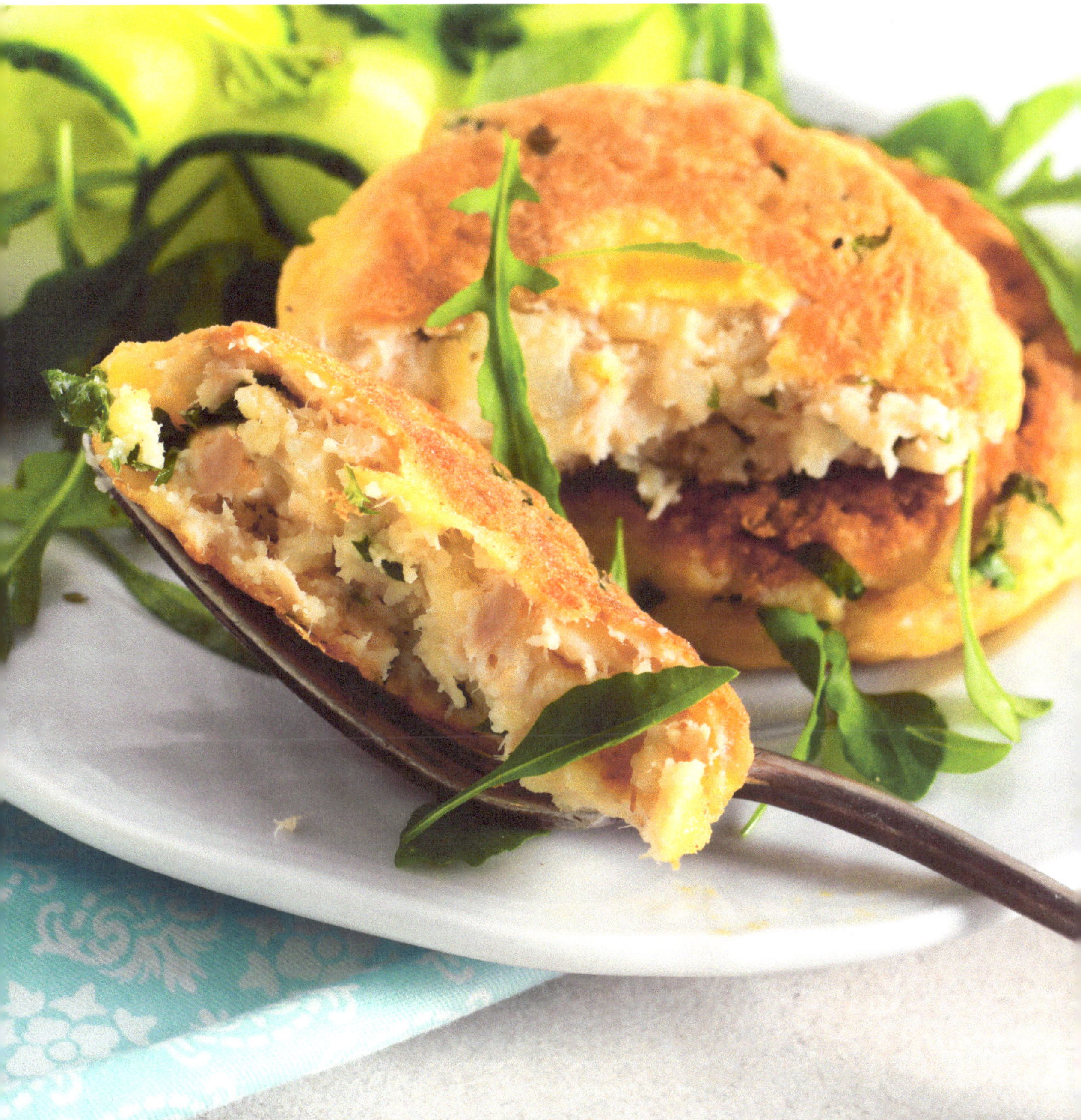

WONTON POCKETS STUFFED WITH CHEESE

Tequeños Rellenos con Queso

DAIRY

60'

60 POCKETS

Tequeños are crunchy, filled with flavor and everyone in Peru loves them. The classic ones are filled with cheese; however, now a days you can find them with a variety of fillings, such as Spicy Creamy Chicken, Beef Stir-Fried, crab with cream cheese, sautéed shrimp, to name a few. The dipping sauces could be endless, being the Huancaina or Rocoto Sauce, my favorites.

Wonton Pockets are one of those appetizers that could be made in advance and frozen. And, it's a lot of fun to make it with your family and friends. A good excuse to get together!

Now it's your turn to make them and try them out!

Ingredients

60 square wonton wrappers
16 ounces cheese (Gouda, Havarti, Monterey Jack)
2 egg whites, beaten
1 cup vegetable or other neutral oil, for frying

Preparation

1. Cut the cheese into sticks about a ¼-inch thick, and no longer than three-quarters of the length of your wonton wrappers.
2. Place one wonton wrapper on your work surface. Cover the remaining wrappers with a bowl or plastic wrap, to keep them from drying out as you assemble the Wonton Pockets.
3. Using your finger, or a small pastry brush, apply a small amount of the egg whites to each edge of the wrapper. Keeping the wonton wrapper flat on your work surface, place a cheese stick on one side of the wonton wrapper—staying away from the edges you've moistened with the egg white—and roll the wrapper to enclose the cheese. When you're near finishing rolling, gently press the long edge to create a good seal. Next, fold over the short edges and press gently but with the tines of a fork to seal. Be careful not to allow the tines of the fork to cut into the edge of the wrapper—press just enough to seal the dough. Repeat the process with the remaining wrappers and cheese.

4. Heat the oil in a large skillet or sauté pan over medium-high heat. Bring the oil to a sizzle and fry several Wonton Pockets at a time (being careful not to crowd the pan). When starting to brown on one side, flip the Wonton Pockets to brown on the other side. Remove them from the pan to drain on a wire rack or paper towels.
5. Serve Wonton Pockets with Huancaina Sauce (see page 112 or 116, Sides & Sauces), guacamole or your favorite dip.

To assemble and preserve the Wonton Pockets ahead
1. Place the pockets in layers in an air-tight container. Lightly dust each layer with cornstarch or rice flour to keep them from sticking together, then place a sheet of parchment or waxed paper on top before adding the next layer, and so on.
2. Cover and refrigerate the appetizers until you're ready to fry them, which should be done just before serving.

A LA MINUTE SOUP

Sopa a la Minuta

SPICY

40'

6 SERVINGS

Winter arrived and it was time to warm up with a "sopita". "Mamama, what shall we cook?" "How do you feel about a good Sopa a la minuta, Cholita?" "Of course! Let's make it!" And we would start having fun in the kitchen. When it was almost ready, we set the table, and placed the one thing that we grew up with: a bread basket. It was always part of setting the table because of my Tata, he loved bread with mostly every meal.

This is what I call a complete meal. It has protein, some veggies, some carbs, and tons of flavor! You can totally adjust it to your preference, and make it more or less brothy and carby. It is absolutely delicious and comforting. You'll love it!

Ingredients

2 tablespoons oil
1 cup red onion, small diced
1 bay leaf
2 tablespoons garlic paste
2 tablespoons Panca hot pepper paste
1 pound ground beef
1–2 tablespoons oregano
3 tablespoons tomato paste
6 cups beef broth
Salt and fresh ground pepper
¼ pound angel hair pasta or capellini
1 cup whole milk, half and half, or evaporated milk (unsweetened)
6 eggs, fried or poached
¼ cup fresh parsley, minced

Preparation

1. Place a pot over medium heat, add oil and sauté the onions and bay leaf till the onions are slightly translucent, add the garlic and Panca hot pepper; cook for 2 minutes.
2. Add ground beef, and with the help of a wooden spoon break it and cook for about 10 minutes.
3. Add oregano, tomato paste, and beef broth. Stir and let this simmer for 8–10 minutes. Taste the soup and season it with salt and pepper as needed.
4. Add the pasta into the pot, mix, and cook almost al dente (read the package instructions).
5. Add the milk, half and half, or evaporated milk.
6. Serve immediately with a fried or poached egg on top, and garnish with fresh parsley.

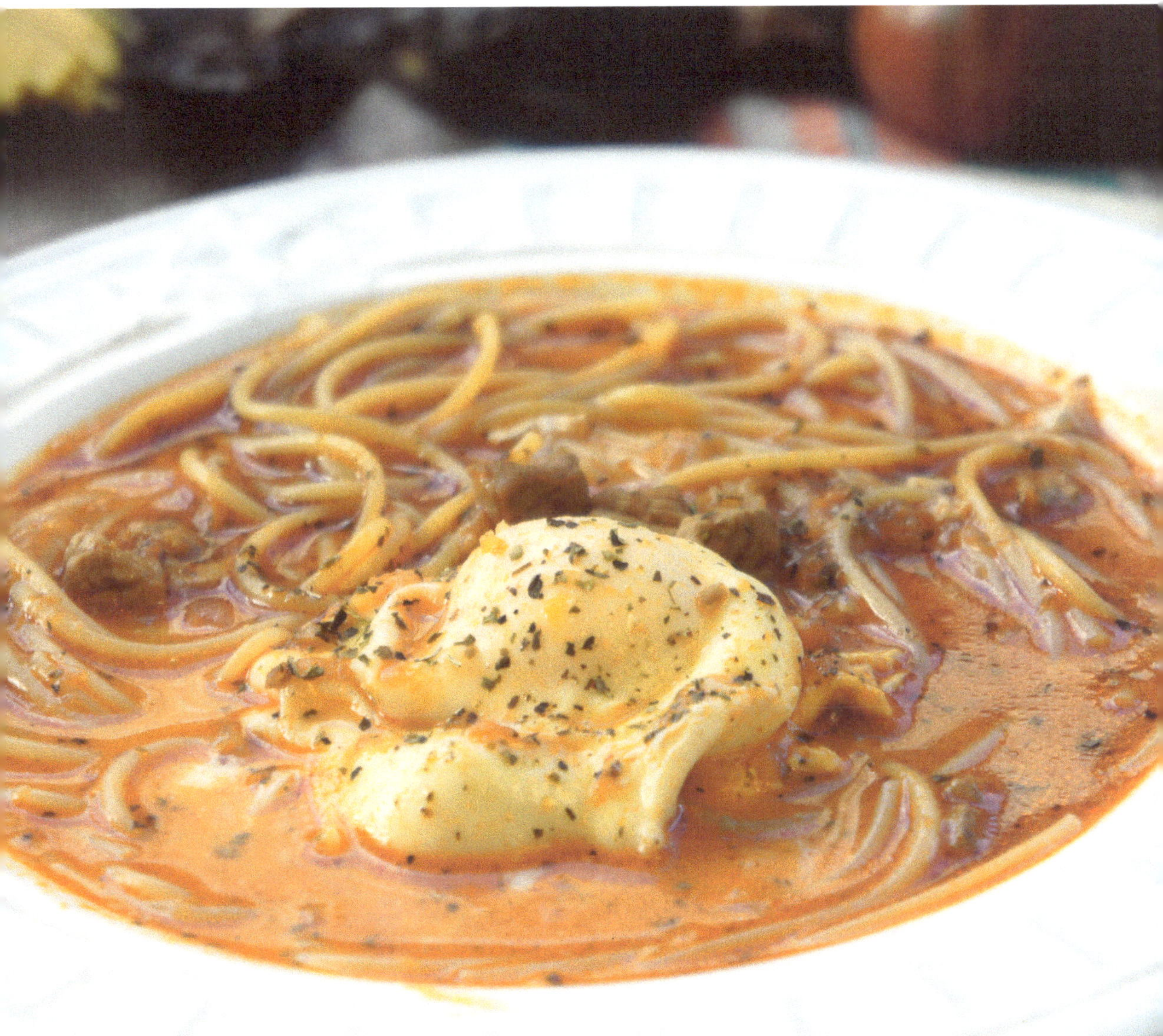

ASPARAGUS SOUP
Crema de Espárragos

GLUTEN FREE

60'

4–6 SERVINGS

In Peru, I grew up eating white asparagus. It wasn't common to find fresh green asparagus in the markets then, at least in Lima. Once, on a business trip I had the opportunity to visit an asparagus farm on the north coast of Peru. There were rows of soil, and under the soil, all snuggled up, were the asparagus. What an experience! The owners served us lunch, sharing some delicious dishes, all made with green asparagus, including a sweet asparagus flan.

If you've had the opportunity to try Peruvian asparagus, you are lucky. If not, try to find some because they are delicious, and so pretty! This soup is perfect for autumn or winter, and I'm sure you'll love it.

Ingredients

2 pounds fresh green asparagus
2 tablespoons olive oil
½ teaspoon each, salt and pepper
3 slices of bacon
2 medium Yukon Gold potatoes, peeled and cut into half-inch dice (about 2 cups)
½ white onion, chopped
2 celery stalks, chopped
1 teaspoon garlic, minced or mashed into a paste
½ cup shredded Parmesan cheese or Parmesan rind
4 cups chicken broth
Additional olive oil, for drizzling over finished soup (optional)

Preparation

1. Preheat the oven to 375 °F.
2. Start by roasting the asparagus: Snap off the woody ends and reserve for vegetable stock or another use. Lay the asparagus spears on a baking sheet and drizzle with 2 tablespoons olive oil, and sprinkle with salt and pepper. Using your hands or tongs, gently toss the asparagus to coat with the olive oil and seasonings. Place the baking sheet in the preheated oven for 15 minutes. Remove and allow to cool. When cool, cut into ¼-inch pieces and set aside.
3. While the asparagus are cooking, brown the bacon in a large stockpot over medium heat. When crispy, remove to a paper towel-lined plate to absorb any excess fat, keeping the drippings in the pot to cook the ingredients in step 4.
4. Add, to the bacon drippings in the pot, the potatoes, onions, celery, garlic and Parmesan cheese rind (if using shredded parmesan, add it at the end, just before blending the soup.) Season

with black pepper, and cook the vegetables for about 5 minutes over medium-high heat, until slightly browned.

5. Add the chicken broth and three quarters of the chopped asparagus (reserve the remaining quarter of the roasted asparagus to top the finished soup). Increase the heat and bring the soup to a boil, then reduce the heat to a simmer and continue cooking until the potatoes are fork-tender, about 15 minutes. Turn off the heat.
6. Remove the remains of the Parmesan rind. Or, if you're using shredded parmesan, add it now to the soup and stir until incorporated.
7. Using an immersion or stand blender, blend the soup until it is creamy.
8. When the soup texture is to your liking, taste and adjust seasonings, adding salt if needed.
9. Garnish with reserved asparagus and bacon crumbles. A finishing drizzle of good olive oil will enhance the flavor!

BUTTERNUT SQUASH SOUP

Crema de Zapallo

DAIRY

60'

6–8 SERVINGS

I have a memory of my Mamama making this recipe of Crema de Zapallo that she prepared from time to time, especially during winter. I really like this soup, it has simple ingredients, and it is kind of savory and sweet, the texture is creamy, you could warm-up in no time. She used to garnish it with homemade croutons, which made this soup even better. Lately, I also garnish it with some crème fraiche, and we all love it!

Ingredients

2 cups vegetable or chicken stock
1 medium (about 3–4 pounds) butternut squash, peeled, seeded, and cut into 1-inch chunks
1 cup carrot, peeled and roughly chopped
1 cup Yukon Gold potatoes, peeled and cut into
large dices
2 celery stalks, roughly chopped
1 teaspoon salt
¼ teaspoon black pepper freshly ground
¼ teaspoon nutmeg
½ cup grated Parmesan cheese
¼ cup butter
½ cup heavy cream

Preparation

1. In a large Dutch oven, or stockpot, combine all the ingredients but the Parmesan cheese, butter and heavy cream, that will be added in step 4.
2. Cook over medium high heat until the butternut squash can be easily mashed with a fork, about 20–30 minutes.
3. Using an immersion blender, purée the soup in the cooking pot, until the texture is smooth. Alternatively, purée the soup in two batches, ladling it into a traditional blender, be extremely careful blending hot liquids; you do not want the blender to be too full (remove the center of the blender lid to allow heat to escape while blending, holding a towel lightly over the lid opening to contain any hot splashes.)
4. Strain the purée into the pot. Add butter, heavy cream, and Parmesan cheese, and continue cooking over medium-low heat until the cheese is fully incorporated.
5. Taste and season. Add additional salt and pepper if needed.
6. Serve and enjoy! Garnish with any of your favorite toppings, such as croutons and crème fraîche.

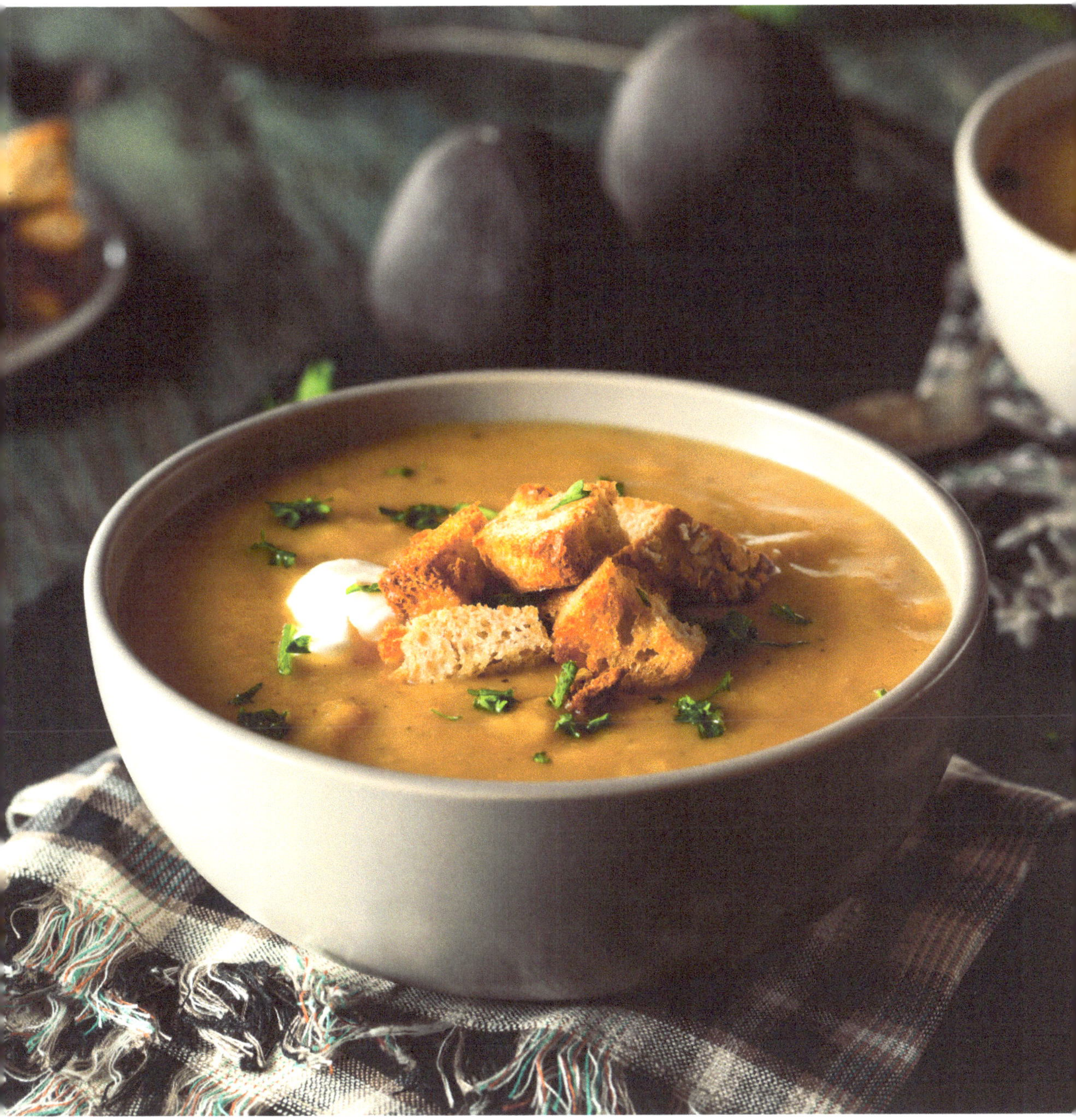

CELERY SOUP

Crema de Apio

DAIRY

60'

6 SERVINGS

Once, our garden put out a huge crop of celery, and I had to come up with a tasty way to use as much of it as I could. That's how this comforting, luscious, and flavorful recipe came to life. Healthy, delicious, and vegan adaptable, I just really looove the flavor, and I think you will, too.

Ingredients

½ cup unsalted butter
½ cup yellow onion, chopped
1 head of celery, chopped (reserve some leaves, to garnish)
1 cup Yukon Gold potatoes, peeled and cut into large dices
3 cups broth, chicken or vegetable
¼ cup fresh dill (fronds only), roughly chopped
½ cup heavy cream
Salt and pepper to taste
Flaky sea salt to finish

Preparation

1. Put the butter in a large saucepan over medium heat, and sauté the onion, celery, and potatoes. Season with a bit of salt and cook for about 10 minutes, stirring occasionally.
2. Add the broth and simmer until potatoes are cooked through, about 10 minutes.
3. Purée the soup in a blender with the dill.
4. Strain the soup back into the pot; add the cream, and heat through.
5. Serve the Celery Soup warm, garnished with celery leaves and a sprinkle of flaky sea salt.

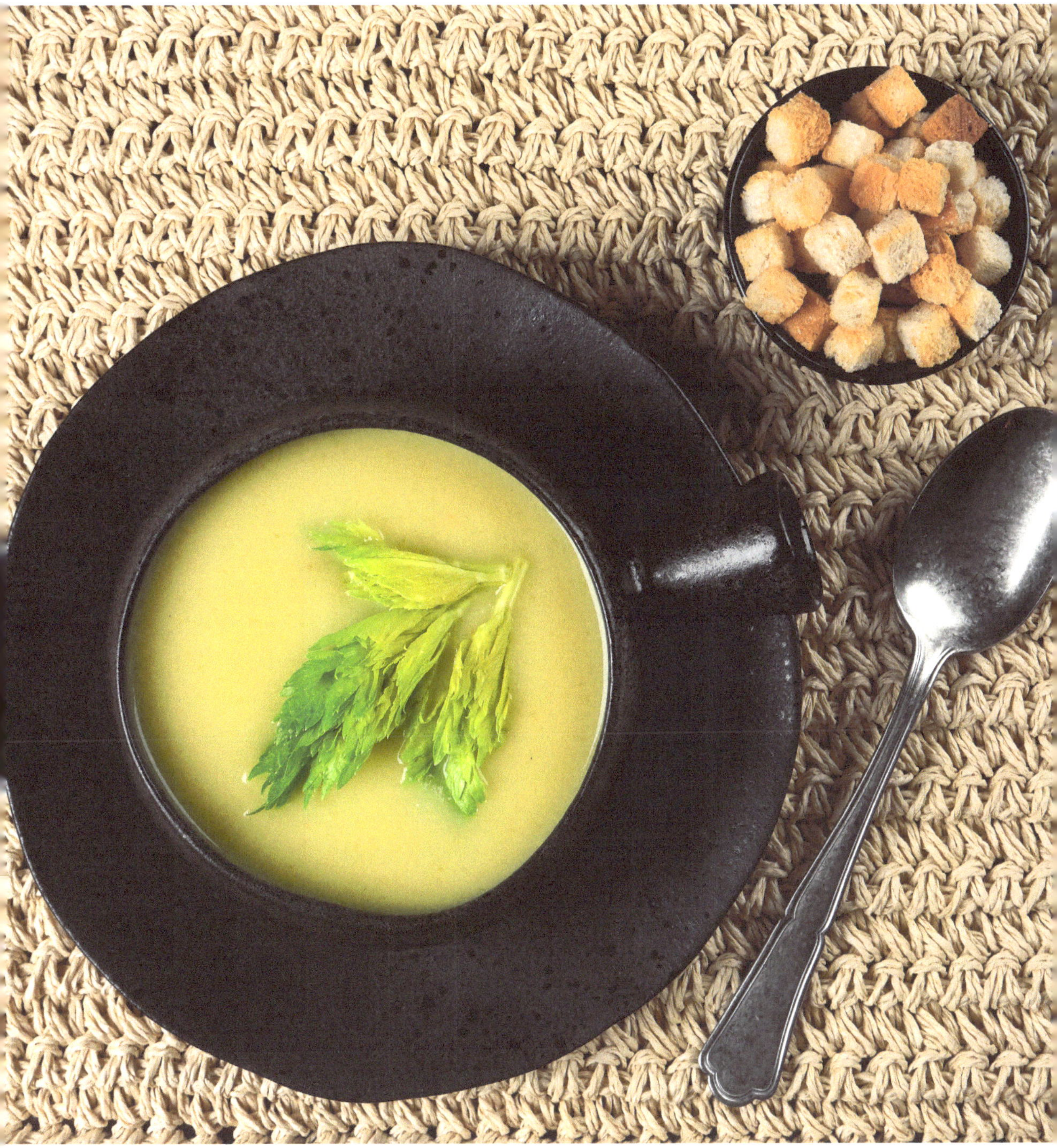

CHICKEN CILANTRO SOUP

Aguadito de Pollo

SPICY

70'

4–6 SERVINGS

Oh, this soup is like one of all grandmothers' soups—a soup to warm not only the body but also the heart! Those soups that make us feel the warmth of home, and perhaps remember a caress from our beloved grandmothers…

In our house, when the Aguadito was prepared, nothing else was served, and the truth is that this is a substantial soup (and not watery as the name suggests). On the contrary, between the chicken, the Yukon Gold potatoes, the rice, and the vegetables, ¡Qué rico! Succulent soup! Even better served with a few drops of lime.

Ingredients

4–6 pieces of chicken (thighs, breast, drumsticks; preferably skinless)
Salt and pepper
¼ cup vegetable oil
2 cups cilantro leaves and some stems, puréed in a blender with ¼ cup cold water
½ cup finely chopped red onion (one small)
¼ cup celery, finely chopped (one stalk)
¼ cup leek finely chopped
3 tablespoons yellow hot pepper paste
1 tablespoon garlic paste, or 3 garlic cloves minced and mashed
6 cups chicken stock
1 cup corn kernels, or hominy
1 cup finely diced carrot (3–4 medium)
1 cup fresh shelled green peas
½ cup long grain white rice
4 medium Yukon Gold potatoes, peeled and quartered
½ red bell pepper, thinly sliced
Fresh lemon or lime juice to squeeze over finished dish (optional)

Preparation

1. Season the chicken with salt and pepper. In a pot, or Dutch oven, large enough to hold the additional ingredients to be added later, heat the oil over medium-heat. Add the chicken pieces, and cook just long enough to sear on both sides (the chicken will cook further when returned back to the pot in step 4). Transfer the seared chicken to a plate, or shallow bowl, and keep warm.
2. In the residual oil and chicken drippings, remaining in the pot, sauté the onion, celery, and leek over medium-heat, until softened and golden. Then stir in the yellow hot pepper paste and the garlic and sauté for an additional minute.

3. Pour the 2 cups of puréed cilantro, into the sauté pot; add the chicken stock, the reserved chicken (and any chicken juices that have accumulated at the bottom of the dish), the corn, carrots, peas, and white rice. Bring to a boil the soup, then, immediately, lower the temperature to medium and keep semi-cover.
4. After 15 minutes, return the chicken pieces back to the pot, add the quartered potatoes and continue cooking just until the potatoes are tender, and the rice is fully cooked, about 12 minutes. Add the sliced red bell pepper at the last minute of cooking.
5. To serve, ladle the hot soup into individual bowls, making sure to include 1 piece of chicken, and a balanced mix of vegetables and broth, in each bowl.
6. If desired, top each serving with a few squeezes of lime, or lemon to brighten and enhance the flavors of the Chicken Cilantro Soup.

BEAN SALAD

Ensalada de Frejoles

LOW FAT

35'

2-3 SERVINGS

Looking for something fresh, healthy, quick and delicious? You can't beat the sweetness of the tomatoes when they are in season. And if you add them to a salad made with your favorite beans, you'll have a tasty, healthy and satisfying result. Best of all, you can make this salad in 10 minutes with just a few ingredients. And if you pair it with a crunchy piece of toast, even better!

Ingredients

1 cup cooked and drained beans: canary, cannellini, chickpeas, pinto, red or black beans (if using canned beans, rinse and drain before using)
2–3 small tomatoes, seeded, small diced
½ cup red onion small diced
1 tablespoon fresh oregano, finely chopped
1 tablespoon fresh parsley, finely chopped
2 tablespoons red wine vinegar
6 tablespoons extra-virgin olive oil
Salt and ground black pepper to taste

Preparation

1. In a small sieve, rinse the diced onion under cold water and allow to drain. (Rinsing removes the sharpness and strong flavor from the onions.)
2. In a medium bowl, combine the beans, tomatoes, onion, and chopped fresh herbs.
3. In a separate bowl, whisk together vinegar, olive oil, salt and pepper.
4. Pour the dressing over the bean mixture and toss gently. Cover and chill.
5. Serve cold and enjoy!

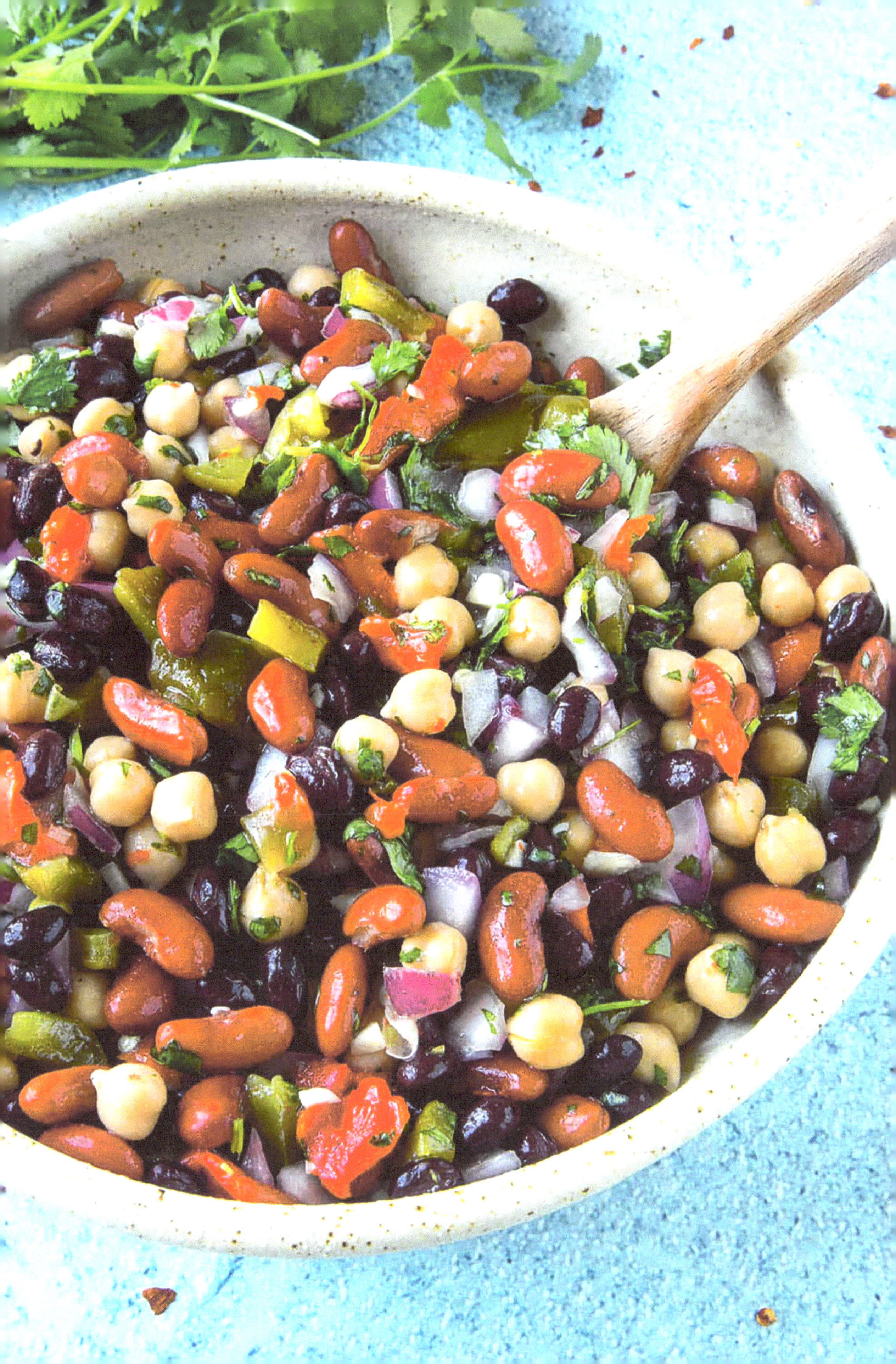

BEET AND POTATO SALAD

Ensalada Rusa

VEGETARIAN

60'

5 CUPS

Did you know that in Peru there's a super popular salad called Russian Salad? Yes! It is a creamy and colorful potato and vegetable salad with mayonnaise dressing. It is served as an accompaniment to many typical dishes in Latin America. In Peru, we have our own version. This delicious salad is a classic for Christmas Eve dinner, Christmas lunch, or New Year's dinner (summer time in Peru). Its bright purple-fuchsia color comes from the beets, which provide a perfect balance for the earthy seasonings.

Ingredients

For the Dressing
2 tablespoons mayonnaise
1 tablespoon white vinegar
1 tablespoon extra-virgin olive oil
1 tablespoon salt
Pinch white pepper

For the Salad
1 cup peas, fresh or frozen
1 cup green beans diced fresh
½ cup carrot diced
1 cup beets (2 medium-size whole beets), diced
2 medium-size Yukon Gold potatoes, peeled and cut into ½-inch cubes
2 hard-boiled eggs, diced
Salt

Preparation

Dressing
- Mix the dressing ingredients in a little bowl and reserve.

Salad
1. In simmering, salted water, cook vegetables separately, beginning with beets and potatoes. Follow with the carrots, peas and green beans. The beets are done when a knife can be easily inserted in the middle and it slides out easily. Drain the beets and set aside to cool before peeling and cutting into medium dice.
2. Once the carrots, peas and green beans turn *al dente*, cool them down quickly by plunging them into a large bowl of ice and cold water.
3. When the potatoes are tender, but not falling apart (about 5 to 7 minutes), drain and set aside.
4. In a large bowl, combine all the vegetables (except the potatoes) with the diced eggs. Add the dressing and mix well, then add the potatoes and gently mix all together. Adjust seasonings if needed and serve the salad.

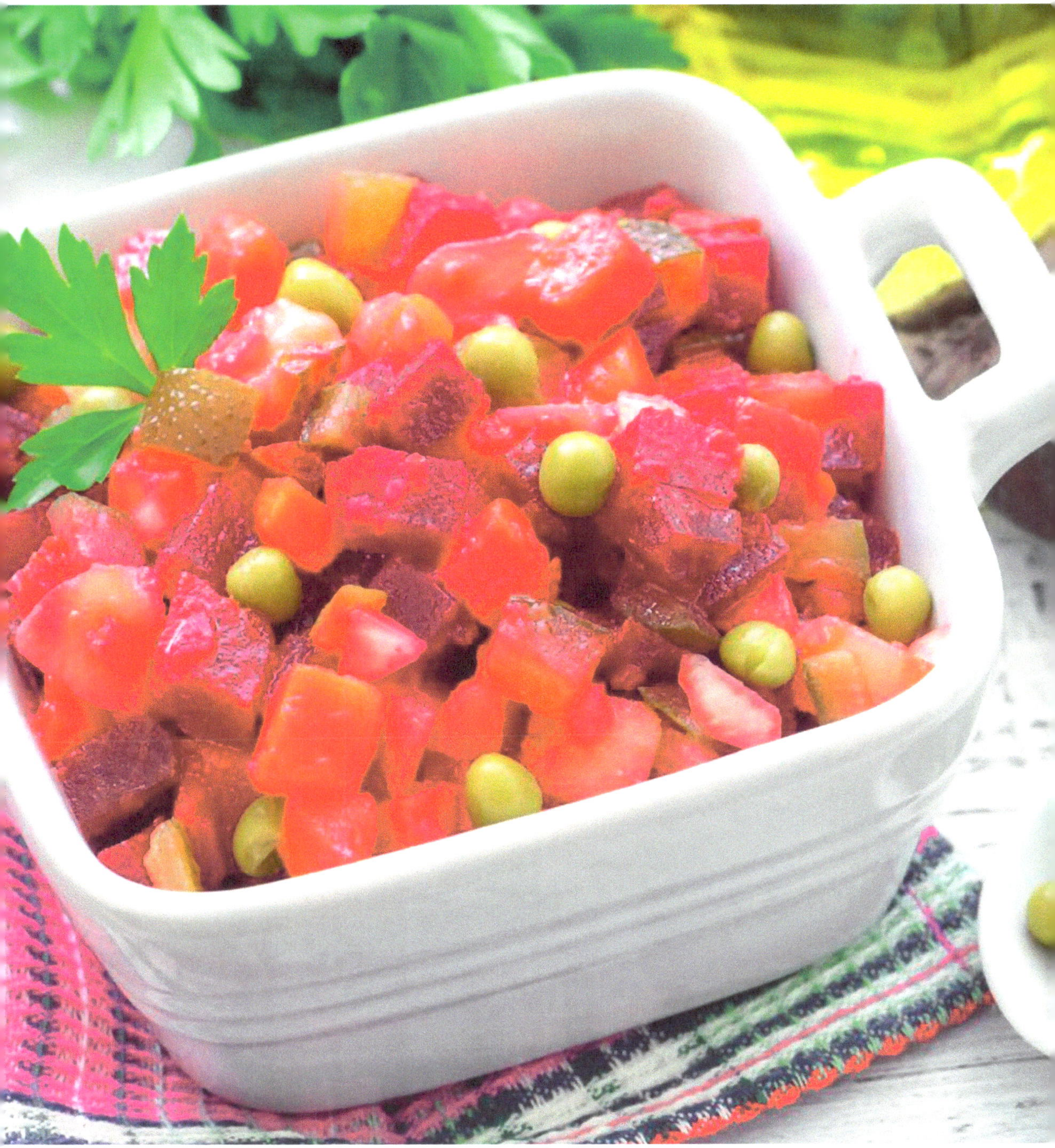

CHICKEN POTATO SALAD

Causa Rellena con Pollo

GLUTEN FREE

60'

6–8 SERVINGS

The name Causa comes from the Quechua word *kausaq*, meaning "that which gives life." Potatoes are a major component of Peruvian cuisine, and there are more than 4000 types of potatoes grown in the region! How amazing is that? In few words, it's a life-giving food.

This dish is both elegant and comforting, and is much beloved by Peruvians. Lemony-spicy cold mashed potatoes are layered in a casserole with a fresh, creamy salad of chicken, crab, shrimp, tuna or veggies, then chilled. When un-molded, it never fails to impress because it looks so pretty. Let me warn you, once you start eating this appetizer, you may not want to stop! Yum!

Ingredients

For the mashed potatoes
4 Yukon Gold potatoes (uncut)
4 Russet potatoes (uncut)
½ cup vegetable oil, or as needed
½ cup yellow hot pepper paste
¼ cup key lime juice
Salt and ground white pepper to taste

For the Chicken Salad
2–3 cups shredded cooked chicken white meat
1 cup mayonnaise
½ cup celery, finely chopped
2 tablespoons yellow mustard or Dijon

Salt and ground black pepper to taste
2 avocados, peeled and cut into thin slices

For the garnish (optional)
2–3 hard-boiled eggs
1 yellow hot pepper, finely chopped
1 handful parsley
6–8 leaves romaine lettuce (not baby), julienned
Huancaina Sauce (see page 116, Sides & Sauces)

Preparation

Mashed potatoes
1. Place all the potatoes in a large pot and cover with water; bring to a boil and add salt. Reduce heat to medium-low and cook until tender, about 20 minutes. Drain.
2. While hot, carefully peel the potatoes and pass them through a ricer or food mill, directly into a large bowl. Gradually stir in oil, until potatoes come together; add the yellow hot pepper paste, key lime juice, salt and pepper.

Chicken Salad
1. In a separate bowl, mix the chicken, mayonnaise, celery, and mustard; season with salt and pepper.

Assemble
2. In a casserole dish, spread half the potato mixture on the bottom of the dish and cover with the avocado slices and all the chicken mixture.
3. Top with the remaining potato mixture; cover with plastic and chill for about 1 hour.
4. When fully chilled, cut and serve.

Note: If desired, place individual servings of the causa over a bed of julienned romaine lettuce. Garnish with a drizzle of Huancaina Sauce
(see page 112 or 116, Sides & Sauces) and a mixture of egg, small diced yellow hot pepper and parsley.

CRAB POTATO SALAD
Causa Rellena con Cangrejo

SEAFOOD

45'

6–8 SERVINGS

It's crab season, and Gramps, like every year, is off to catch some gorgeous and exquisite Dungeness crab. Luckily, he shares it gladly with us, and we've decided to make Causa. Made with potatoes, yellow hot pepper paste, and lime juice. Simple yet tricky to get the right texture and flavor. In contrast with Dungeness crab, which is sweet, tender, and unique, as unique as the one in Peru.

One thing I have to tell you: when Crab Potato Salad is well prepared, you'll remember it forever.

Get your potato ricer and make this recipe that will deliver a great experience! "A pillow from heaven."

Ingredients

<u>For the mashed potatoes</u>
4 Yukon Gold potatoes
4 Russet potatoes
½ cup vegetable oil, or as needed
½ cup yellow hot pepper paste
½ cup key lime juice, or regular lime juice, divided in 2 quarters
Salt and freshly ground white pepper

<u>For the Crab Salad</u>
1 pound cooked crab meat
1 cup green onions finely diced (optional)
1 cup mayonnaise, divided in 2 parts
2 ripe avocados, peeled and cut into thin strips (optional)
Salt and freshly ground white pepper

Preparation

<u>Mashed potatoes</u>
1. Place the 8 potatoes (whole, uncut) into a large pot and cover with water; bring to a boil and add salt. Reduce heat to medium-low and simmer until tender, about 20 minutes. Drain.
2. Carefully peel potatoes while still hot, place the potatoes in the ricer, and rice the potatoes into a large bowl. Gradually stir in oil until the mashed potatoes come together; add the yellow hot pepper paste, ¼ cup of the key lime juice, salt and pepper.

<u>Crab Salad</u>
1. In a separate bowl, mix the crab meat, green onions, the other ¼ cup key lime juice, and season with salt and pepper.

Assemble

1. Line a casserole dish with plastic wrap. Spread half the mashed potatoes on the bottom of the dish.
2. Spread ½ cup of mayonnaise over the layer of mashed potatoes; spread the crab mixture over the mayonnaise, and place the avocado slices in a single layer on top of the crab mixture (optional). Spread the remaining mashed potatoes over the avocados, and top with remaining ½ cup of mayonnaise.
3. Cover casserole dish with plastic wrap and refrigerate until firm, about 30 minutes.
4. When fully chilled, invert the casserole dish onto a serving platter; remove plastic wrap, cut, and serve cold.

Note: It could be assembled individually portioned as well.

FAVA BEAN SALAD

Solterito de Habas

VEGETARIAN

60'

4–6 SERVINGS

This recipe originated in the city of Arequipa in Peru. The word *solterito* means 'young single man.' Peruvian fava beans are so tender and sweet that they seem to melt in your mouth, melding with, and balancing the zesty and salty flavors of the other ingredients in the salad. Because this fava bean salad is nutritious, quick and simple to make, it's the perfect meal for a bachelor to make, and so the inspiration for the name of the dish. This fresh and filling salad is great as a side dish or a small treat to serve guests as an appetizer. Easy peasy!

Ingredients

<u>For the Salad</u>
1 ½ cup baby fava beans, fresh or frozen
1 ½ cup corn kernels, fresh or frozen
1 small diced red onion, rinsed thoroughly before and after dicing
1 small Roma tomato, diced
1 handful fresh parsley, chopped
1 tablespoon chopped fresh oregano
1 yellow hot pepper, minced
½ cup sliced olives, Botija or Kalamata
1 cup Queso Fresco (Casero or Cotija), small diced

<u>For the Dressing</u>
5 tablespoons key limes, or regular fresh lime juice
¼ cup extra-virgin olive oil
1 tablespoon white wine vinegar
Salt and pepper

Preparation

<u>Salad</u>
1. In a medium saucepan, bring water to a boil; add salt and the fava beans and cook until just firm-tender.
2. In a separate pot, boil the corn kernels in unsalted water for about 15–20 minutes.
3. In a large bowl, combine the cooled fava beans and corn kernels, diced onion, diced tomato, chopped parsley, oregano and minced yellow hot pepper.

<u>Dressing</u>
1. In a little bowl, whisk together the dressing ingredients.
2. Assemble
3. Add the dressing to the salad and toss to combine.
4. Plate and serve topped with diced olives and Queso Fresco.

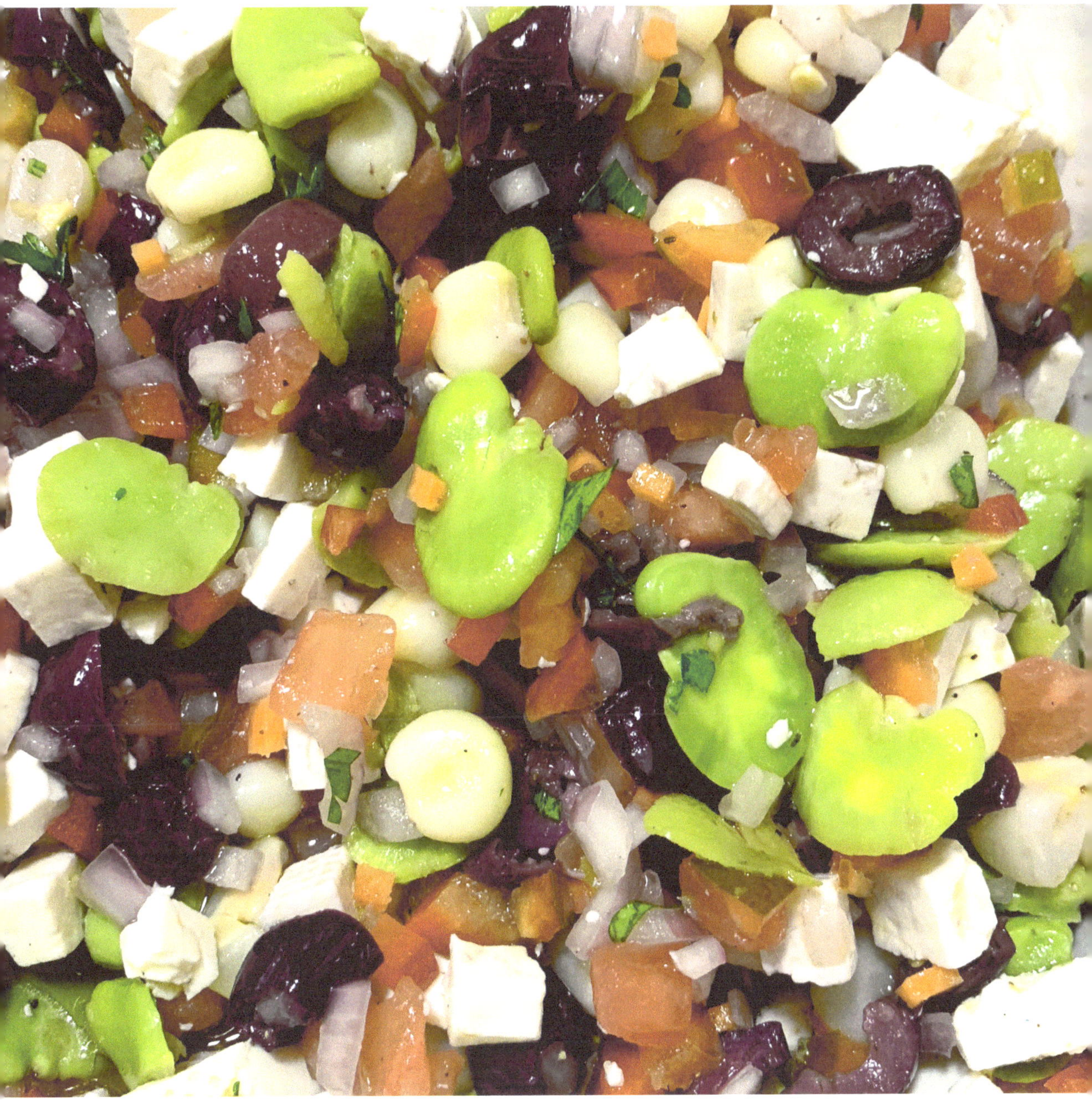

SHRIMP STUFFED AVOCADO

Palta Rellena con Camarones

I have always loved Palta (avocado). It's flavor and creaminess are so distinctive, especially the ones in Peru. I remember being a little girl, and my Tata coming into the kitchen in the evening, and cutting an avocado in half, removing the pit, sprinkling some salt, and pouring a small amount of olive oil. Then he grabbed a spoon and started eating it directly from the peel. He gave me a bite to taste, and since that day I've been hooked for life.

My husband and children also love avocado, and we enjoy it at any time of the day, either with toasts or crackers. And of course, as guacamole when my husband makes nachos.

Anyhow, this is one of those dishes that will help you on those hot summery days, and you will be grateful. You just make your salad, stuff your avocado and done! Lunch or dinner is ready!

Ingredients

For the Shrimp Salad
2 cups cooked shrimps
1 cup mayonnaise
¼ cup green onion, diced
¼ cup yellow hot pepper paste
White pepper and salt
¼ cup cilantro freshly chopped (divided)
¼ cup freshly squeezed key lime juice (plus an additional tablespoon)

For the avocados
3 ripe semi-soft avocados
6 large lettuce leaves or a handful of mixed baby greens, chilled

Preparation

Shrimp Salad
1. In a bowl, combine the shrimps, green onion, mayonnaise, yellow hot pepper paste, half of the chopped cilantro, salt and pepper. If making ahead of time, cover the salad and keep chilled until ready to fill the avocados and serve.
2. When ready to serve, add the quarter cup fresh key lime, or regular lime juice to the salad.

Avocados
1. Slice avocados in halves, remove pits and peel carefully. Drizzle with lime juice to keep the fruit from turning brown. Slice a bit off the bottom halves so the avocados can sit without tipping over, and put the slice on.

Assemble
1. On each serving plate, place a lettuce leaf, or a mound of mixed baby greens; top with an avocado half, and fill each half with shrimp salad. Garnish with the remaining chopped cilantro and serve immediately.

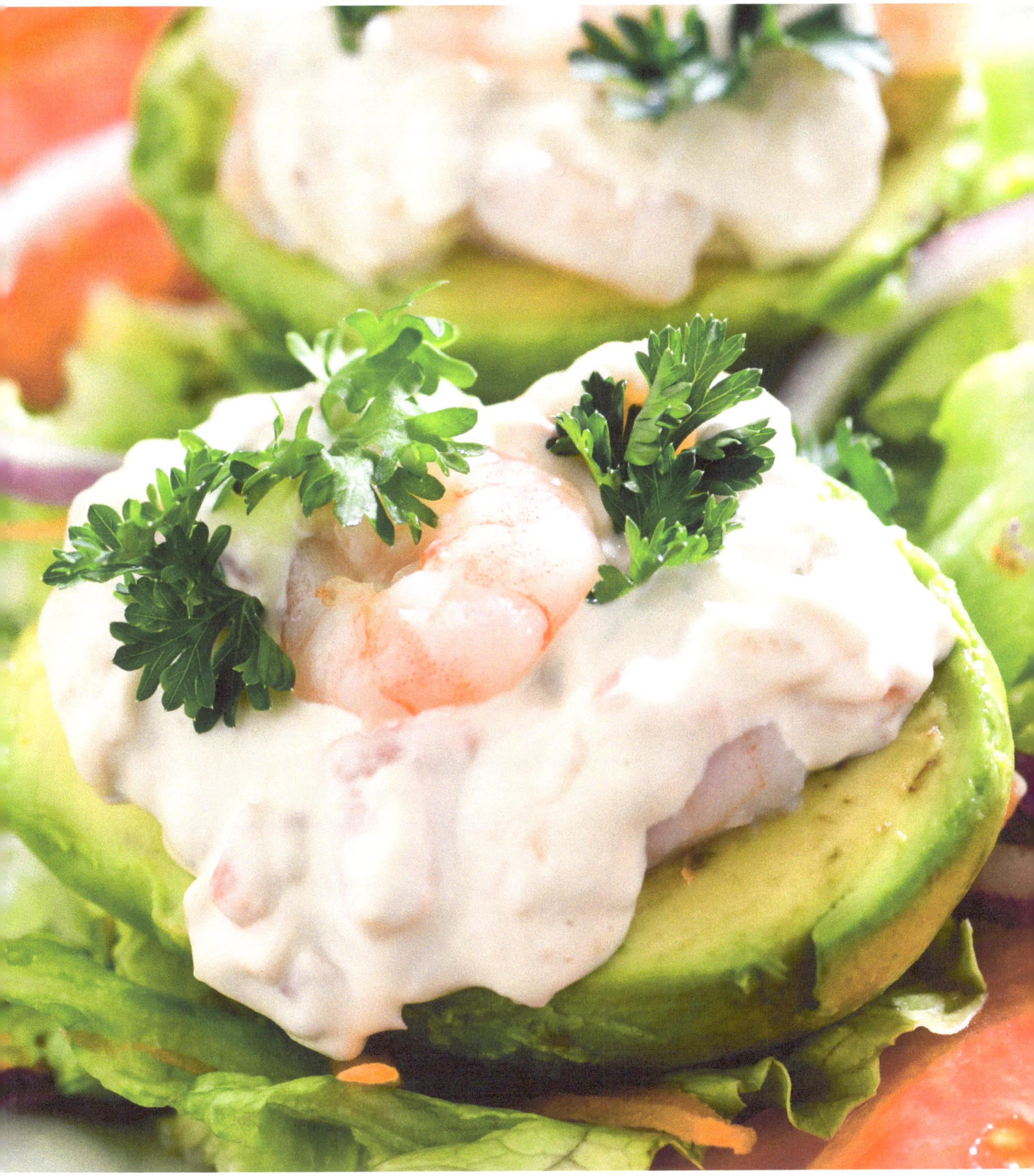

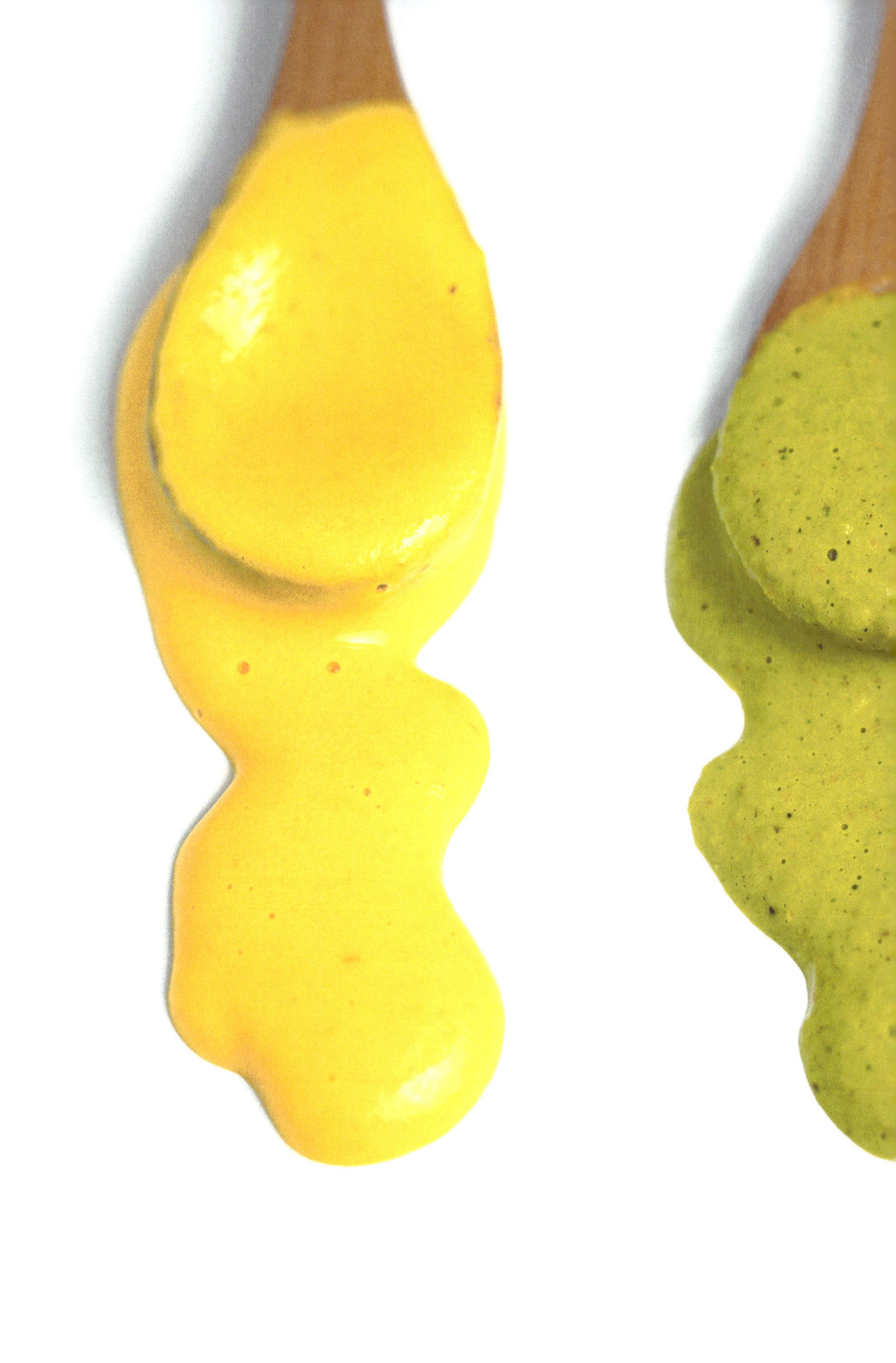

Sides & Sauces

APPLE SAUCE
Puré de Manzana

When Christmas approaches, a tasty dinner with succulent dishes is part of the tradition. In Peru, applesauce is a classic Christmas dinner side dish. The sweet and tart flavors of apples are perfect to accompany your main entrée, be it turkey, pork or chicken.

When I became a mom, I decided to incorporate this purée in my repertoire, and now we have it often at home. My favorite apples for this dish are Gravenstein. They are the best apples to achieve a perfect balance between tanginess and sweetness. And with the warm spices… heavenly!

Ingredients

4 pounds of apples (about 8 to 10 apples, depending on size). Choose good cooking varieties, such as Granny Smith, Gravenstein, McIntosh, Fuji, or Golden Delicious
1 cup water
½ cup of light brown sugar
1–3 tablespoons fresh lemon juice, or apple cider vinegar (to desired tartness)
1 lemon zest
1 cinnamon stick
½ teaspoon salt
¼ cup unsalted butter

Preparation

1. Peeled, core and quarter the apples and place in a large pot. Add the water, the brown sugar, the lemon juice, or vinegar, the lemon zest, the cinnamon stick and salt. Bring to a boil over high heat, then lower the temperature, cover the pot, and maintain a low simmer for 15–20 minutes, until the apples are completely tender and cooked through.
2. When the apples are cooked, remove the pot from the heat; and remove the cinnamon stick.
3. Using a potato masher, mash the cooked apples in the pot to create a chunky sauce. For smoother applesauce, you can either run the cooked apples through a food mill, or purée them using a stick blender, or a standing blender. (If you use a standing blender, purée in small batches and do not fill the blender carafe more than halfway.)
4. Last but not least, add the butter and mix in until totally melted and incorporated. Serve warm or cold. May be kept refrigerated for up to 1 week, if you can make it last that long!

Note: This sauce can be served as a snack or dessert but is also a perfect complement for savory dishes like pork and roasted turkey.

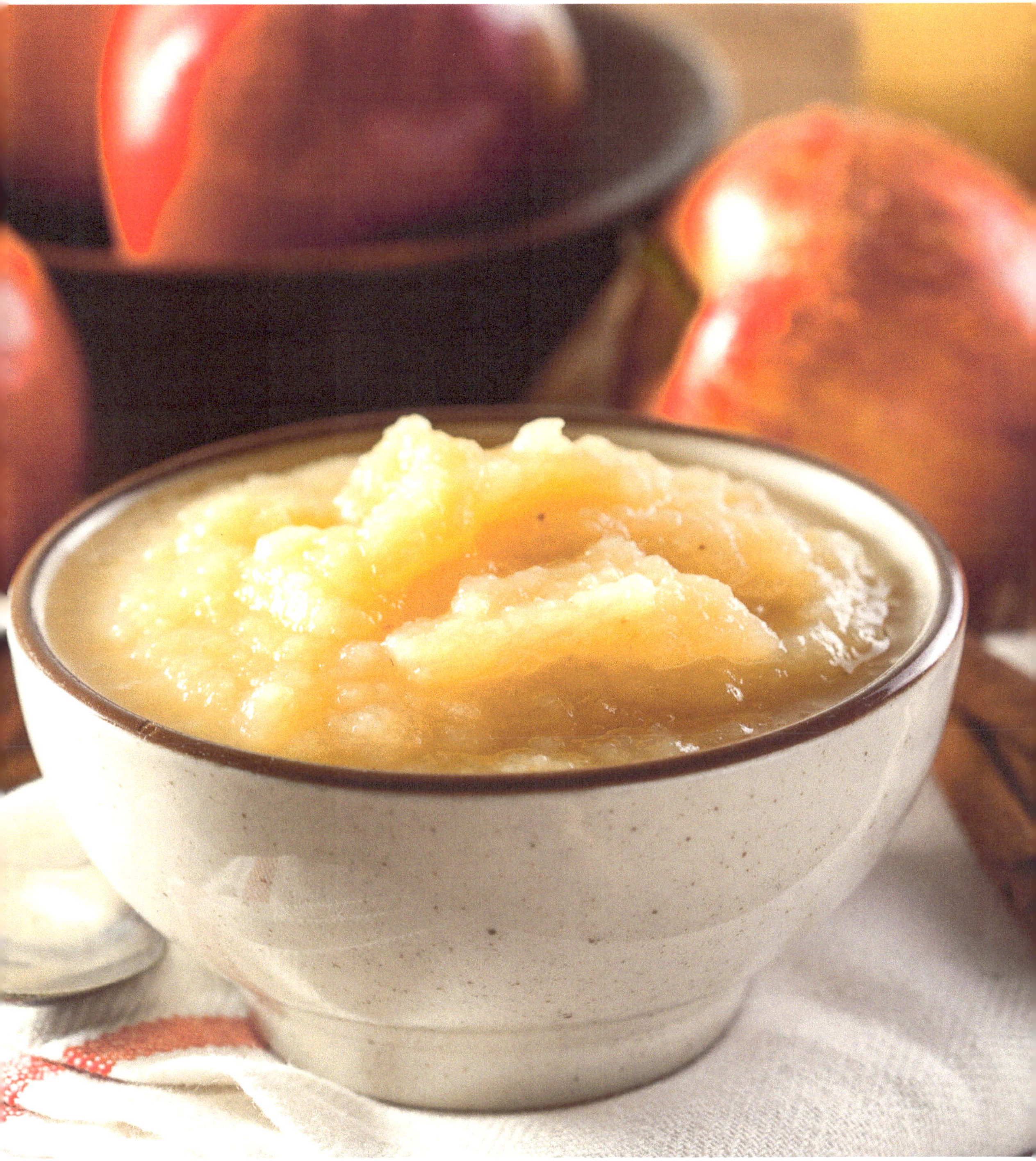

ARABIC RICE
Arroz Árabe

Have you ever tried Arabic Rice? If not, I can tell you that this is one of the classic holiday dishes in Peru. We always make certain modifications to the recipe, enhancing it even more. This rice is very flavorful paired with turkey or pork.

I invite you to discover this delicious recipe, with its unique sweet and savory balance. It's a simple way to vary everyday rice dishes, while being special enough for your holiday table.

Ingredients

4 tablespoons vegetable oil
½ cup angel hair pasta, broken in 1-inch pieces
2 teaspoons garlic paste, or minced and mashed garlic
2 heaping teaspoons salt
2 cups basmati rice
½ cup golden raisins
2 cups water
1 cup Cola
½ cup toasted and chopped pecans or walnuts
½ cup toasted and laminated almonds
2 tablespoon butter (optional)

Preparation

1. Heat 2 tablespoons of the vegetable oil in a large saucepan over medium heat. Add the angel hair pasta and fry until golden brown. Remove the fried pasta from the pan and set aside in a bowl.
2. Using the same pan, add the remaining 2 tablespoons of oil; when heated, stir in the garlic, salt and rice, and cook for about 2 minutes, or until the rice starts to turn opaque.
3. Add the raisins, the cup of Cola, the water, and the fried pasta. Stir briefly and bring to a boil. Cover the pan with a fitted lid; lower the heat and simmer, undisturbed, for about 20 minutes, or until the rice is tender. Remove from the heat and let the rice rest in the covered pan for 10 minutes.
4. If desired, add a couple of tablespoons of butter to the rice; fluff with a fork and add the nuts. Serve immediately.

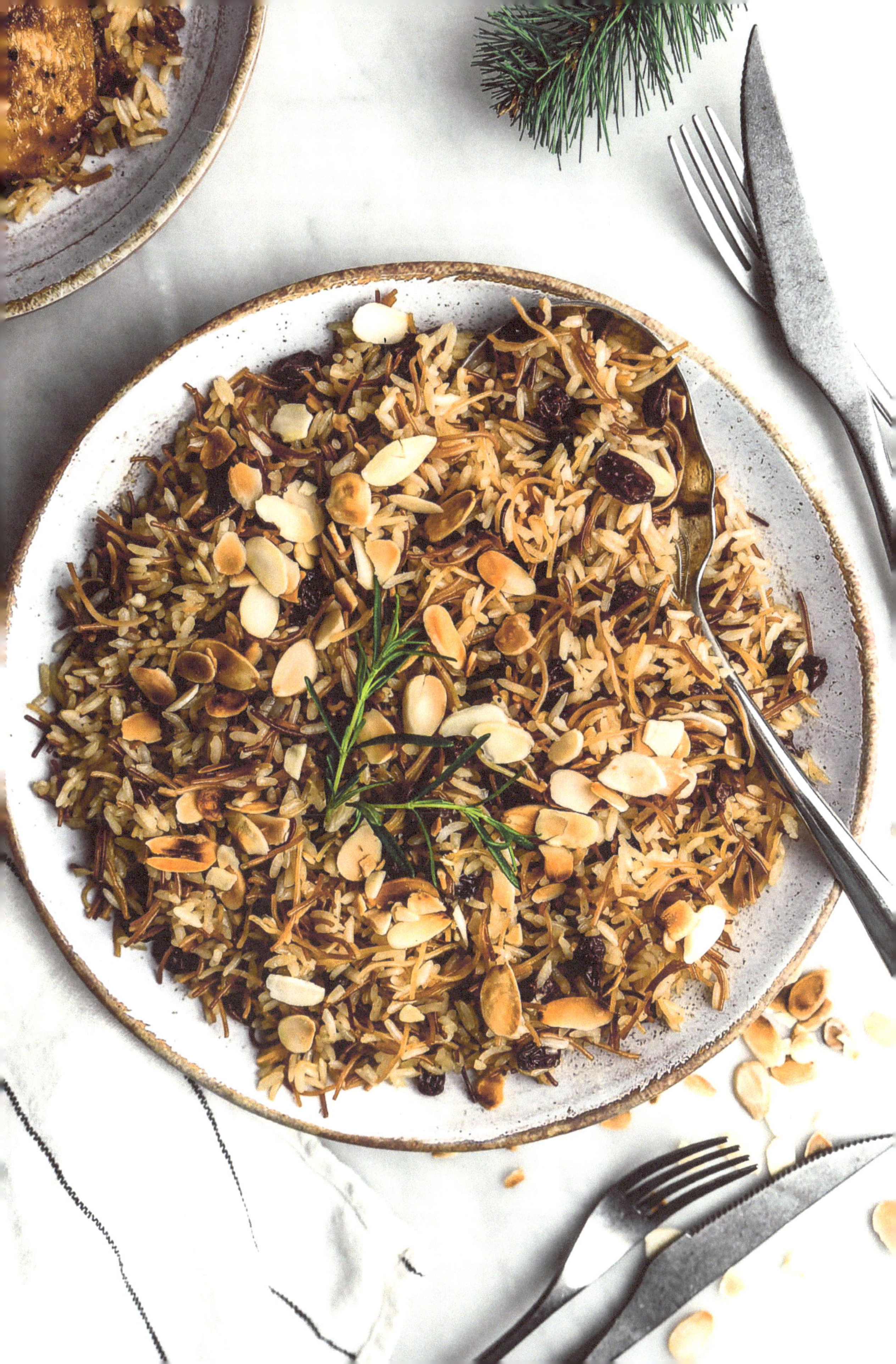

CANARY BEANS WITH BACON

Frejol Canario con Tocino

Canario, Mayocoba or Peruano, all are names for these creamy and tender beans which absorb all the flavors of the ingredients added to them. That's why a good amount of bacon with garlic and properly cooked onions will make these stewed beans a dream come true.

GLUTEN FREE — 24h — 8 SERVINGS

Ingredients

- ½ pound canary beans (available at supermarkets and online)
- 2 bay leaves
- ½ pound bacon, diced
- 1 red onion, diced small (about one cup)
- 3 tablespoons garlic paste, or minced and mashed garlic
- 2 tablespoons tomato paste
- 1 tablespoon dried oregano
- ½ teaspoon ground cumin
- Salt and ground black pepper
- 3 tablespoons extra-virgin olive oil (for a finishing drizzle)

Preparation

1. The day ahead, put the beans in a large bowl, and cover the beans with cold water by two inches; soak overnight (no more than 12 hours).
2. The next day, drain the beans, cover with fresh water, add the bay leaves and bring to a boil.
3. Reduce the heat, and with the lid slightly ajar, simmer the beans until tender, approximately 2–4 hours. Periodically skim off any foam that rises to the surface.
4. When the beans are cooked, fry the bacon over medium heat for about 5 minutes (do not let crisp) in a large pot or Dutch oven. Add the onion, when onion is translucent, add the garlic, oregano and cumin; stir together for a minute, then add the tomato paste.
5. When the beans are fully cooked (tender and creamy), add them and their cooking liquid to the bacon and onion mixture pot. Check seasonings and add salt and pepper to taste; drizzle with extra-virgin olive oil.

Note: These beans are perfect to accompany a good Adobo Pork Stew (see page 128, Main Courses) or Beef Cilantro Stew (see page 130, Main Courses)... mmm... And don't forget the Onion Relish (see page 114, Sides & Sauces)!

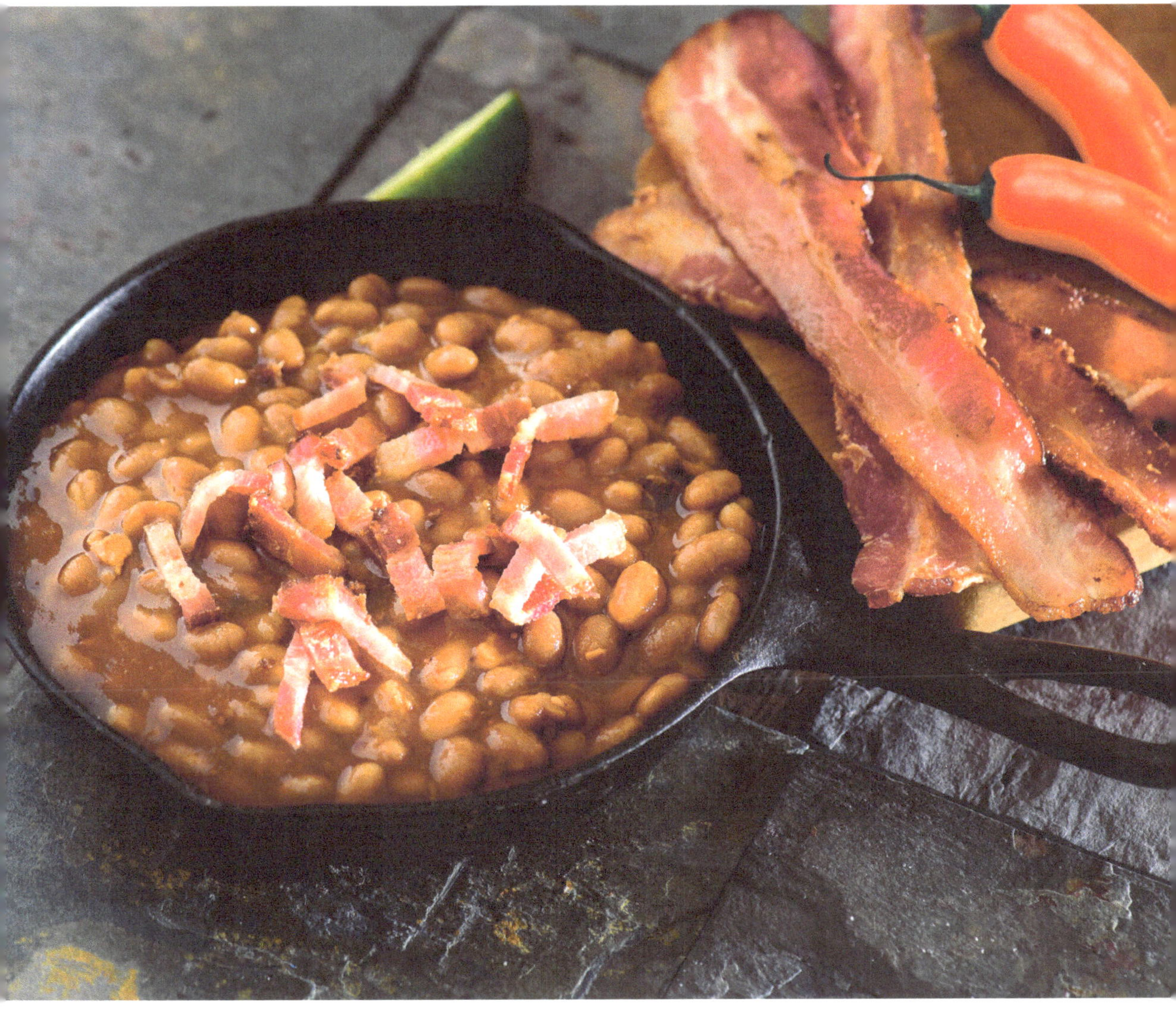

CREAMY POLENTA

Polenta a la Crema

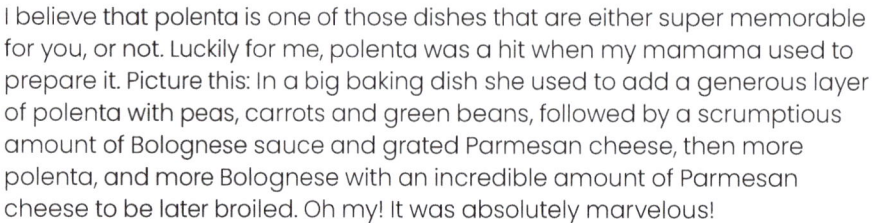

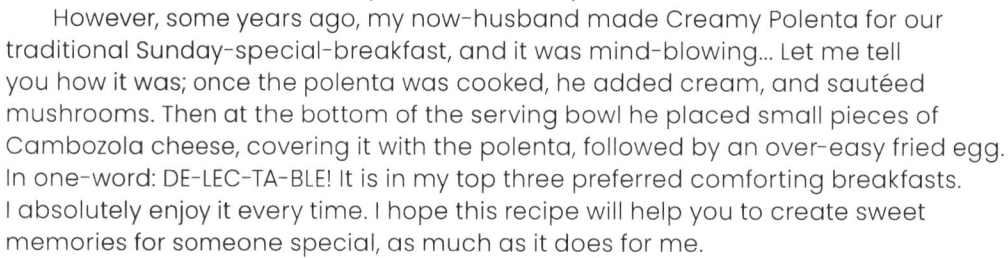

DAIRY

35'

4–6 SERVINGS

I believe that polenta is one of those dishes that are either super memorable for you, or not. Luckily for me, polenta was a hit when my mamama used to prepare it. Picture this: In a big baking dish she used to add a generous layer of polenta with peas, carrots and green beans, followed by a scrumptious amount of Bolognese sauce and grated Parmesan cheese, then more polenta, and more Bolognese with an incredible amount of Parmesan cheese to be later broiled. Oh my! It was absolutely marvelous!

However, some years ago, my now-husband made Creamy Polenta for our traditional Sunday-special-breakfast, and it was mind-blowing… Let me tell you how it was; once the polenta was cooked, he added cream, and sautéed mushrooms. Then at the bottom of the serving bowl he placed small pieces of Cambozola cheese, covering it with the polenta, followed by an over-easy fried egg. In one-word: DE-LEC-TA-BLE! It is in my top three preferred comforting breakfasts. I absolutely enjoy it every time. I hope this recipe will help you to create sweet memories for someone special, as much as it does for me.

Ingredients

6 cups low-sodium or unsalted chicken or vegetable broth/stock
1 teaspoon salt
1 cup dry polenta
½ cup heavy cream (or whipping cream)
2 tablespoons unsalted butter
½–1 cup freshly grated Parmesan cheese
Additional salt and finely ground black pepper to taste

Preparation

1. In a large saucepan, bring the broth and salt to a boil over high heat. Slowly (as in a gentle rain) pour the polenta into the boiling broth, whisking constantly until all the polenta is mixed in, and there are no lumps.
2. Reduce the heat to low and simmer, uncovered, whisking often, until the polenta begins to thicken, about 5 minutes. The polenta should still be slightly loose. Continue to simmer for 30 minutes, whisking every 3 to 5 minutes. The polenta is done when the texture is creamy, and the individual grains are tender.
3. When the polenta is cooked and thickened, add the cream and stir in well, to incorporate.
4. Turn off the heat and gently stir the butter into the polenta until the butter is partially melted; add the Parmesan cheese and stir in until thoroughly melted and incorporated; taste for salt and pepper, adding more if needed before plating into a serving bowl.

Note: Polenta is delicious on its own, topped with an additional dusting of grated Parmesan, and as a side or main dish complemented with many other additions: sautéed mushrooms; tomato sauce; a fried egg; gorgonzola or blue cheese; a good drizzle of truffle oil; Bolognese sauce; Ossobuco, or your favorite accompaniment.

GARDEN RICE
Arroz a la Jardinera

Colorful and packed with vegetables, this savory rice is garlicky and pillowy fluffy. It complements so many dishes, from stews, medleys, veggies and beans to roasted or grilled meats. Even with a humble fried egg, this rice is absolutely heavenly and will fulfill your carb cravings without inducing too much guilt. It not only tastes delicious, but looks bright and beautiful on your plate. And the turmeric adds a crazy-good anti-inflammatory bonus!

Ingredients

2 tablespoons vegetable oil
½ cup red onion finely diced
1 cup white Basmati rice
1 tablespoon minced garlic
1 teaspoon ground cumin
1 teaspoon ground turmeric
1 ½ teaspoons kosher salt
1 ½ cups vegetable stock or water
½ cup carrot finely diced (fresh or frozen)
½ cup corn kernels (fresh or frozen)
½ cup petite peas (fresh or frozen)

Preparation

1. Choose a pot that has a fitted lid, and preheat over medium heat. When hot, add oil and onion. Cook for about 5 minutes. Increase the burner heat to medium-high. Add the rice and the garlic, and cook for 1 minute.
2. Add the cumin, the turmeric and the salt; then, the water and the vegetables. The corn kernels, and carrots and the petite peas may be added frozen.
3. Bring to a full boil, turn the heat to low and cover the pot. Simmer for 20 minutes without opening the lid.
4. Remove the pan from the heat as soon as the rice has cooked. Let the rice rest in the covered pan for 10 minutes. Then, uncover and pluff the rice with a large fork.

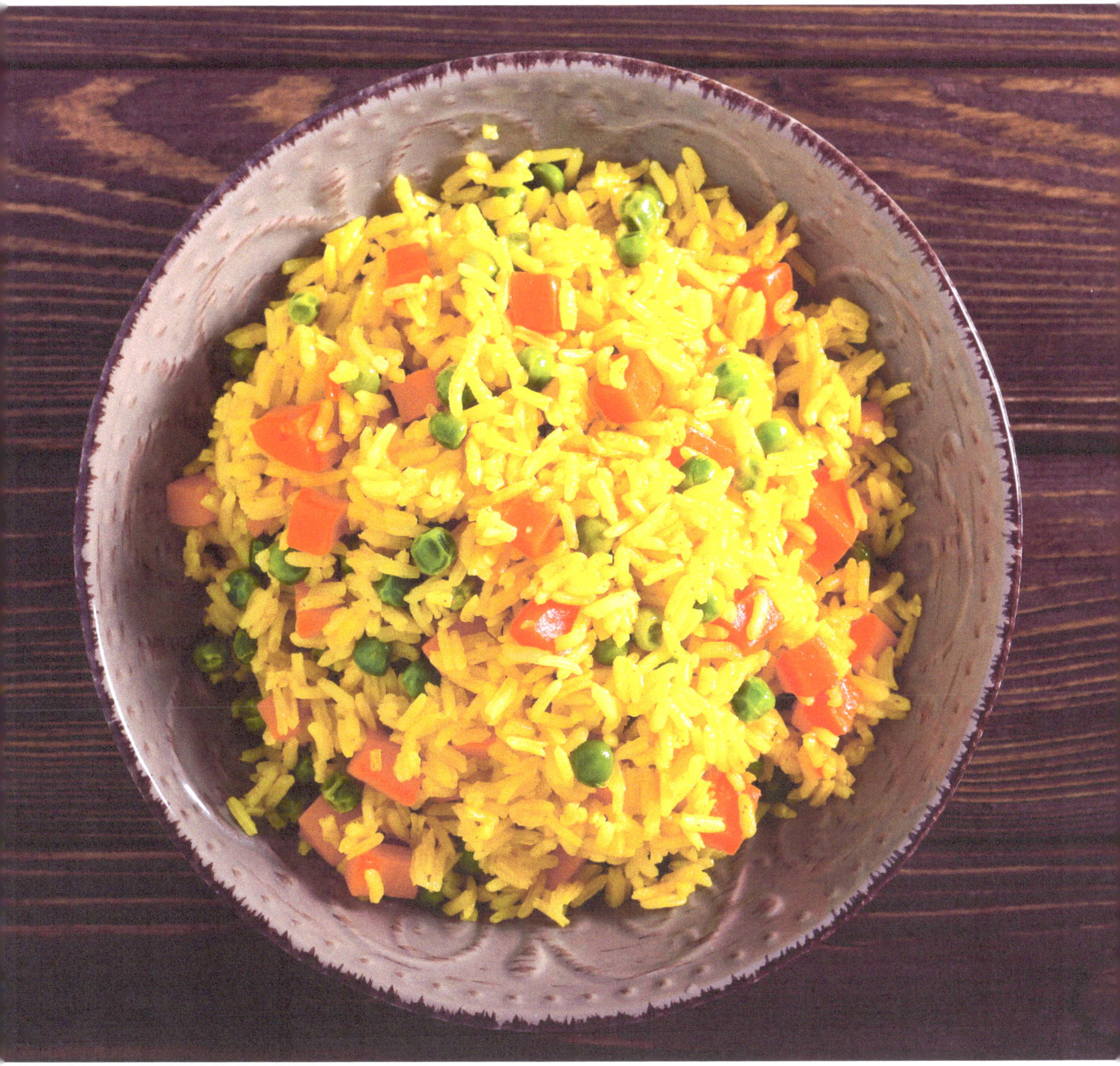

LENTILS
Lentejas

GLUTEN FREE · *120'* · *8 SERVINGS*

One of my traditional family beliefs, as in many other Peruvian households, was that if you eat lentils every Monday, you'll always be blessed by having money in the house.

This dish can be eaten unembellished, or paired with a piece of steak, a fish fillet, a fried egg, a side or garlicky rice, or some Onion Relish. Let your taste buds be your guide!

Ingredients

- ½ pound dried green lentils
- 1 pound mild Italian sausages, cut into half-inch rounds (or 1 pound diced bacon)
- Vegetable oil, if needed
- 1 red onion finely diced
- 3 tablespoons garlic paste, or minced and mashed garlic
- 1 tablespoon dried oregano
- 1 teaspoon ground cumin
- 1 cup tomato sauce
- 1 dried bay leaf
- Salt and pepper to taste
- 3 tablespoons extra-virgin olive oil

Preparation

1. Cover the lentils with cold water and soak for about 1 hour.
2. Just before the lentils finish soaking, preheat a Dutch oven, or large heavy-bottomed pot, over medium-high heat; sauté the sausage until golden brown. Remove the sausage from the pan and set aside, leaving the rendered sausage fat in the pan.
3. Reduce the heat to medium and add the onion to the fat in the pot. Sauté until golden brown, about 7 minutes.
4. Add the garlic and cook for about 1 minute. Next, add the tomato sauce, the cumin and the oregano, and cook for an additional couple of minutes.
5. Add the drained lentils to the pan with 3 cups of water, and bring to a boil. Reduce the heat to low and cook covered for 20–30 minutes, stirring occasionally, just until the lentils are tender. Then, season with salt and pepper, and drizzle with extra-virgin olive oil.

Note: This hearty lentil recipe can be enjoyed as a main dish or served as a side.

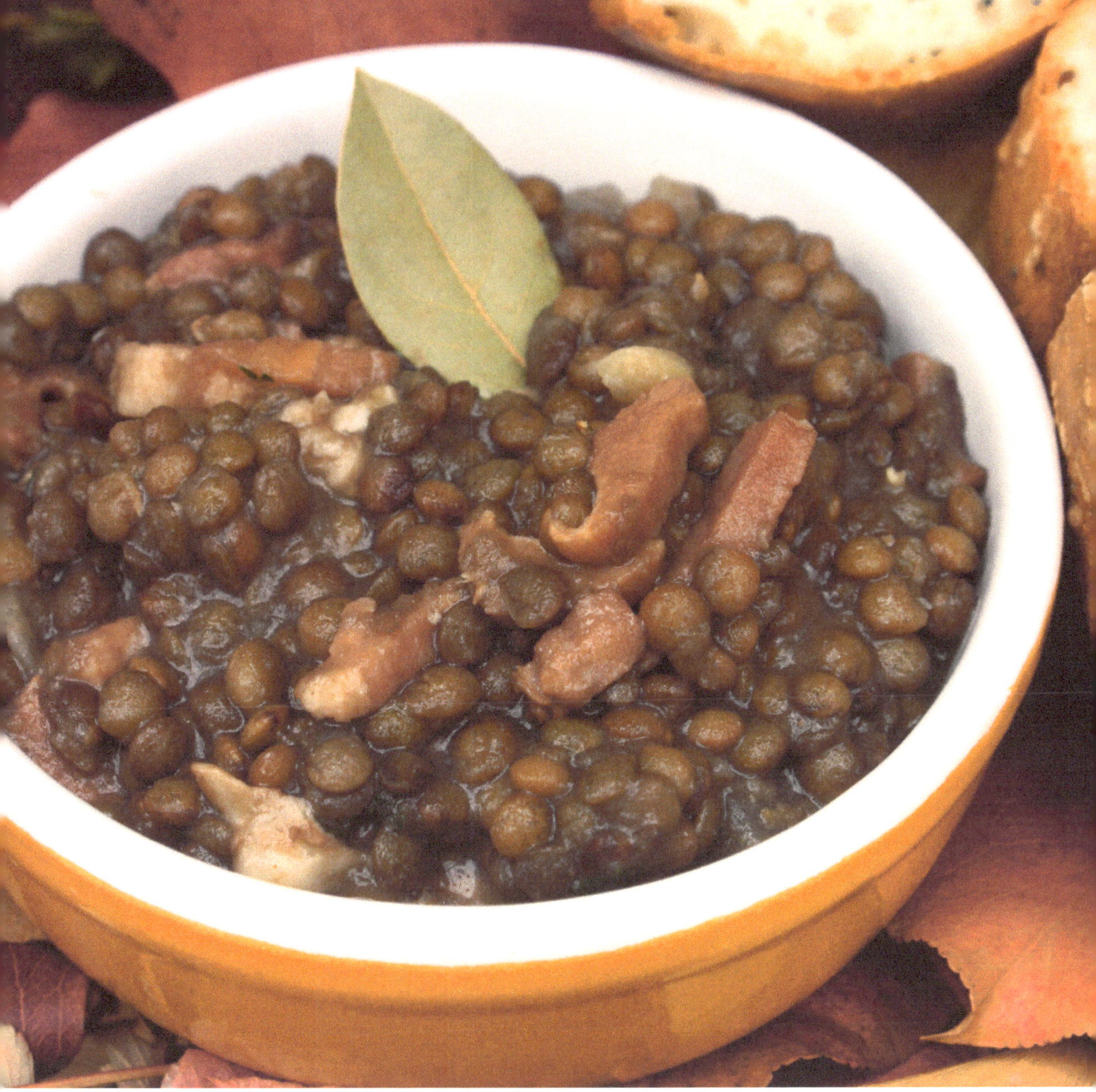

MASHED POTATOES WITH SPINACH

Puré de Papas con Espinacas

VEGETARIAN

45'

6 SERVINGS

For me, one of the most comforting things in the world is a good bowl of mashed potatoes. And if it has spinach, even better. This recipe is smooth, buttery, and fluffy. And if you are up to a little extra preparation, you can add some chopped, raw spinach for more texture. Either way, they are both comforting and tasty.

If you make patties, or roasted chicken, beef, or pork, this is a perfect and satisfying side dish.

Ingredients

1 ½ pounds potatoes (Russet or Yukon Gold), peeled and quartered
6 tablespoons butter
1 tablespoon minced fresh garlic
8–10 ounces fresh spinach
Salt and pepper
½–1 cup whole milk, heated
Pinch of nutmeg

Preparation

1. In a large pot, bring the potatoes to a boil in salted water. Lower the heat and simmer until fork-tender, but not falling apart.
2. While the potatoes are cooking, preheat a large sauté pan and add 3 tablespoons of butter and the garlic. Add the spinach, season with salt and pepper, and sauté for about 3 minutes, or until fully wilted.
3. When the spinach is cooked, transfer it to a blender with ½ cup of milk and the nutmeg. Purée and set aside.
4. Drain the potatoes and mash with a ricer until smooth. Add the puréed spinach mixture and the remaining 3 tablespoons butter. Mix together until the potatoes are moist and fluffy, adding more milk, if needed. Season with pepper, and additional salt if necessary.

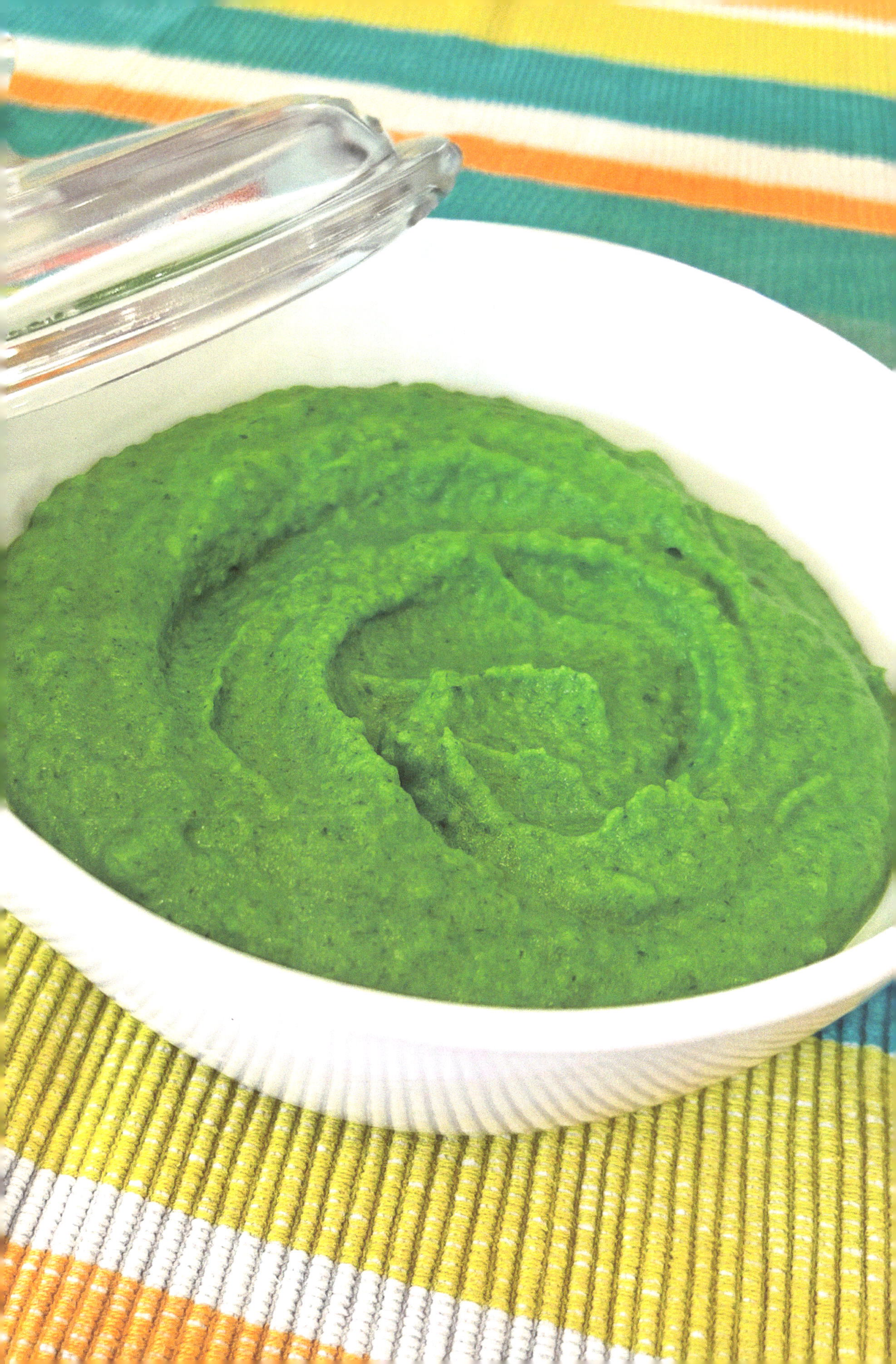

MASHED SWEET POTATOES

Puré de Camote

VEGETARIAN

50'

8 SERVINGS

One of my boys loves sweet potatoes in just about every kind of preparation, whether simply boiled, steamed, roasted, or as in this recipe, mashed. Like most kids, he has a sweet tooth and this hits the spot when I add maple syrup to it. He can eat it all, hot or cold! The warm notes of cinnamon and clove, fresh-citrus orange and rich maple syrup are the perfect companions to join this dish, and they meld beautifully. I like to add a pinch of salt towards the end. It doesn't just taste good—the smell is also so inviting... *Delicioso!*

Ingredients

3 cups orange juice
3 ½ pounds sweet potatoes, cut into large chunks
2 cinnamon sticks
6 cloves
3 tablespoons butter
¼ cup maple syrup
¼ teaspoon salt

Preparation

1. In a large pot with a cover, add the orange juice, the sweet potatoes chunks, the cinnamon and cloves, too. Cover and bring to a boil, then lower the temperature and let the sweet potatoes simmer for about 20 minutes, or until fork tender, but not falling apart.
2. Remove and discard the cloves and the cinnamon; add the butter, the maple syrup and the salt. Mash until smooth with a potato masher or ricer.
3. Transfer the mashed sweet potatoes to a casserole, or baking dish.

Note: If desired, top with candied pecans or walnuts. Alternatively, top with mini marshmallows and broil briefly until the marshmallows are glossy and browned.

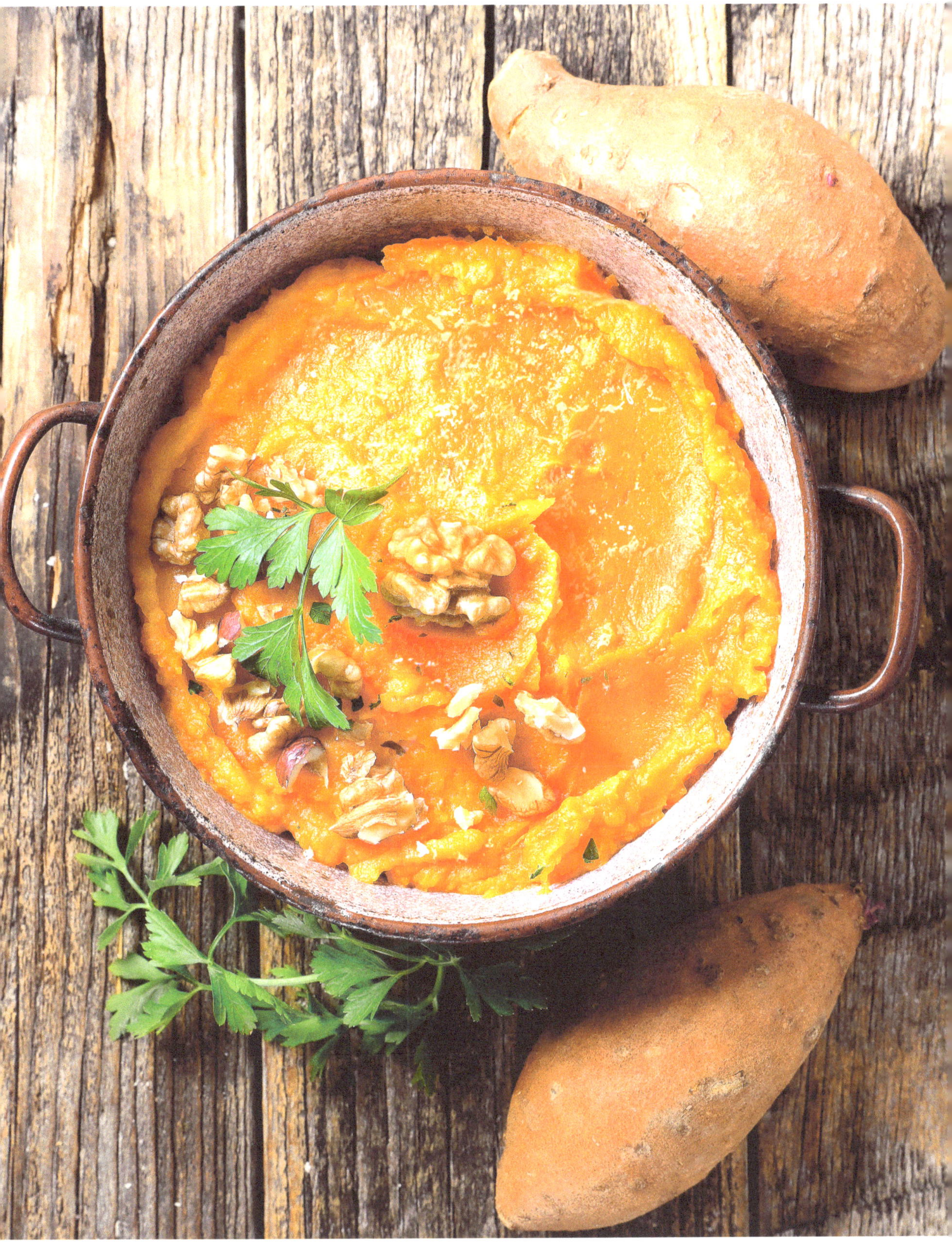

ORANGE GLAZED SWEET POTATOES

Camotes Glaseados con Naranja

VEGETARIAN

60'

10 SERVINGS

Good dishes are all about balanced flavors, and a sweet element often helps even the ratios. This sweet potato recipe is bright and invigorating. It could be served as a side to many dishes, or, as one of my kids does, eat this Orange Glazed Sweet Potatoes by itself.

It's almost effortless to make and it tastes great! Delicious and healthy! It complements nicely pork, ham, and turkey dishes. A great side dish for potlucks, holiday meals, and summer cookouts. Use fresh squeezed orange juice and it'll make a huge difference. It is always a hit!

Ingredients

6 medium-size sweet potatoes (about 4 pounds)
¼ cup firmly packed dark brown sugar
½ teaspoon orange zest
1 cup fresh orange juice or orange soda
2 tablespoons melted butter
¼ teaspoon kosher salt

Preparation

1. Preheat oven to 325 °F.
2. Peel sweet potatoes, and cut into 1 ½-inch-thick slices; arrange in a single layer in two lightly buttered 13 x 9 inches baking dishes.
3. Mix the brown sugar with the orange zest, the orange juice, the butter and salt; pour the sugar mixture over the sweet potato slices.
4. Cover the baking dishes with aluminum foil and bake at 325 °F for 45 minutes, or until the potatoes are fork-tender. Uncover and bake 5 more minutes or until the glaze becomes syrupy.

Note: To make ahead: Follow preparation steps 1 and 2 above. Cover and chill the cooked sweet potatoes up to one day ahead. To bake, let stand at room temperature 1 hour, then place it in the oven covered with foil, at 325 °F for 45 minutes.

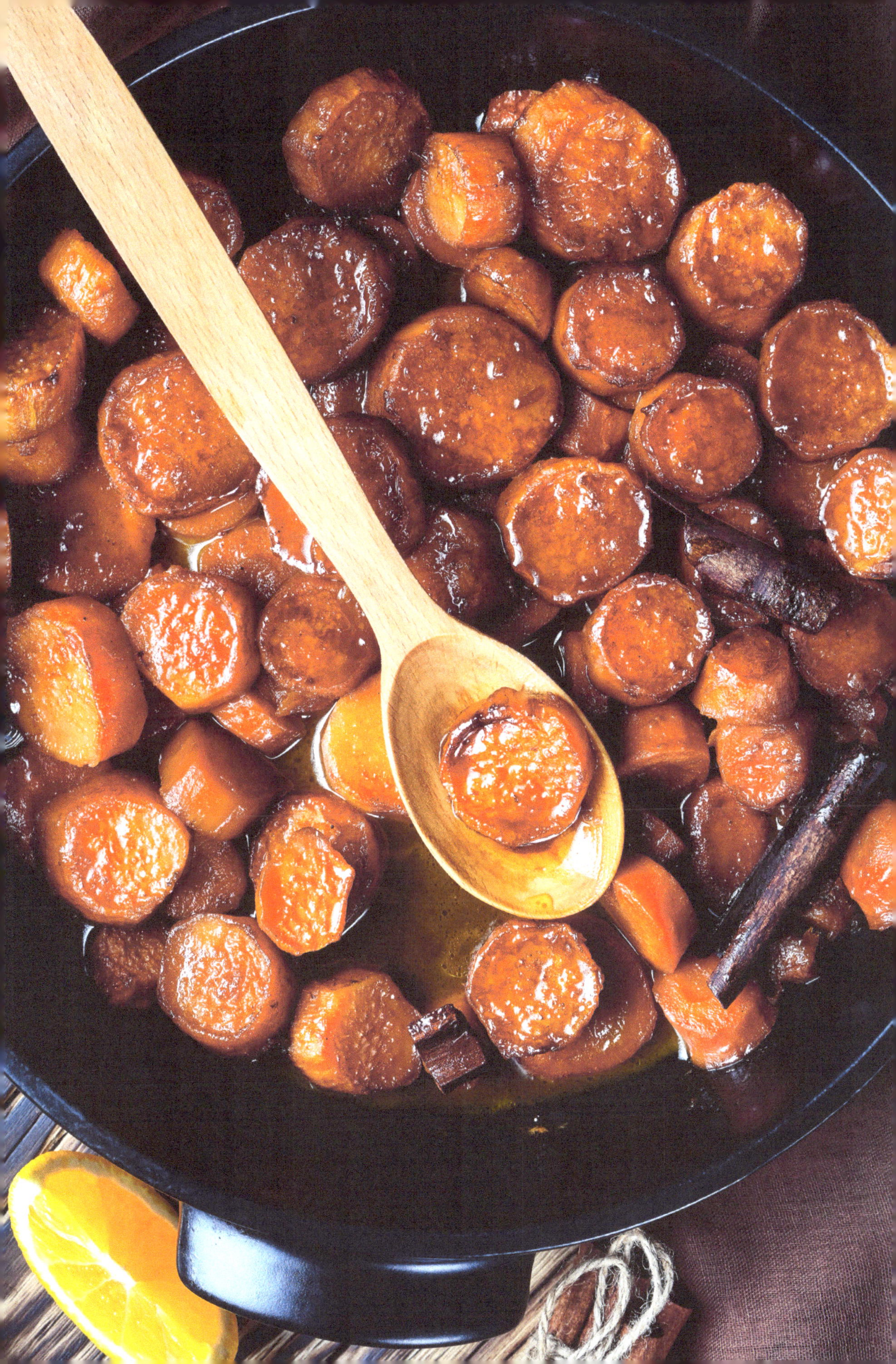

PECAN RICE CROWN

Corona de Arroz con Pecanas

Since the first time I made this crown, this impressive rice dish has been a must at our special celebrations and at Thanksgiving, Christmas and New Year meals.

My family loves rice dishes of all kinds, and this is a special one because of the sauce. Just imagine the flavors of a silky sauce made from pecans and Parmesan cheese. The presentation is also pretty and dramatic, with a sort of lava cake effect.

Just thinking of this rice crown makes me want one of those special festive days to come soon, or maybe this dish alone is reason enough to start a celebration!

Ingredients

For the Sauce
5 cups pecans
4 cups low-sodium chicken broth
2 tablespoons room temperature butter
1 ½ cup Parmesan cheese

For the Rice
3 tablespoons olive oil
5 cups jasmine rice
5 tablespoons garlic paste, or minced and mashed garlic
1 tablespoon sea salt
6 cups low-sodium chicken broth
2 tablespoons melted butter
2 tablespoons fresh, chopped parsley, to garnish the "crown"

Preparation

1. The day before making the rice, soak the pecans overnight in chicken broth and reserve.
2. Next day, in a large (4–5 quart) saucepan with a tight-fitting lid, heat the oil. Add the rice and stir constantly, until the rice just begins to turn opaque. Add the garlic and salt, and continue to cook, stirring, until the rice turns a deep white color. Briefly stir in the chicken stock and bring to boil. Reduce the heat, cover the pan with the lid and cook, undisturbed, for 20 minutes at a low simmer.
3. When the rice is done, remove the pot from the heat. Without removing the lid, let the rice rest in the pot for 10 minutes. Then, uncover and fluff the rice with a large fork.
4. While the rice is resting, pour the pecans and the chicken stock soaking liquid into a blender and purée until smooth.
5. Transfer the blended pecan mixture to a saucepan over medium heat; add 2 tablespoons of butter. When the mixture is heated and the butter is melted, turn off the heat and stir in the Parmesan cheese until completely incorporated.

To Mold
1. Coat the inside of the Bundt pan with 2 tablespoons of melted butter. Add the warm rice, distributing it evenly in the pan. With the back of a large spoon, press the rice firmly into the pan, evening out the surface, as the surface will become the base of the crown when the rice is un-molded.
2. To un-mold, invert the crown onto a rimmed serving platter deep enough to hold the sauce.
3. Pour the hot pecan sauce generously over the top of the crown, and into the center hole.
4. Garnish with fresh parsley.

Note: This festive and delicious dish makes an impressive addition to your special celebrations or holiday table.

PURPLE CORN RICE
Arroz Morado

This dish will give you the perfect reason to search for purple corn, make some Chicha Morada, and reserve some of the very concentrated purple liquid to make this recipe.

As I've already shared with you, Peruvians love rice in all its variety and versions, so we find this purple corn rice not only beautiful, but also delicious and unique. The nuttiness of the corn combined with onion, yellow hot pepper and garlic makes it a real treat.

Look for your closest Latin Market or search online, or even better, book a trip to Peru!

Ingredients

2 tablespoons vegetable oil, bacon fat or lard
½ yellow onion finely diced
1 tablespoon yellow hot pepper paste
2 tablespoons minced garlic
2 teaspoons salt
2 cups long-grain white rice
3 cups unsweetened Purple Corn Drink concentrate (see page 294, Cocktails & Drinks)
2 tablespoons extra-virgin olive oil

Preparation

1. In a sauté pan, or 3-quart pot, preheat the oil over medium heat. Add the diced onion and sauté until golden brown. Add the yellow hot pepper paste, the garlic and the salt; sauté for an additional minute.
2. Stir in the rice and the Purple Corn Drink concentrate. Bring to a boil, cover, and adjust to a low simmer for 20 minutes. Do not stir or remove the lid from the pot while the rice is cooking.
3. When the rice has finished cooking, remove the pan from the heat. Keep it covered for 10 minutes. Then fluff with a fork.

Note: Take advantage of the fact that you boiled purple corn to make a delicious Purple Corn Drink.

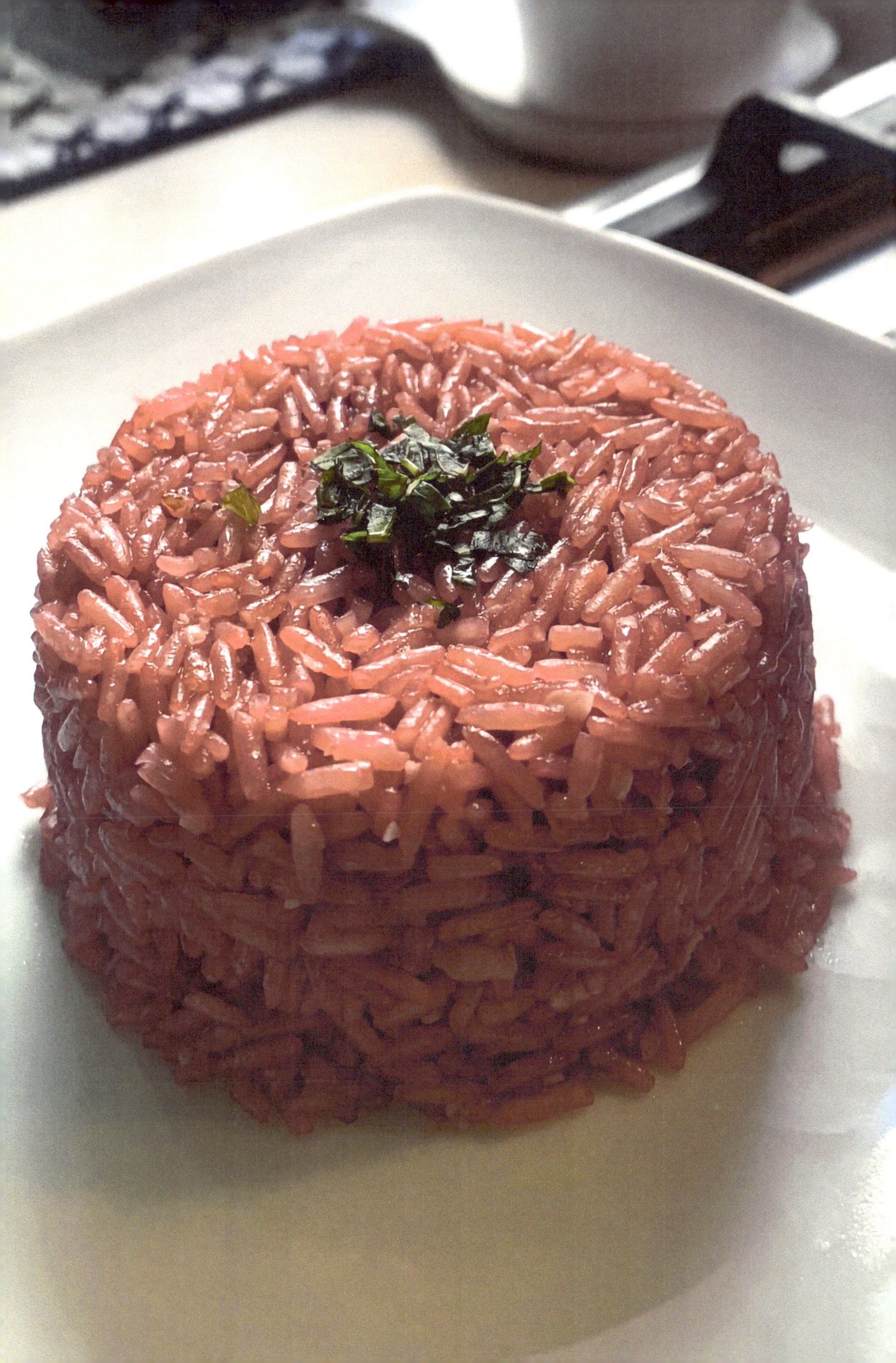

TURMERIC RICE

Arroz Amarillo (con Palillo)

VEGAN

35'

6–8 SERVINGS

Some time ago, a dear friend from school in Peru came to visit us with her husband and son, from the Dominican Republic. We love them all, they are super fun and good hearted.

We were talking about our Peruvian gastronomy, and he mentioned something that was actually very accurate. He said, "don't you guys get tired of the same white, boring-looking rice?" And since that moment, his comment got stuck in my mind. That's why sometimes I feel like my plate needs some color, and when that's the case I add a little bit of turmeric to my rice, it's not only going to make your rice look prettier, but also it will taste better, and as a plus it will help with any inflammation going around.

It's an easy way to add color to your rice, and life!

Ingredients

¼ cup vegetable oil
2 cups long-grain white jasmine or basmati rice
Salt to taste
2 tablespoons garlic paste, or minced and mashed garlic
2 teaspoons turmeric powder
2 ½ cups water

Preparation

1. In a large saucepan, heat the oil over medium heat, and add the rice and salt. Sauté the rice in the oil until it becomes an opaque, deep white color; add the garlic paste and sauté for about 1 minute.
2. Increase the heat to high and add the water and the turmeric powder; stir briefly, just to combine. As soon as the rice comes to a boil, reduce the heat and cover the pot with a tight-fitting lid. Let the rice simmer for 20 minutes, with the lid on. Do not remove or lift the lid while the rice is cooking!
3. After 20 minutes, remove the pot from the heat. Do not remove the lid. Keep covered and let the rice rest, undisturbed, for 10 minutes. Remove the lid, fluff the rice with a fork and enjoy!

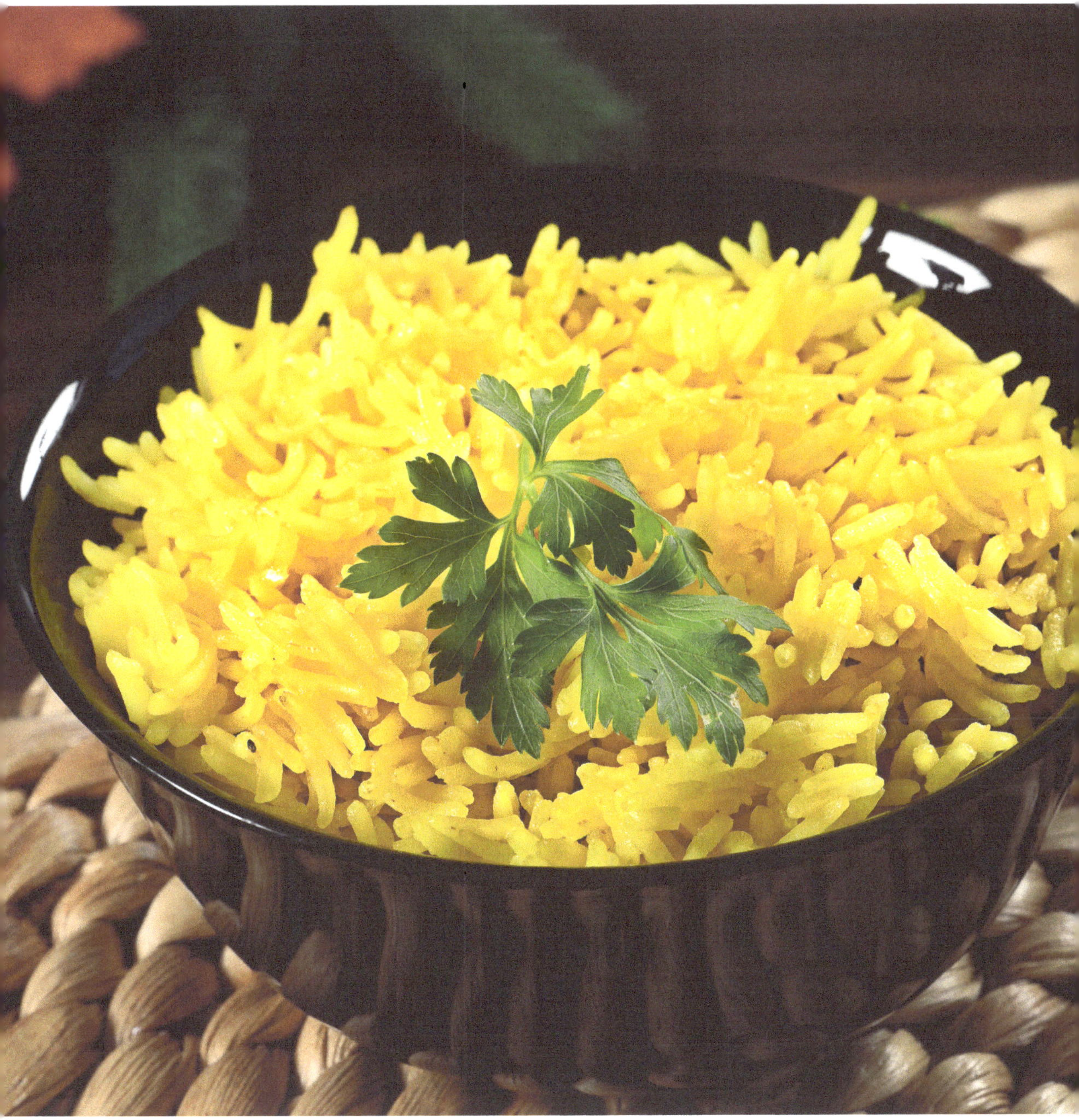

WHIPPED MASHED POTATOES

Puré de Papas Batido

DAIRY

45'

4-6 SERVINGS

Since I can remember, one of my favorite dishes has been mashed potatoes. Nothing compares to the authentic-native creaminess of the Papa Amarilla (yellow Peruvian potato). I must confess that when I was in Peru, in my apartment, I loved to eat Whipped Mashed Potatoes in a little bowl with a teaspoon. Its creamy texture made with ingredients such as butter and warm milk make this side dish one of the yummiest and most requested at home! Also it looks awesome served at the table!

Here is my recipe so you can delight and surprise all your family and friends.

Ingredients

2 ½ pounds Russets or Yukon Gold potatoes
¾ cup heated milk or half and half
½ cup unsalted butter, room-temperature
1 teaspoon finely minced garlic
¼ teaspoon mustard powder
Salt and pepper to taste

Preparation

1. Cut the potatoes into similar sized chunks and place them in a large pot; cover with water about 1 inch. Add salt and bring to a boil. Reduce the heat to a simmer and continue to cook until just fork-tender, but not falling apart.
2. Drain the potatoes and add the heated milk, the butter, minced garlic, mustard powder, salt and pepper.
3. Mash the potatoes with a potato masher until very smooth and fluffy, adding a little extra milk or half and half, if needed. If preferred, use an electric-hand-mixer for a smoother consistency, but be sure not to overbeat to avoid a gluey consistency.
4. Taste for seasonings, adding more salt and pepper, if needed.

Note: There are many optional ingredients you can add to Whipped Mashed Potatoes to make them taste even more amazing: Fresh greens: green onions, chives, thyme, parsley or rosemary.
Dairy: sour cream, crème fraîche, cream cheese, Parmesan, blue, cheddar.
Meat: Bacon, ham, pancetta.

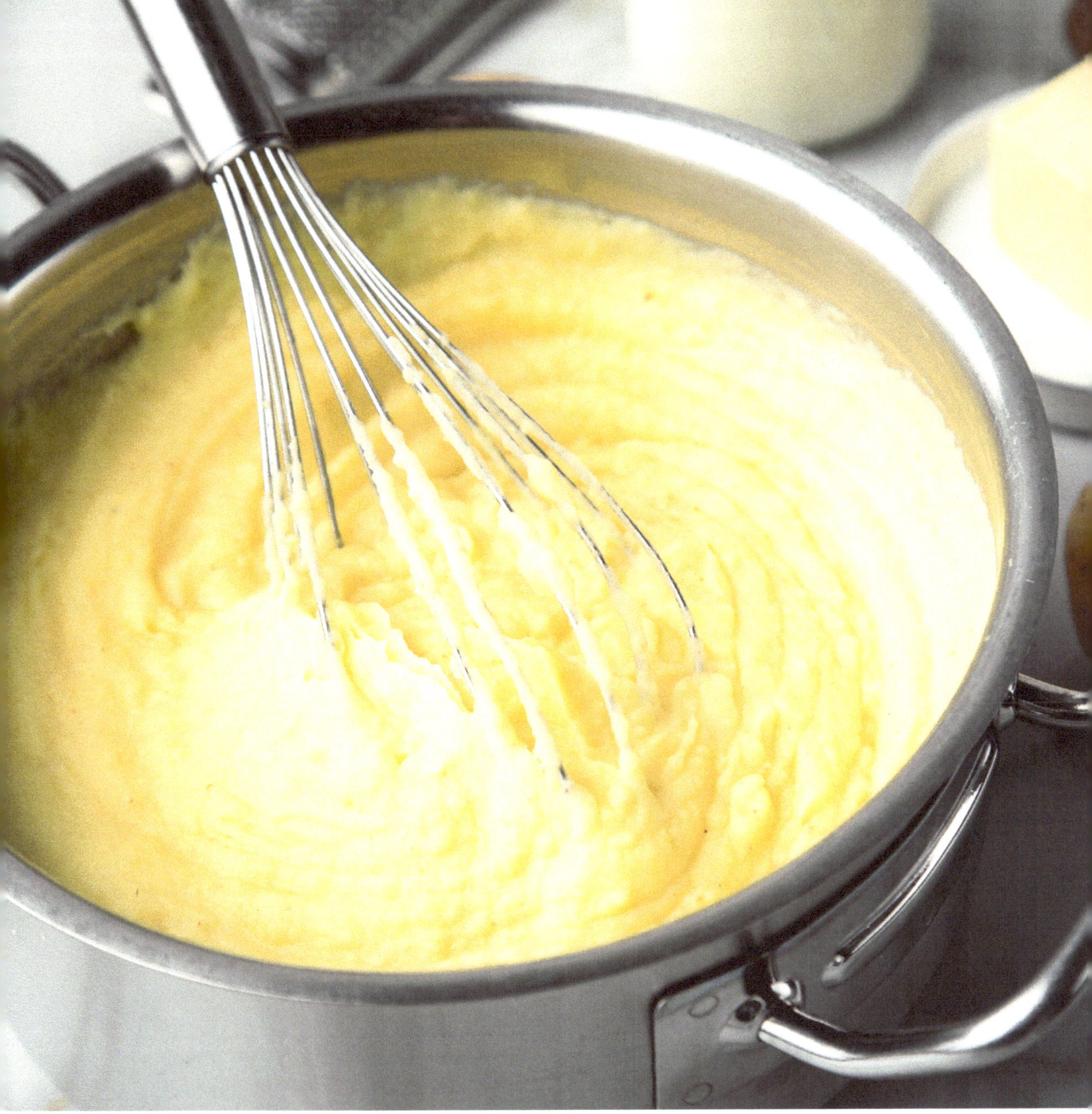

WHITE GARLICKY RICE
Arroz Blanco

GLUTEN FREE

35'

6–8 SERVINGS

My Tata loved rice so much! He used to come home for lunch, first he kissed my Mamama on her forehead, then off to freshen up, after which he quickly landed in the kitchen, grabbed a spoon, opened the pot of warm rice and started digging out generous spoonsfuls as quickly as possible. Until my Mamama asked him to leave the kitchen. On his way out, he would wink an eye at me, acknowledging that he was in a little bit of trouble…

There's nothing like a good side of *arroz graneado*, which means exactly the opposite of mushy rice. Most of our dishes are complemented with a generous portion of this magnificent—but never mushy—fluffy rice.

My personal reflection: Rice and a lot of Peruvian dishes are like best lovers together!

Ingredients

¼ cup vegetable oil
2 cups long-grain white basmati or jasmine rice
2 teaspoons salt
3 tablespoons garlic paste, or minced and mashed garlic
2 ½ cups water

Preparation

1. In a large saucepan, heat the oil over medium heat and add the rice and salt. Sauté the rice in the oil until it becomes an opaque, deep white color; add the garlic paste and sauté for about 1 minute.
2. Increase the heat to high and add the water; stir briefly, just to combine. As soon as the rice comes to a boil, reduce the heat and cover the pot with a tight-fitting lid. Let the rice simmer for 20 minutes. Do not be tempted to lift the lid while the rice is cooking!
3. After 20 minutes, remove the pot from the heat. Keep it covered and let the rice rest, undisturbed, for 10 minutes. Remove the lid, fluff the rice with a fork and enjoy!

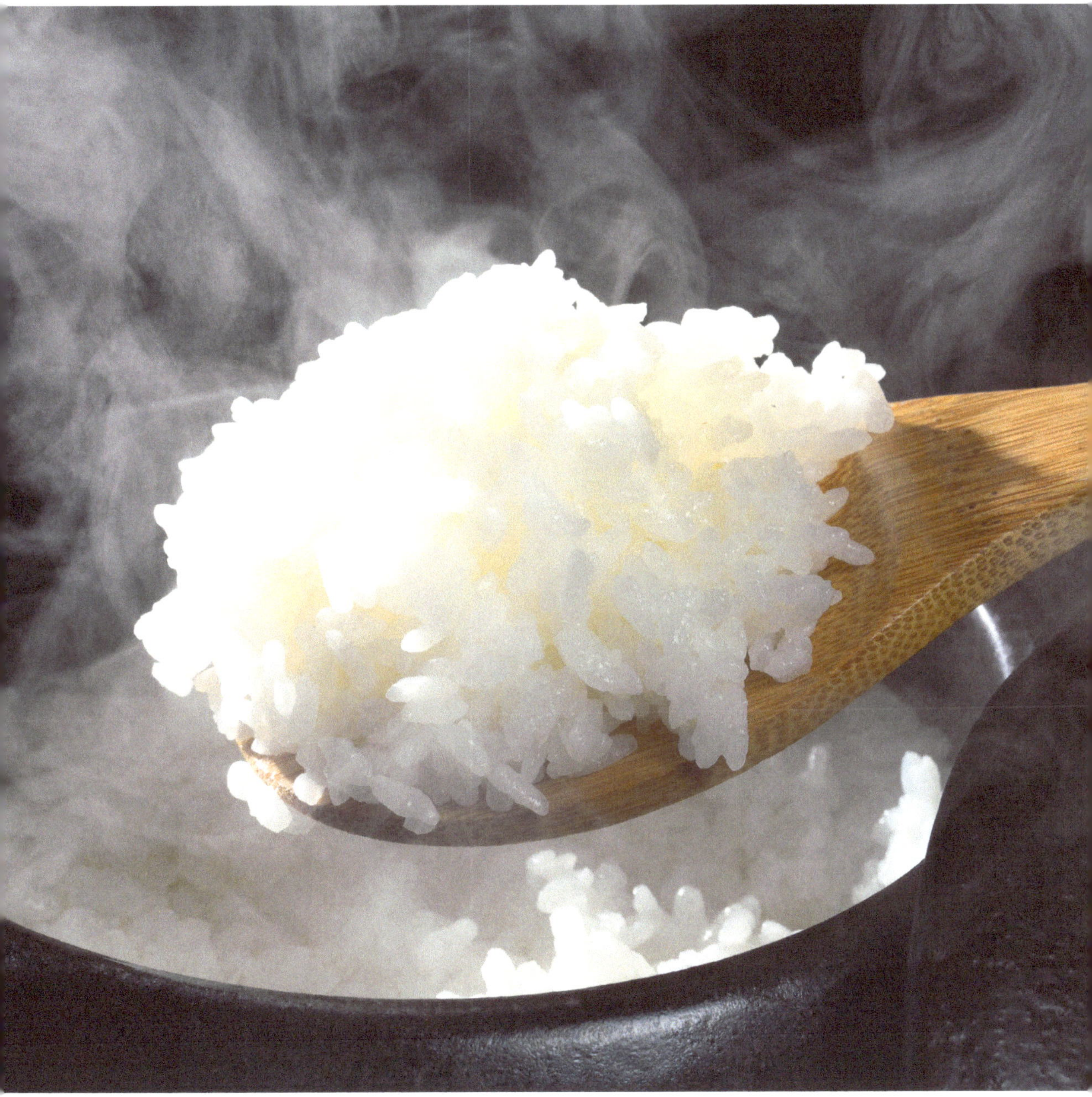

ANTICUCHERA SAUCE

Salsa Anticuchera

SPICY · 10' · 1 ¼ CUPS

Anticuchos, shish kebabs, brochettes. Around the world, there's a wide variety of meats cooked on sticks and skewers. This marinade is used to tenderize and season the meat, such as beef heart, beef, chicken, pork, seafood, either to grill, roast or pan fry. In Peru, Anticuchos are a popular street food that has now also been elevated to fine dining fare served in some of the best restaurants.

I love the Anticuchos in any of their forms. But the true star here is this potent and explosively flavorful marinade. And if you can find some Inca Kola® soda to go with your Anticuchos, mmm… even better!

Ingredients

½ cup Panca hot pepper paste
2 tablespoons garlic paste, or minced and mashed garlic
1 tablespoon soy sauce
1 tablespoon dried oregano
1 tablespoon ground cumin
½ cup vegetable oil
4 tablespoons red wine vinegar
Salt and pepper to taste

Preparation

Combine all the ingredients in a bowl and mix well.

Note: The Anticuchera Sauce is a marinade that pairs well with pork, chicken, beef and seafood, grilled, roasted or pan fried.

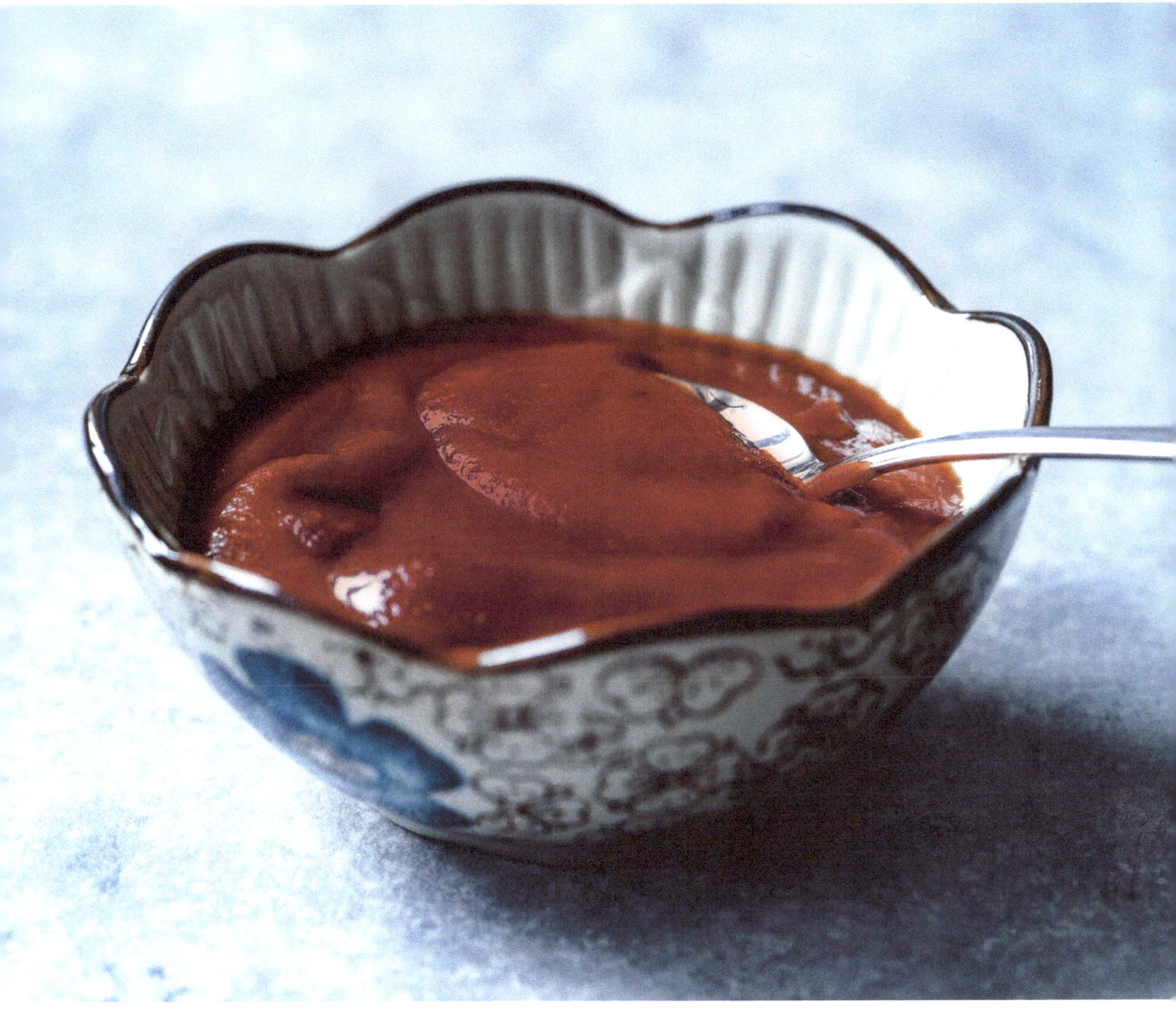

BLACK MINT SAUCE

Salsa de Huacatay

CONTAINS NUTS

25'

2 CUPS

With a unique mint-like flavour that can be difficult for some to identify, Huacatay (wah-ka-tie) or Peruvian black mint is an Andean herb, and the star of this flavor-packed, spicy green sauce. It's very popular in Peru, served as a dipping sauce to complement meats, rotisserie chicken, grilled proteins and vegetables, boiled, roasted, or fried potatoes, and many other dishes.

You can adjust the level of spiciness to your liking. This recipe is not very spicy, but you can add more yellow hot pepper if you really want to feel the heat.

If using frozen black mint leaves, the true flavor will develop and become more pronounced a few hours or the following day after you've made it. In my opinion this sauce is indispensable, and a keeper!

Ingredients

¼ cup vegetable oil, divided
3–5 yellow hot peppers, fresh or frozen
½ chopped shallot
¼ cup evaporated milk (unsweetened)
⅓ cup roasted and salted peanuts
¼ cup black mint leaves (available frozen in some Latin markets)
10 ounces Queso Fresco (Casero, or Cotija), cut into cubes
Pinch of salt
2–4 saltine crackers, if needed*

*If the sauce is not as thick as you'd like, blend in 2–4 saltine crackers, one a time, until the sauce reaches your desired consistency.

Preparation

1. Remove the stems from the yellow hot peppers. Discard the stems and cut the peppers into chunks. If frozen, there's no need to defrost.
2. Heat a sauté pan over medium heat and add 2 tablespoons of the oil. When hot, add the yellow hot pepper chunks and the shallot, sauté for about 5 minutes.
3. When cooked, transfer the sautéed vegetables to a blender. Add the evaporated milk, the peanuts, the black mint leaves and blend until very smooth. Next, add the Queso Fresco; when incorporated, remove the smaller center blender cover, and with the blender still running, slowly add the oil in a stream. Blend until the sauce is silky. Taste for salt, and add if needed.
4. Use immediately or store in a glass jar with a lid and refrigerate up to 5 days.

Note: Use as a dipping sauce for French fries or sweet potato fries, fried yuca, chicken, grilled vegetables, crudités, and as a garnish for pumpkin soup, or butternut squash soup.

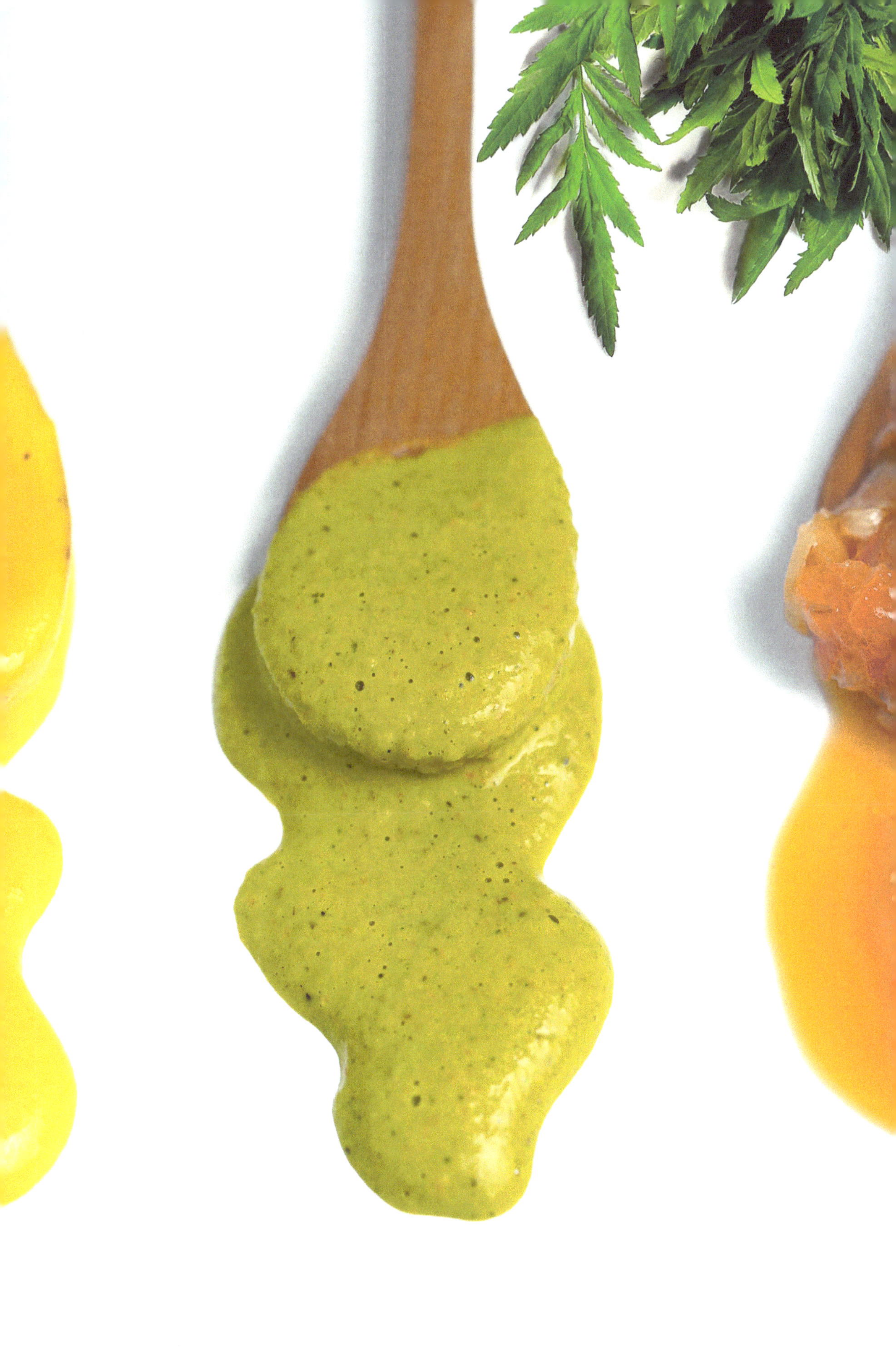

GARLIC PASTE

Pasta de Ajo

Garlic paste played an essential role in my grandparents' kitchen, where it was always stored in the refrigerator, in its own special container, with its own designated spoon. It was nothing fancy, just a simple thick, plastic container, jade green with a white lid, joined by its sidekick plastic spoon. But without garlic, we would have been wandering in a culinary desert.

My Mamama always had a kettle with boiling water on her stove, and another thing that had to be available at all times was this jar of garlic paste. Why? Well, because when you cook every day and most of your dishes require garlic, you can abbreviate the prep time by having garlic paste at hand, with no need to mince.

Before becoming a mother, I used to mince my garlic whenever I needed or wanted to cook, but now, I have to cook daily, so it's imperative that I have my garlic paste handy. Its practical, and I don't have to think twice before cooking, because it's always ready to be used, which in my case is generously!

Ingredients

2 cups peeled garlic cloves
½ cup vegetable oil
1 tablespoon salt

Preparation

1. Place all the ingredients in a food processor.
2. Pulse, pulse, pulse, until the mixture reaches your desired consistency (from finely minced to purée texture).
3. Transfer the garlic paste to a glass jar with a lid and store in the refrigerator, where it will last for about 2 weeks.

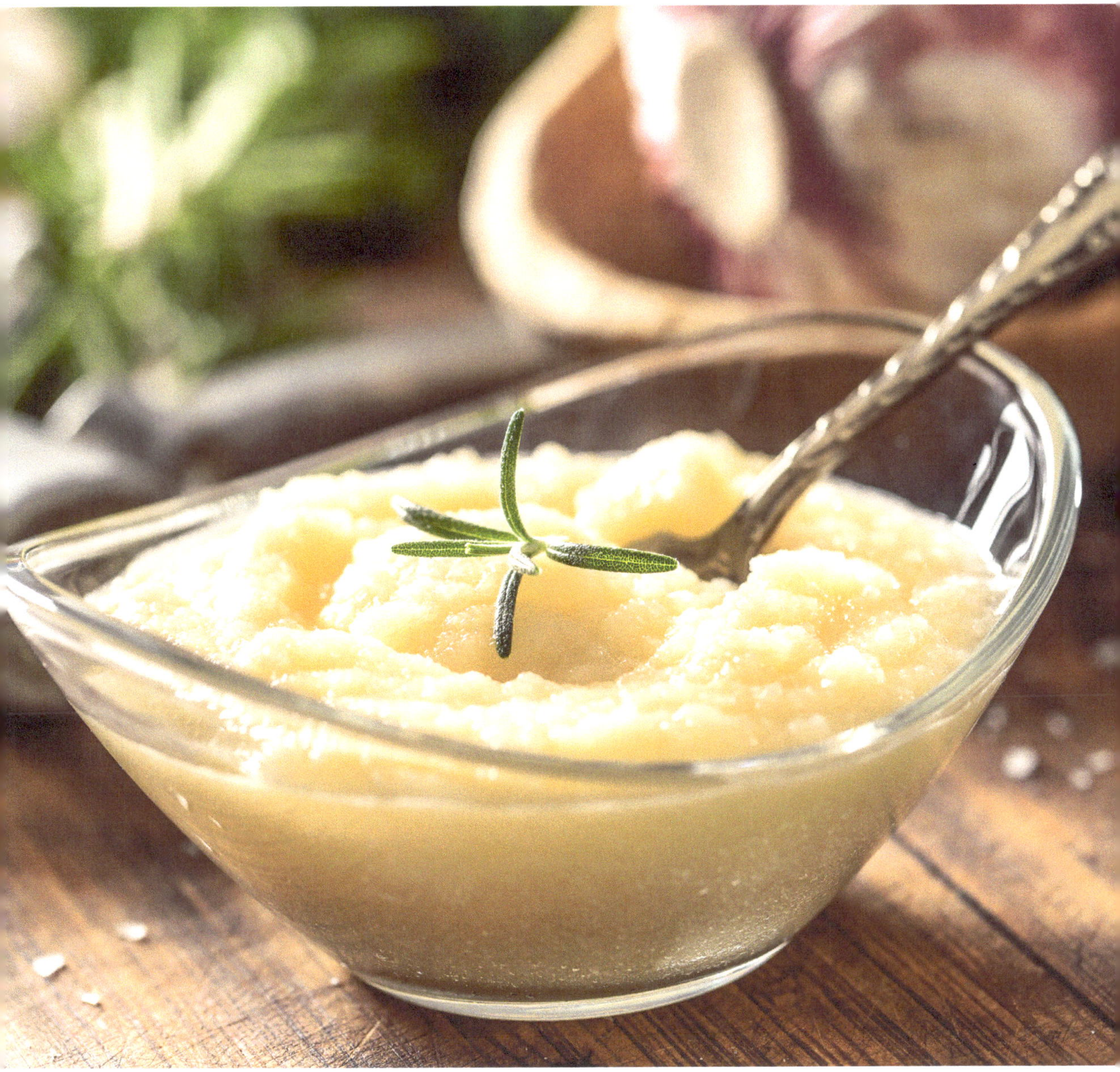

GOLF SAUCE
Salsa Golf

There are several recipes for Golf sauce, but it is mostly always mayonnaise with ketchup and a few other ingredients. Mine gets a little kick from a bit of brandy and a grating of fresh orange zest which makes it very aromatic, and complements the sweetness of prawns and shrimp.

This is a pink and silky sauce that is a pleasure to enjoy with our "adopted" Shrimp Cocktail. It's a showstopper, and all the elements complement each other: the shrimp, the avocado, and the Golf sauce are a delicate, sweet, savory gift to the senses.

Ingredients

1 cup mayonnaise
½ cup ketchup
2 teaspoons Worcestershire sauce
¼ cup chopped capers
1 orange zest
2 teaspoons brandy (optional)

Preparation

1. In a bowl, stir together the mayonnaise and the ketchup.
2. Add the Worcestershire sauce, chopped capers, orange zest and brandy (if using), and mix in until well combined.
3. Cover the sauce and keep it refrigerated.

Note: This Golf sauce is best when made a day in advance, allowing the flavors to marry. It is the traditional sauce used for the Shrimp Cocktail (see page 38, Appetizers).

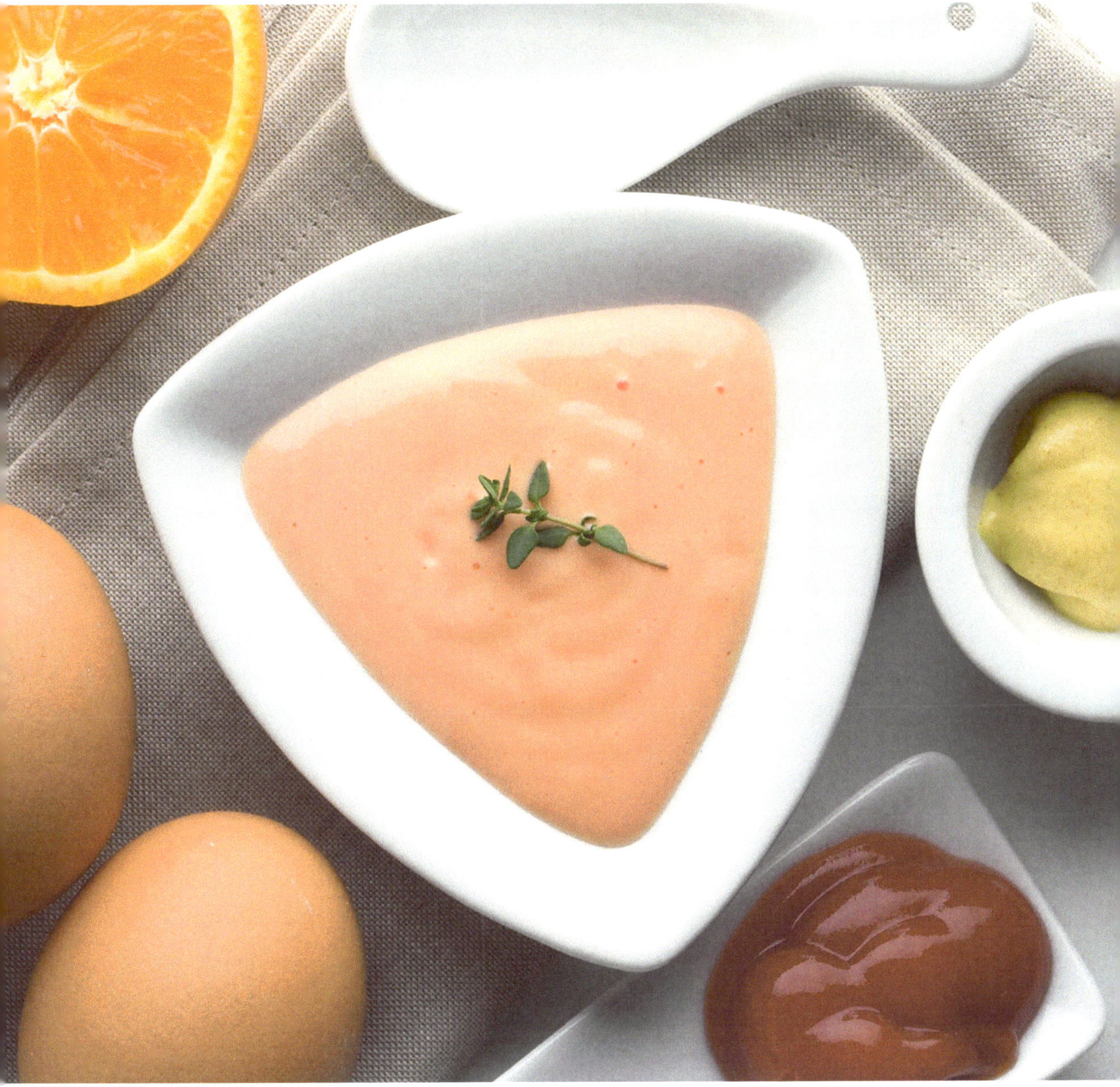

OLD FASHIONED HUANCAINA SAUCE

Salsa a la Huancaína de Antaño

SPICY

30'

2 CUPS

When you blend fresh yellow hot peppers, Queso Fresco, milk and *sofrito* you'll get a silky, spicy, savory sauce with which to bathe warm slices of potatoes, or to eat with tender corn on the cob, or to toss with pasta... the tasty possibilities are endless.

Originally from the beautiful Andean town of Huancayo, this easy recipe is a staple sauce you can find throughout Peru. Its unctuous texture and spicy yet mellow flavor will win you over!

A little bit of advice: if you really want to get the best, most authentic results with this recipe, please try to find the correct Peruvian ingredients. It's not the same with feta cheese or cream cheese, or habaneros, or jalapeños. I beg you—no, no, no!

And if you have a little bit of trouble with the pronunciation, and you want to say it like a Peruvian, let me help you here. Do you remember the film "Willy Wonka and the Chocolate Factory"? Well, Huancaina is pronounced like /Wonka-yina/.

Ingredients

¼ cup vegetable oil, divided

3–5 yellow hot peppers, fresh or frozen

¼ cup roughly chopped red onion

2 whole garlic cloves, peeled, or 1 teaspoon minced garlic

½ cup evaporated milk (unsweetened)

10 ounces Queso Fresco (Casero or Cotija) cut into chunks

Pinch of salt

2–4 saltine crackers, if needed*

*If the sauce is not as thick as you'd like, blend in 2–4 saltine crackers, one a time, until the sauce reaches your desired consistency.

Preparation

1. Remove the stems from the yellow hot peppers. Discard the stems and cut the hot pepper into chunks. If frozen, there's no need to defrost.
2. Heat a sauté pan over medium heat, and add 2 tablespoons of oil. When the oil is hot, add the yellow hot pepper chunks and the onions and sauté until golden brown. Next add the garlic for an additional minute.
3. When cooked, transfer the sautéed vegetables to a blender; add the milk and blend until very smooth. Next, add the Queso Fresco; when the cheese is incorporated, remove the smaller center blender cover, and with the blender still running, slowly add the remaining oil in a thin stream. Blend until the sauce is silky. Taste for salt, and add if needed.
4. Use immediately or store in a glass jar with a lid and refrigerate, for up to 5 days.

Note: This versatile recipe can be used as a dipping sauce for Fried Yuccas (see page 22, Appetizers), Wonton Pockets (see page 50, Appetizers), French fries, sweet potato fries and crudités. It also makes a deliciously creamy, spicy pasta sauce or a flavorful complement to grilled meats and fried fish.

ONION RELISH
Sarza Criolla

In Peru, this salad, or relish, is traditionally made with thinly sliced red onions, fresh yellow hot pepper, parsley, cilantro and lime juice.

The key to making the best Onion Relish is to soak the sliced onions in cold water with salt, and then rinse them thoroughly under cold water. This process tones down the sharp onion flavor (sulfuric acid) and will make them more mellow and pleasant on the palate.

We enjoy this relish as a side or garnish in many, many dishes, such as Adobo Pork Stew, Beef Cilantro Stew, beans, seafood, or sandwiches, to name just a few. The citrusy-spicy-crunchy elements of the relish complements either earthy or fish dishes. It will wake up so many of your favorite foods—please give it a try!

Ingredients

2 red onions, sliced in very thin half moons (Julienne)
1–2 yellow hot peppers (depending on size), fresh or frozen (if using frozen, defrost partially)
2 tablespoons chopped cilantro or parsley, or both
½ cup fresh lime juice
Salt and pepper to taste

Preparation

1. Slice the onions and soak in cold salted water, for 10 minutes.
2. While the onions are soaking, seed and slice the yellow hot peppers into very thin matchsticks.
3. Using a sieve, drain the onions well, removing as much liquid as possible. Transfer the onions to a bowl and stir in the remaining ingredients.
4. Let it rest for 3 minutes and serve!

Note: This Onion Relish is also the perfect accompaniment for rich meat dishes like Adobo Pork Stew (see page 128, Main Courses), Beef Cilantro Stew (see page 130, Main Courses) or Crispy Pork Belly (see page 150, Main Courses). Also for seafood and sandwiches.

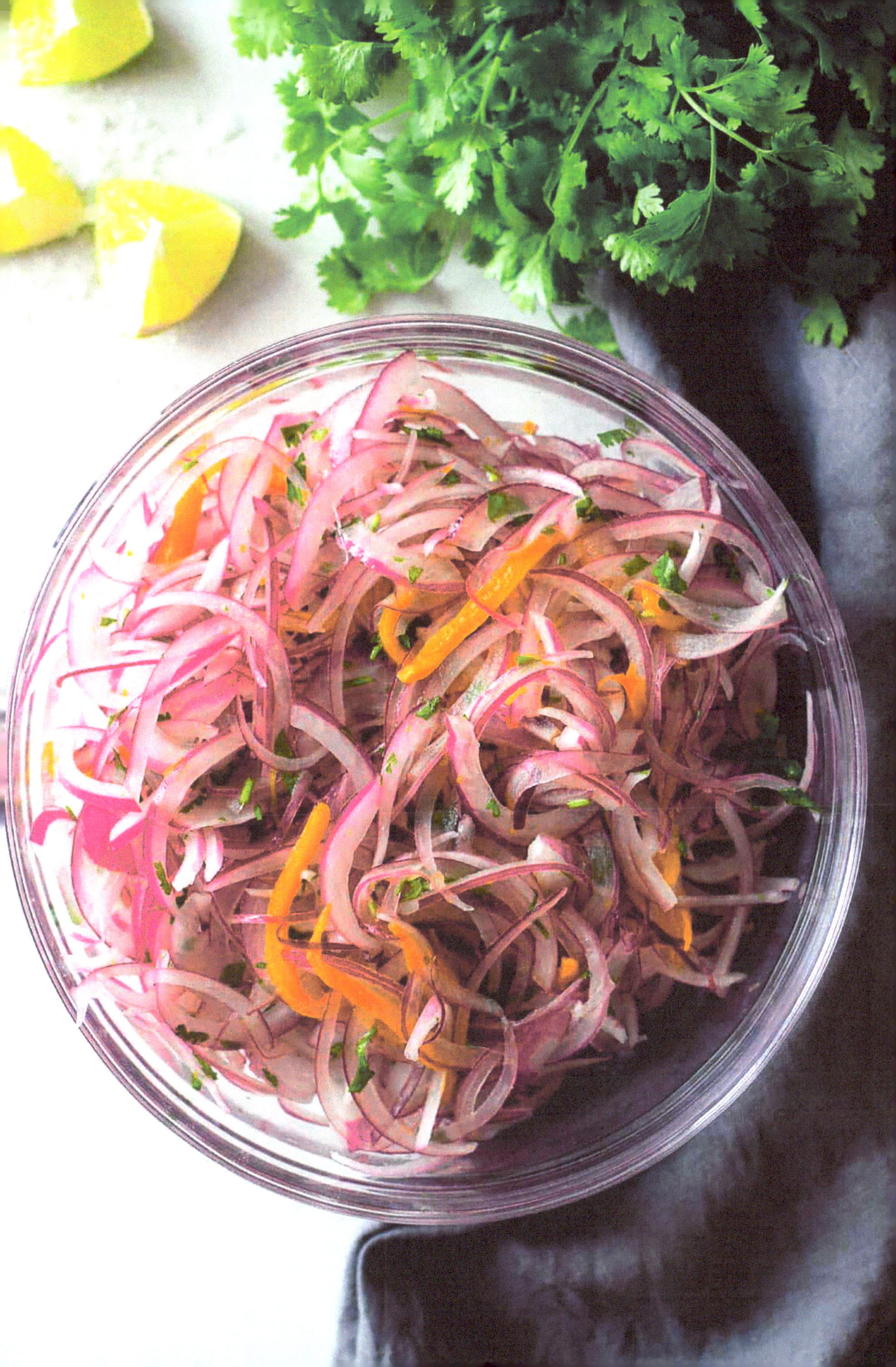

QUICK HUANCAINA

Salsa Huancaína

SPICY • *20'* • *2 CUPS*

We've all been in a situation where we don't have all the time in the world to cook, right? So, I offer this quick and simple version of Peru's unique and famous Huancaina Sauce. You just combine all the ingredients in a blender, whizz it up, and done! It doesn't require the *sofrito* from the traditional, old fashioned version, and it will give you that creamy, spicy, cheesy dip that you are craving. It's simple, and you can have it ready in 5 minutes!

Ingredients

3–5 yellow hot pepper, fresh or frozen
½ cup evaporated milk (unsweetened)
10 ounces Queso Fresco (Casero or Cotija) cut into chunks
¼ cup vegetable oil
Pinch of salt
2–4 saltine crackers, if needed*

*If the sauce is not as thick as you'd like, blend in 2–4 saltine crackers, one a time, until the sauce reaches your desired consistency.

Preparation

1. Remove the stems from the yellow hot peppers. Discard the stems and cut the hot peppers into chunks.
2. In a blender, process the yellow hot pepper chunks with the milk for about 2 minutes or until well incorporated.
3. Add the cheese and blend for about 1 minute, or until smooth. When it is fully incorporated, remove the smaller center blender cover, and with the blender still running, slowly add the oil in thin stream. Blend until the sauce is silky. Taste for salt, and add if needed.
4. Use immediately or store in a glass jar with a lid and refrigerate for up to 5 days.

Note: This versatile recipe can be used as a dipping sauce for Fried Yuccas (see page 22, Appetizers), Wonton Pockets (see page 50, Appetizers), French fries, sweet potato fries and crudités. It also makes a deliciously creamy spicy pasta sauce, or a flavorful complement to fried fish.

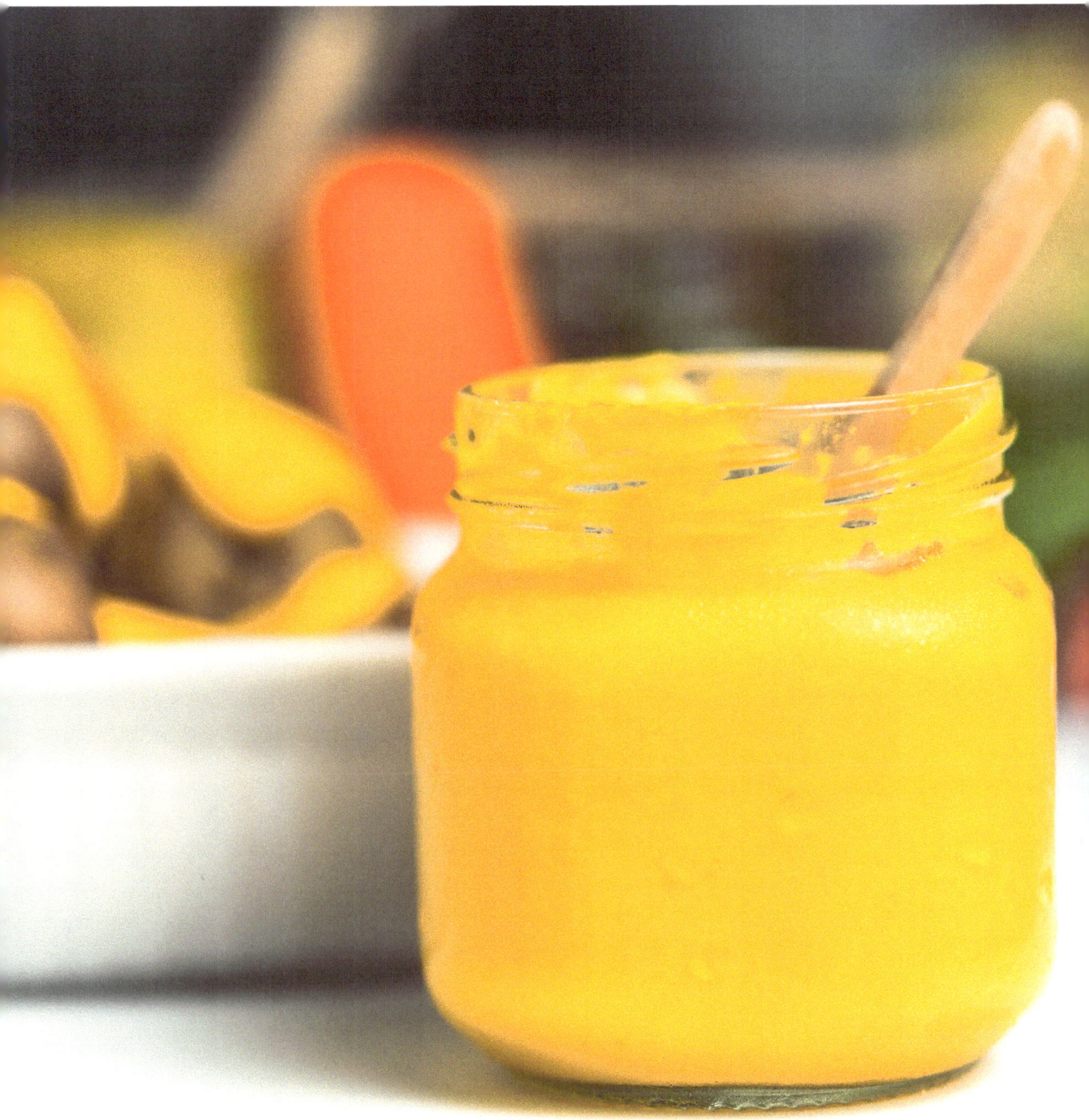

ROCOTO SAUCE

Salsa de Rocoto

SPICY

20'

2 CUPS

When I was teaching a class at a cooking school, I wanted to share this recipe with the students. I began by explaining that Rocoto is from Peru and may resemble a red bell pepper or a tomato in shape, but that it's truly one pungent-packed hot pepper full of surprises. Then, I gave them the recipe, and started guiding them through the process, beginning by telling them to be sure to wear gloves while removing the Rocoto stems and seeds.

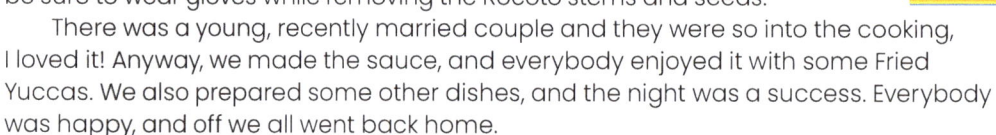

There was a young, recently married couple and they were so into the cooking, I loved it! Anyway, we made the sauce, and everybody enjoyed it with some Fried Yuccas. We also prepared some other dishes, and the night was a success. Everybody was happy, and off we all went back home.

The following day around noon my phone rang, and there was a timid voice asking for me: "Hi Chef, you remember we were in your class yesterday? Well, we're having a little situation here." I was so worried! "Yes," I said, "tell me what's going on?" The timid voice replied, "Well, my husband and I were working on the Rocoto sauce and his hands are still burning and we don't know what to do." I took a deep breath and asked: "Did he wear gloves?" With an almost imperceptible voice she answered, "No." "Well, "I said, "did he wash his hands after he worked with the Rocotos?" And she started laughing like crazy. The poor guy! I felt so bad for him that I shared with her all my tricks to get rid of the burning.

The question for you my friend is, can you imagine what happened that night? I can! So, don't let that happen to you! Practice safe hot peppering and always wear gloves!

Ingredients

2 Rocoto hot peppers
2 tablespoons vegetable oil
2 small shallots roughly chopped
1 teaspoon garlic paste, or minced and mashed garlic
½ cup evaporated milk (unsweetened)
½ teaspoon salt
10 ounces Queso Fresco (Casero or Cotija) cut into cubes
¼ cup extra-virgin olive oil

Preparation

1. Remove and discard the stems, seeds and veins of the Rocoto and cut in chunks.
2. Heat the vegetable oil in a skillet over medium heat; sauté the Rocoto and the shallot for about 3 minutes. Add the garlic and cook for another minute.
3. Transfer the sautéed Rocoto and aromatics to a blender; add the milk and the salt and pulse for about 2 minutes, or until well incorporated.
4. Add the cheese and blend for about 1 minute or until smooth. When it is fully incorporated, remove the smaller center blender cover, and with the blender still running, slowly add the oil in a thin stream. Blend until the sauce is silky.

Note: This spicy, silky sauce is perfect for dipping Fried Yuccas (see page 22, Appetizers), Wonton Pockets (see page 50, Appetizers), French fries, sweet potato fries and crudités. It also makes a flavorful complement to grilled vegetables, poultry, meat and fish.

STREET HOT PEPPER SAUCE

Ají Carretillero

SPICY

15'

1 ½ CUPS

Peruvians are very resourceful and creative. As in many countries, there are street food vendors whose food is prepared, carried, and served in *carretillas*—small carts equipped with all that is needed.

The Ají Carretillero sauce is a zesty addition to many of your favorite dishes, such as rotisserie chicken, brochettes, Anticuchos, in any of its varieties, grilled meats or vegetables, a good sandwich, you name it. It will spice up your game for sure!

Ingredients

3 Rocoto hot peppers
2 tablespoons vegetable oil
1 teaspoon salt
1 teaspoon lime juice
Pinch of ground cumin
2 whole garlic cloves
2 tablespoons minced parsley
¼ cup finely chopped green onions
¼ cup finely diced red onion

Preparation

1. Remove the stems and seeds from the Rocoto hot peppers, cut into rough chunks.
2. In a blender, process the chunks with the oil, salt, lime juice, cumin and garlic, until smooth.
3. Transfer to a bowl and mix in the parsley and the green and red onions.
4. Refrigerate until ready to use.

Note: This sauce makes a lively accompaniment for grilled meats or vegetables.

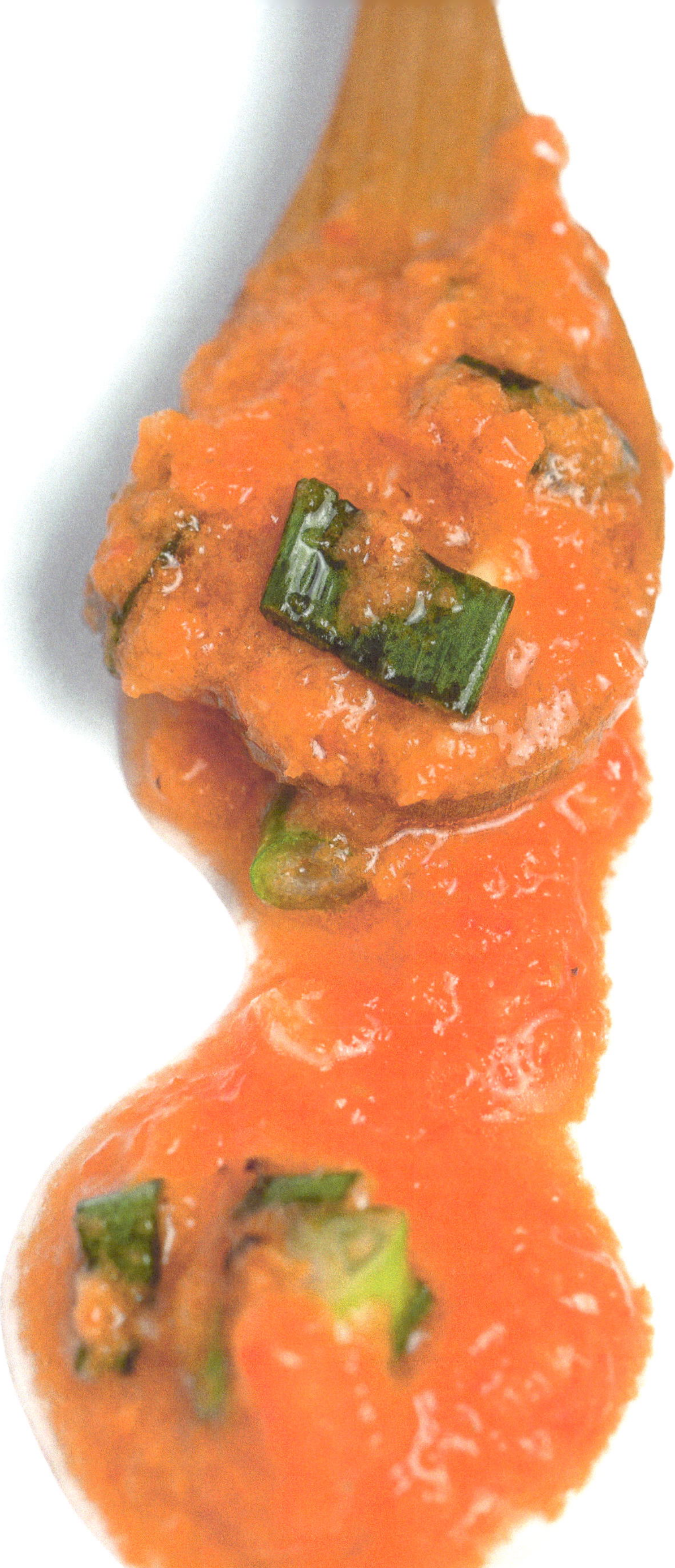

TARTAR SAUCE

Salsa Tártara

Qué rico! This sauce is a must when I want to enjoy some fish fritters, or as we call them in Peru: Chicharrón de Pescado.

This creamy, mildly piquant Tartar Sauce is so easy to make with simple ingredients that you likely already have on hand. Rich and tangy, it's the perfect accompaniment to simply prepared seafood.

After making this recipe you won't be tempted to buy anymore tartar sauce from the store. And when you make it at home, there are no icky stabilizers or preservatives, and it will last for a while in the fridge.

GLUTEN FREE

25'

1 ½ CUPS

Ingredients

2 hard-boiled eggs finely chopped
1 cup mayonnaise
2 tablespoons minced capers
1 tablespoon minced fresh parsley
1 tablespoon fresh lemon juice
Dash of Tabasco sauce
¼ teaspoon garlic paste, or minced and mashed garlic
¼ teaspoon finely ground black pepper
Salt

Preparation

1. In a bowl, combine the chopped eggs, mayonnaise, capers, parsley, lemon juice, Tabasco, garlic, salt and pepper. Stir well. Taste for seasoning and add salt, if needed.
2. Cover the sauce and chill for at least 1 hour before serving, to allow the flavors to meld.

Serving suggestions: Tartar Sauce and fried fish are a well-known combination, but you can also serve it as a tasty complement to fried calamari, french fries and Fried Yucca, and as a spread for fish sandwiches.

Note: Tartar Sauce can be stored for up to 3 days in the refrigerator.

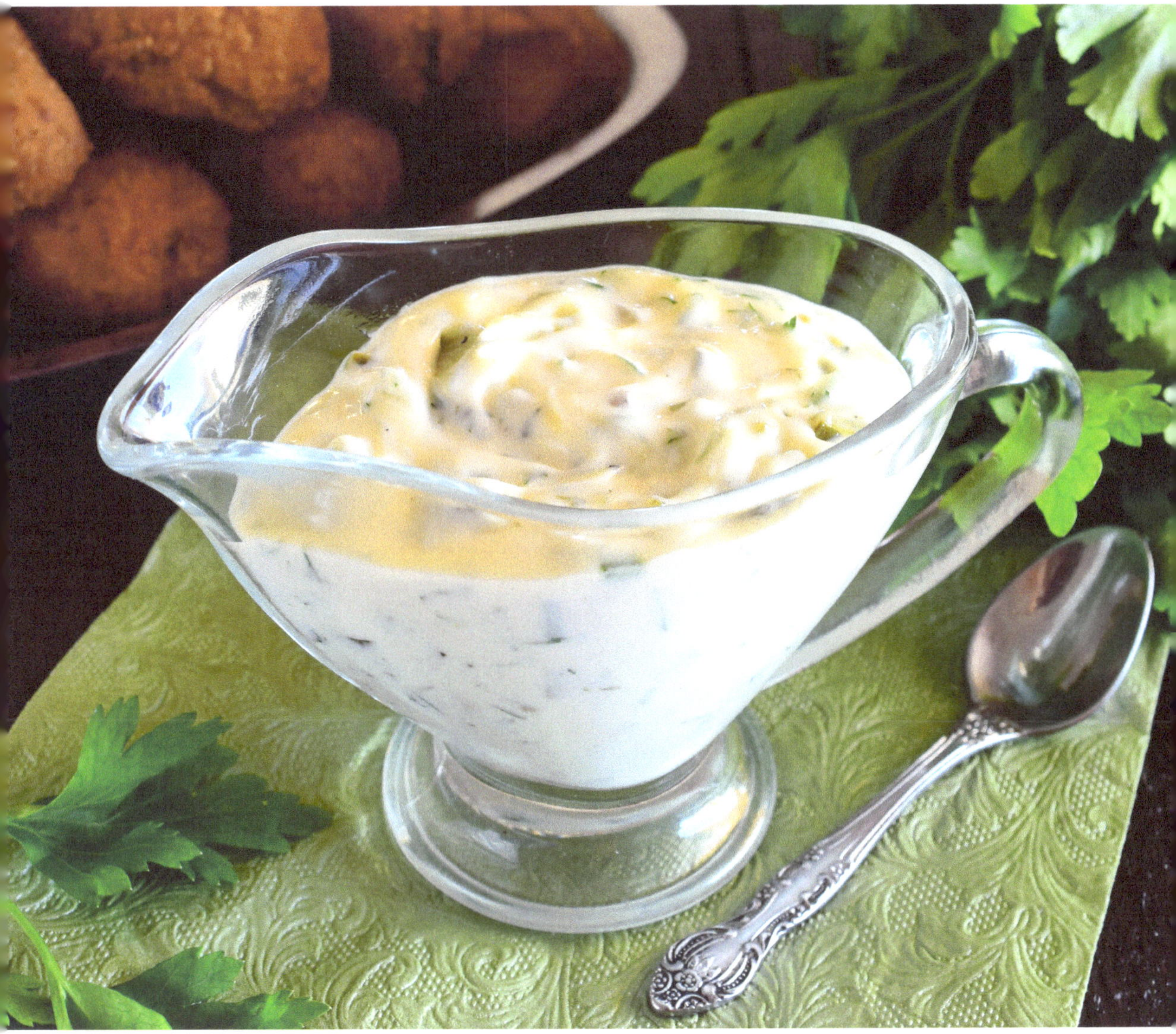

YELLOW HOT PEPPER PASTE

Pasta de Ají Amarillo

SPICY

15'

1 ½ CUPS

Considered the pillar of Peruvian gastronomy, yellow hot peppers have their origins in ancient Peru and across the Andean region of South America. Unknown to many in the world, this flavorful hot pepper will entice your palate. It has a bright orange color when ripe, a subtle aroma, and a mellow spicy flavor that will enhance your dishes.

In Peru, the yellow hot pepper is considered part of a trilogy of key ingredients that—along with onions and garlic—make up the basic aromatics of Peruvian cuisine.

The best Yellow Hot Pepper Paste is the one you make at home. Fresh, aromatic, with no chemicals and no citric acid to alter its unique, fresh flavor. It's a super simple recipe that you can make and enjoy any time!

Ingredients

6 yellow hot peppers (fresh or frozen)
3 garlic cloves
½ cup vegetable oil
Pinch of salt

Preparation

1. Remove the stems of the yellow hot peppers and cut in chunks without removing the seeds. If using frozen peppers, there's no need to defrost all the way.
2. Put the chunks of yellow hot pepper into a blender with the garlic, oil and salt, and process for 2 minutes, or until you get a smooth paste.
3. For a silkier smoother texture pass through a fine mesh strainer.
4. Refrigerate the Yellow Hot Pepper Paste in a covered glass container. It will keep for 7–10 days.

Note: This easy-to-prepare hot pepper paste is great to have in hand, as Yellow Hot Pepper Paste is used in many Peruvian dishes. For an even smoother texture, press it through a strainer and enjoy!

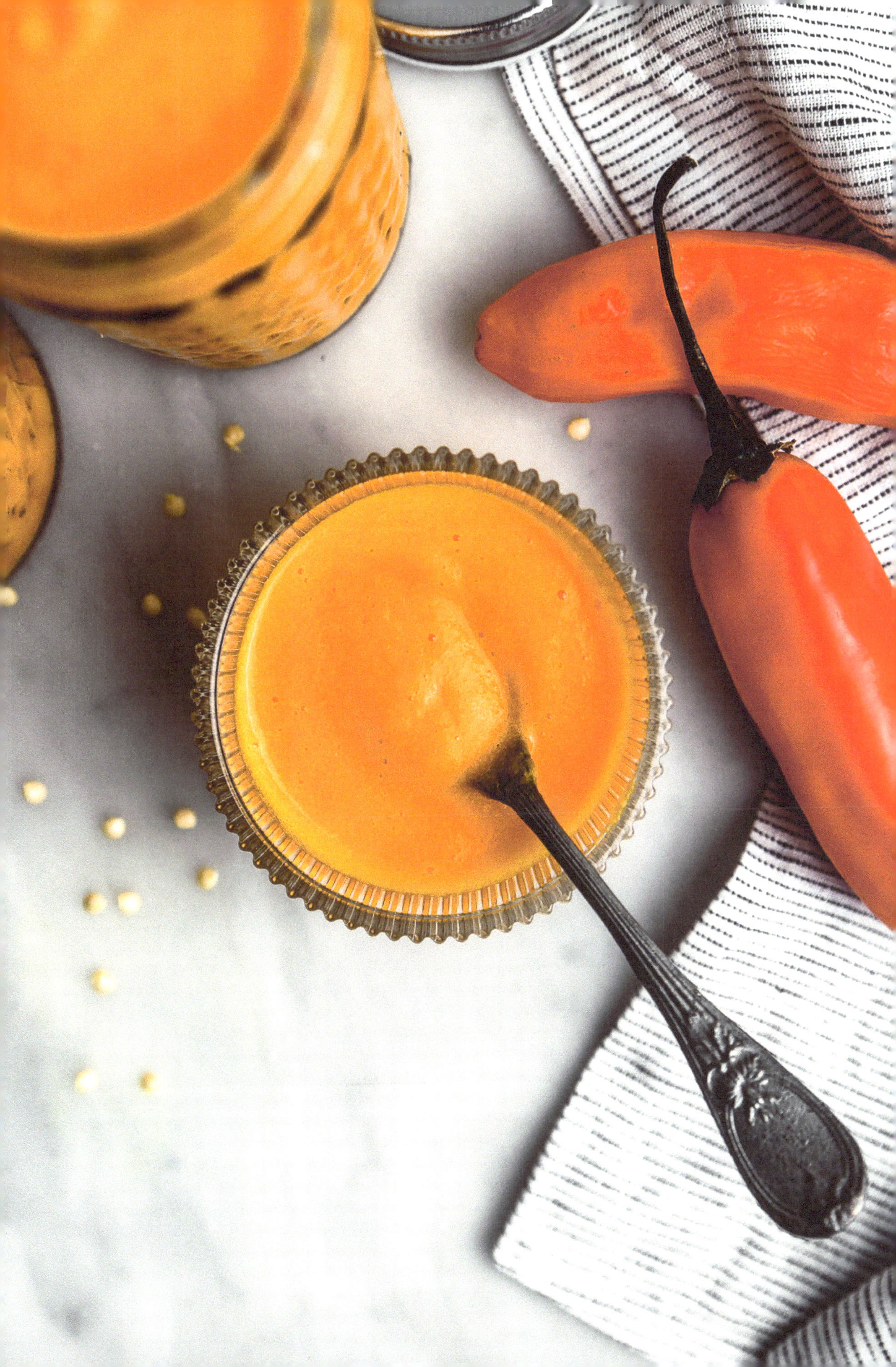

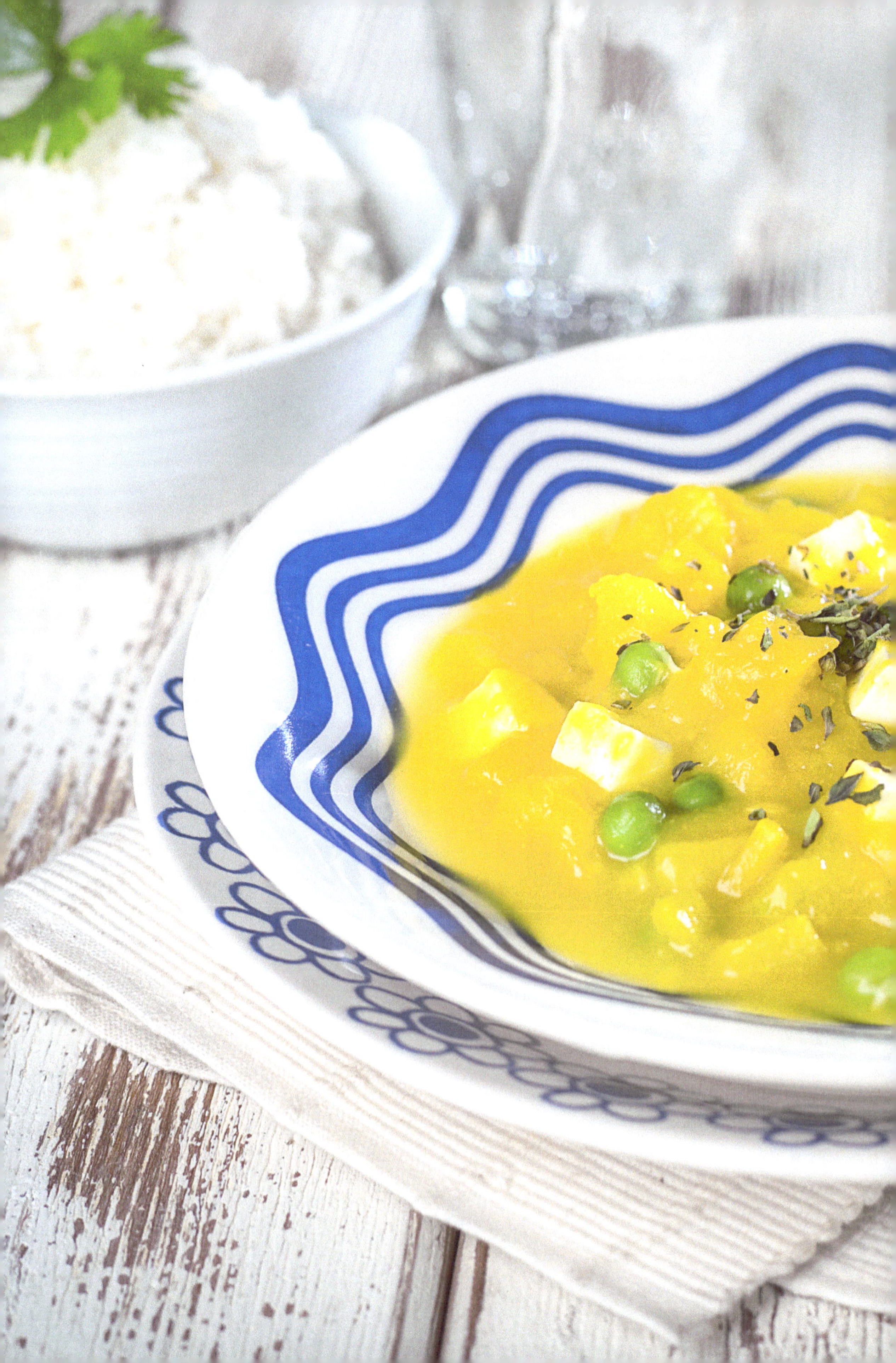

Main Courses

ADOBO PORK STEW

Adobo de Cerdo

SPICY

36h

8 SERVINGS

When I was a child, there were two requirements to prepare this dish; one was to go to Juanita, the lady who sold Anticuchos and Picarones, and get the Chicha de Jora she made, a Peruvian drink made with germinated fermented corn dating back to Tupac Inca Yupanqui times, before the Spanish arrived to America. The other requirement was going to the market and buying freshly made Colorado hot pepper paste which they used to sell in small plastic bags. One would get to the stand and say: "Good morning, *Caserita*, please, could you give me Fifty cents of Panca hot pepper paste?" And so, you took your little bag home to cook.

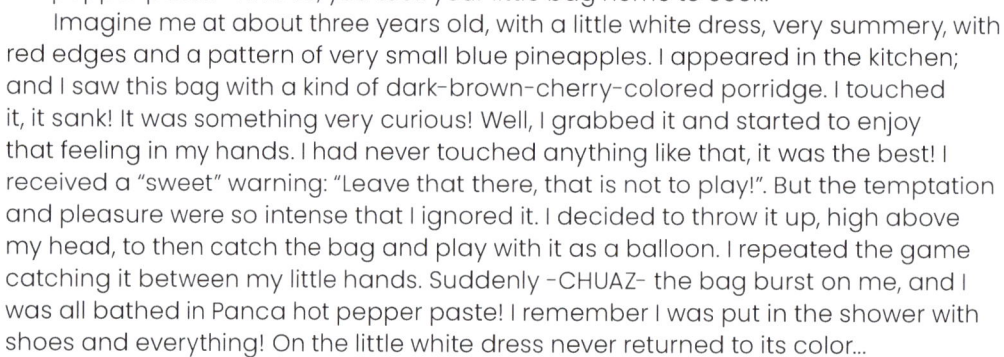

Imagine me at about three years old, with a little white dress, very summery, with red edges and a pattern of very small blue pineapples. I appeared in the kitchen; and I saw this bag with a kind of dark-brown-cherry-colored porridge. I touched it, it sank! It was something very curious! Well, I grabbed it and started to enjoy that feeling in my hands. I had never touched anything like that, it was the best! I received a "sweet" warning: "Leave that there, that is not to play!". But the temptation and pleasure were so intense that I ignored it. I decided to throw it up, high above my head, to then catch the bag and play with it as a balloon. I repeated the game catching it between my little hands. Suddenly -CHUAZ- the bag burst on me, and I was all bathed in Panca hot pepper paste! I remember I was put in the shower with shoes and everything! On the little white dress never returned to its color…

But regardless of the bursted bag, those Adobos that my Mamama or my Nana Mery prepared were finger licking good! And if there is a little leftover for the next day, even better!

Ingredients

3 pounds pork butt, or shoulder, trim excess fat, cut into 3-inch cubes

For the Adobo Marinade
(the day before)
¾ cup red wine vinegar
¼ cup Panca hot pepper paste
3 tablespoons minced garlic
2 tablespoons salt
1 tablespoon ground black pepper
1 teaspoon cumin powder
1 teaspoon dried oregano
Cooking spray for browning pork

Cooking day
1 large red onion, finely chopped
½ cup vegetable oil, divided
5 tablespoons garlic paste
5 tablespoons Panca hot pepper paste
3 tablespoons yellow hot pepper paste
8 tablespoons red wine vinegar
2 tablespoons Mirasol hot pepper paste
(sun-dried yellow hot pepper)
2 tablespoons dried oregano
1 tablespoon cumin powder
3 teaspoons salt
1 teaspoon fresh ground black pepper
1 ½ cup Chicha de Jora (or your favorite ale)

Preparation

1. The day before, in a large bowl, mix the pork cubes with the marinade ingredients and refrigerate overnight.
2. Next day, when ready to cook, preheat a Dutch oven, add ¼ cup of oil, and heat on medium-high. Sear the meat in batches until just golden brown. Remove and keep warm.
3. Using the same pot, reduce the heat to medium, add the remaining oil quarter, and cook the onion until soft, about 5–7 minutes. Add the Panca, Mirasol and yellow hot pepper pastes, cumin and oregano. Sauté for a couple of minutes to bloom the spices.
4. Add the garlic and cook until fragrant, about 1 minute.
5. Then pour the vinegar, the browned pork and the Chicha de Jora, or ale. Bring to a boil for 5 minutes. Reduce to a simmer, cover tightly and cook over low to medium heat, for about 3–4 hours, until the pork is tender.

Serving suggestion: This dish can be served with Canary Beans with Bacon (see page 80, Sides & Sauces), White Garlicky Rice (see page 102, Sides & Sauces), and Onion Relish (see page 114, Sides & Sauces).

BEEF CILANTRO STEW
Seco de Carne

SPICY

5h

4 SERVINGS

If you are a cilantro lover, this recipe is for you! Imagine the most tender piece of meat cooked in cilantro and other super flavorful spices for a slow and long period of time. The meat will fall apart, and I am sharing all the secrets especially with you in order for you to have the most pleasant experience. There's no way that you could resist a well prepared Seco de Carne.

This dish has so many wonderful rich-deep-flavors, and if you ask me, it is a must-try during the colder months! It is traditionally served with Canary Beans, White Garlicky Rice and Onion Relish, Yum!

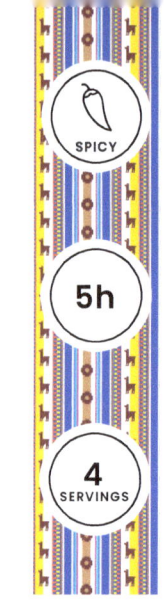

Ingredients

½ cup corn oil
1 ½ pound boneless beef short ribs, 6 ounces each
2 cups small diced red onions
4 tablespoon yellow hot pepper paste
1 tablespoon Panca hot pepper paste
4 tablespoon garlic paste
1 cup spinach
3 cups cilantro leaves
½ cup water
2 cans of beer (pale Ale, Sierra Nevada or similar)
2 cups beef stock (if necessary)
2 cups peas
1 cup butternut squash
Salt and pepper

Preparation

1. Heat the oil in a saucepan over high heat, sear the beef pieces until they are golden brown. Reserve.
2. In the same pot, sauté the onions until translucent. Add the yellow hot pepper paste, Panca hot pepper and garlic, stir and let them cook for 1 minute.
3. Put the spinach and cilantro in the blender and process with ½ cup cold water. Reserve.
4. Pour ½ of the mix into the sautéed onion mix, and add the seared short rib pieces (cilantro is going to get a dark green color). Pour the beer, add the squash and simmer over medium low heat for 3-4 hours, with the lid on. Check eventually and add beef broth if necessary.
5. When the meat is fork tender add green peas, and cook uncovered until they are tender.
6. The stew is ready! Time to add the other ½ of the blended cilantro, stir, and serve.

Serving suggestion: Serve with White Garlicky Rice (see page 102, Sides & Sauces), Onion Relish (see page 114, Sides & Sauces), and if desire with Canary Beans (see page 80, Sides & Sauces). Enjoy!

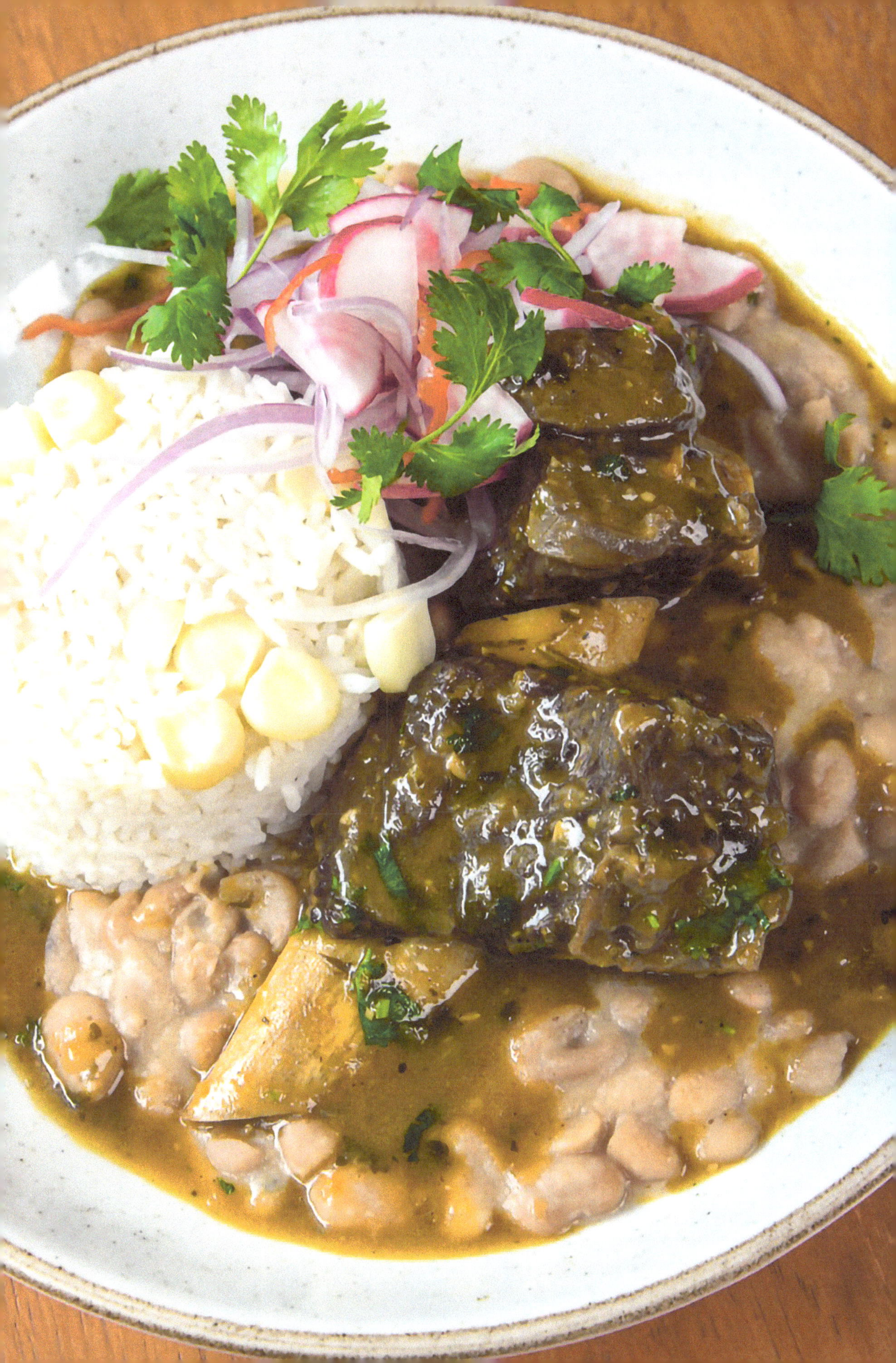

BEEF MILANESE

Bistec Apanado

DAIRY FREE

30'

4-6 SERVINGS

Not long ago, I called my Nana (nannie) and asked her how she made those super memorable Bistec Apanado when I was a little kid. She shared all the details, so I went to my kitchen and did as she told me. OMG! My husband, who loves this dish, was so quiet, and my kids were so happy, because I don't usually cook many fried foods at home. They even asked if I could cook the same thing the following day.

This versatile Beef Milanese can be served in different ways: as a main course paired with rice or mashed potatoes, with a salad or roasted veggies, or in a sandwich—you name it! Try it and you'll see why my family and I love it. I'm sure you will, too.

Ingredients

2 pounds beef top sirloin
2 eggs
3 tablespoons water
1 teaspoon garlic paste, or minced and mashed garlic
1 teaspoon ground cumin
4 cups dry plain bread crumbs, or more as needed
1 tablespoon salt + 1 teaspoon
1 teaspoon ground black pepper + 1/4 teaspoon
½ cup vegetable oil, or as needed

Preparation

1. Slice the beef about ⅛ inch thick across the grain. You can also ask the butcher to slice it very thinly for you. Set aside.
2. Whisk the eggs, garlic, cumin, 1 teaspoon salt and 1/4 teaspoon ground black pepper, and water together in a shallow bowl.
3. Spread the breadcrumbs out onto a large sheet of aluminum foil or parchment paper, and sprinkle with salt and pepper. Mix all the crumb ingredients together until well combined.
4. Dip each piece of beef into the egg mixture, then thoroughly coat with crumbs. Place the coated slices in a single layer onto a baking sheet covered in parchment or waxed paper. Place another sheet of parchment or waxed paper over the first layer, and continue the breading process.
5. Heat the vegetable oil in a large heavy skillet until shimmering, and pan-fry the beef slices—without crowding the pan—until golden brown, about 2 minutes on the first side and 1 minute on the second side. After each batch is cooked, put the slices on a paper towel-lined baking sheet, and keep warm in the oven set at the lowest temperature, while you continue to fry the remaining beef slices.

Serving suggestion: Serve as a main course, or with your favorite side dishes, such as Creamy Pesto Pasta (see page 148, Main Courses), Whipped Mashed Potatoes (see page 100, Sides & Sauces), Beet and Potato Salad (see page 64, Appetizers, Soups & Salads). Add your favorite sauces.

BEEF STIR-FRIED

Lomo Saltado

DAIRY FREE

30'

4 SERVINGS

The name Lomo Saltado comes from the way the beef was prepared by the Chinese who immigrated to Peru. They used a wok, sautéing several ingredients at the same time. Also, sauté in Spanish is *saltear*. Hence the name *saltado*!

Over time, red onions, tomatoes and yellow hot peppers were introduced to the dish. It is traditionally served with delicious, crunchy french fries!!! Oh my, oh my! And in addition to the fries, it's also paired with a portion of fluffy White Garlicky Rice. And if you're in the mood, don't hesitate to add a fried egg! This wonderful stir-fry is a tribute to the "marriage" of both Peruvian and Chinese food cultures. It's an unforgettable experience, so give this recipe a try!

Ingredients

1 pound beef tri-tip or filet mignon, cut into ⅛ to ¼-inch slices
Salt and pepper to taste
Vegetable oil, as needed
1 large red onion, cut into ½-inch slices
1 tablespoon minced fresh ginger
1 tablespoon garlic paste, or minced and mashed garlic
3 large Roma tomatoes, cut into ½-inch slices
1 yellow hot pepper, deveined, stems removed and julienned
3 tablespoons red wine vinegar
¼ cup low-sodium soy sauce
2 tablespoons chopped fresh parsley

Preparation

1. Season the sliced meat with salt and pepper to taste.
2. Preheat the oil in a skillet or wok over high heat. Sear the meat for 1 minute until just cooked, when the juices begin to be released. Remove the meat from the pan and set aside. Retain the oil and meat juices in the pan.
3. If needed, add more oil in the pan with the meat juices, and add the onion slices. Sauté the onions for 1 minute. Add the ginger and garlic and cook for no more than 1 minute.
4. Stir in the tomato and the yellow hot pepper; cook for about 30 seconds to 1 minute. Add vinegar and soy sauce. Season to taste with salt and pepper, and sprinkle with chopped parsley to serve.

Note: This dish is traditionally served with a side of french fries and White Garlicky Rice (see page 102, Sides & Sauces).

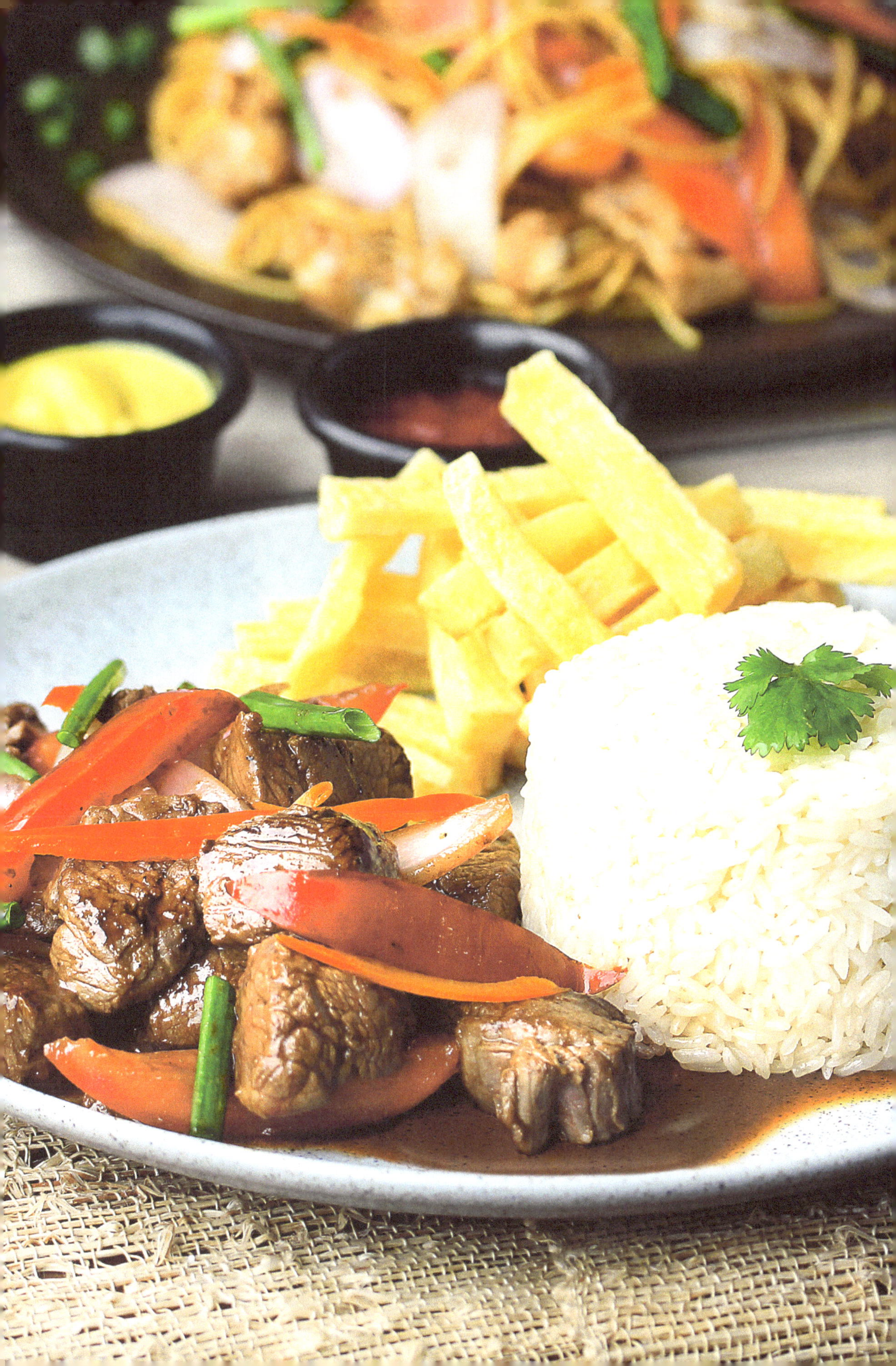

BUTTERNUT SQUASH MEDLEY

Locro de Zapallo

DAIRY

40'

6 SERVINGS

Uf! I love Locro! It is such a comforting dish. Maybe because it's a hearty vegetarian stew, authentic cold weather comfort food, or because of the different ingredients that combines butternut squash, potatoes, corn kernels, peas, fava beans, onion, garlic and yellow hot pepper, with some cheese towards the end. All together with a portion of white rice, or not. You can accompany Butternut Squash Medley with a fried egg, a fried fish fillet, a piece of fried or grilled meat. The possibilities are endless, and the truth is that it comes packed with flavor.

Ingredients

¼ cup vegetable oil
1 cup red onion small diced
1 tablespoon garlic paste, or minced and mashed garlic
1 cup yellow hot pepper paste
3 cups butternut squash, peeled and cut into 1-inch chunks
½ teaspoon ground cumin
1 teaspoon ground turmeric
1 cup vegetable stock
4–5 medium Yukon Gold potatoes cut into 1-inch pieces (about 4 cups)
1 cup shelled fava beans (fresh or frozen)
1 cup frozen corn kernels (uncooked)
1 cup peas (fresh or frozen)
Salt and ground black pepper
1 cup roughly chopped fresh black mint (available in the frozen section of Latin markets)
¼ cup evaporated milk (unsweetened)
10 ounces Queso Fresco, cut into ¼ inch cubes (about one cup)

Preparation

1. Preheat a Dutch oven, or large heavy-bottomed pot, over medium heat. Add the oil and sauté onions for about 5 minutes, then add the garlic and cook for an additional 2 minutes.
2. Reduce the heat to low; stir in the yellow hot pepper paste, the cumin and turmeric; cook for about 5 minutes.
3. Add the butternut squash and broth; cover and cook for 20 minutes, stirring occasionally.
4. Then, add the potatoes, fava beans, corn kernels and peas, with a little bit of salt, pepper, and the black mint.
5. Continue to let cook at a low boil, stirring occasionally, until the vegetables are tender. Stir in milk and cheese cubes; remove the pan from the heat and serve.

Note: This dish pairs well with White Garlicky Rice (see page 102, Sides & Sauces).

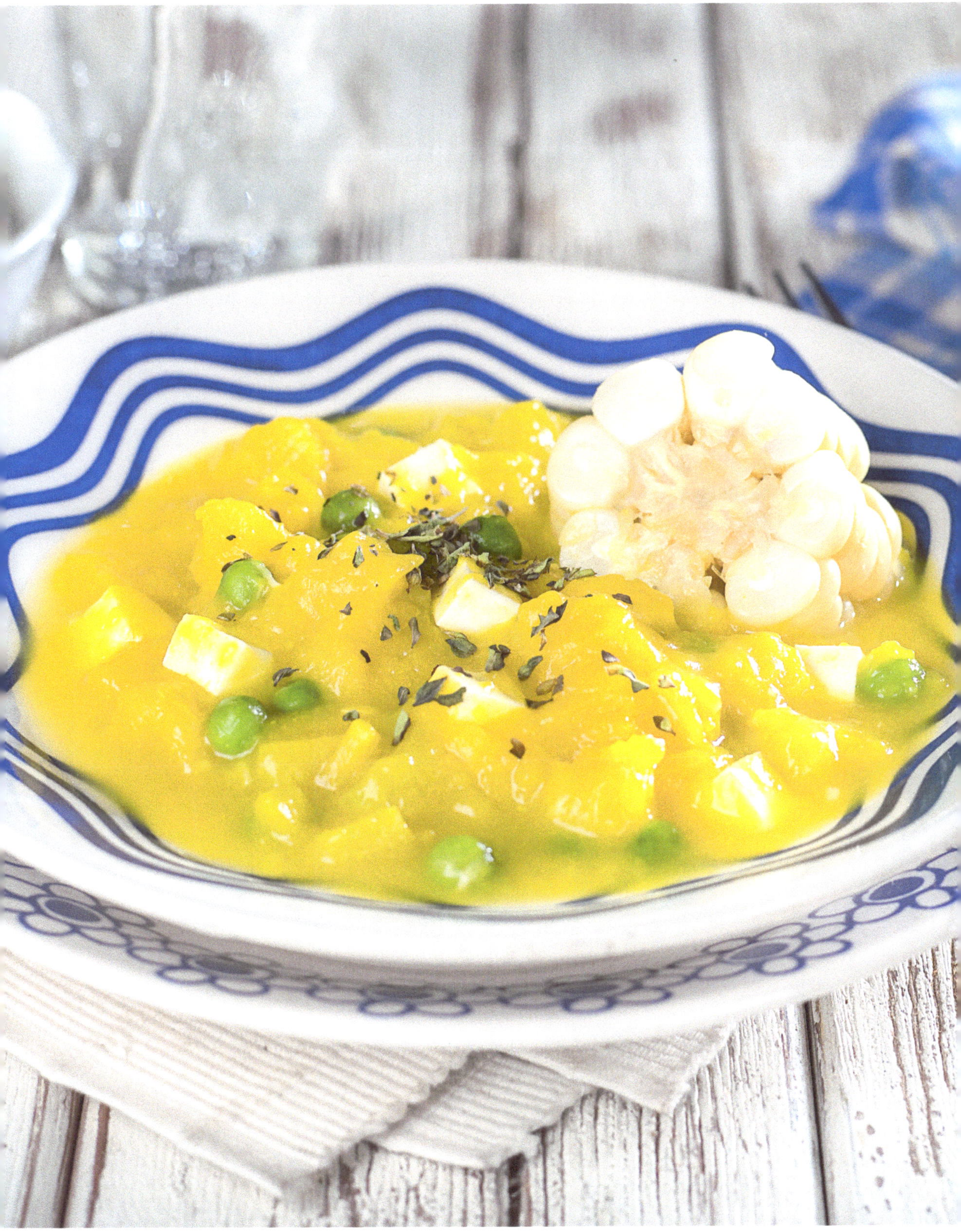

CHICKEN CAU-CAU

Cau-Cau de Pollo

SPICY

60'

4 SERVINGS

Cau-Cau is one of those dishes that can awaken pleasant or unpleasant childhood memories, depending on whether one enjoyed it, or suffered languishing at the table... This typical stew originated with the arrival of Africans, brought as slaves by the Spanish. At that time, slaves were not allowed the same food as their masters, so they cooked with what they were given. So, it was usually tripe, or the stomach of the cow, that starred in their version of this unique stew. But over the years, the dish has taken on a different character, and is now also made with other proteins in place of tripe. Now, chicken or seafood Cau-Cau is popular. And the diced potatoes cooked in the sauce are spectacular! As with many Peruvian main courses, it's also served with a good portion of rice, which absorbs the juices—delicious to the last bite!

At home, whenever my Mamama prepared Chicken Cau-cau, that day was a party! And it's the same way today when I prepare it for my dear family.

Ingredients

4 tablespoons vegetable oil
1 ½ pound skinless chicken and boneless breast, cut into ¾-inch pieces
1 small red onion finely diced
2 tablespoon garlic paste, or minced and mashed garlic
5 tablespoons yellow hot pepper paste
½ teaspoon ground cumin
1 teaspoon ground turmeric
2 cups chicken stock
4 cups medium diced red potatoes
6 sprigs fresh mint
2 teaspoons fresh lime juice
Salt and ground black pepper

Preparation

1. Add the oil to a Dutch oven, or large pot, preheated over medium-high heat. Sauté the chicken pieces until golden brown. Remove the chicken from the pot and reserve, leaving the remaining oil and chicken juices in the pot.
2. Using the same pot, sauté the onion until tender. Next, add the garlic and the yellow hot pepper paste, cook for one minute. Add cumin and turmeric, and stir all together.
3. Return the reserved chicken to the pot and add the chicken stock, the potatoes, salt and pepper. Cover and let cook over low heat until done, about 15 minutes.
4. Check for seasonings, add more salt and pepper if needed. Stir in the finely minced mint leaves, then turn off the heat and add the lime juice.

Note: This dish is normally served with White Garlicky Rice (see page 102, Sides & Sauces). Yum!

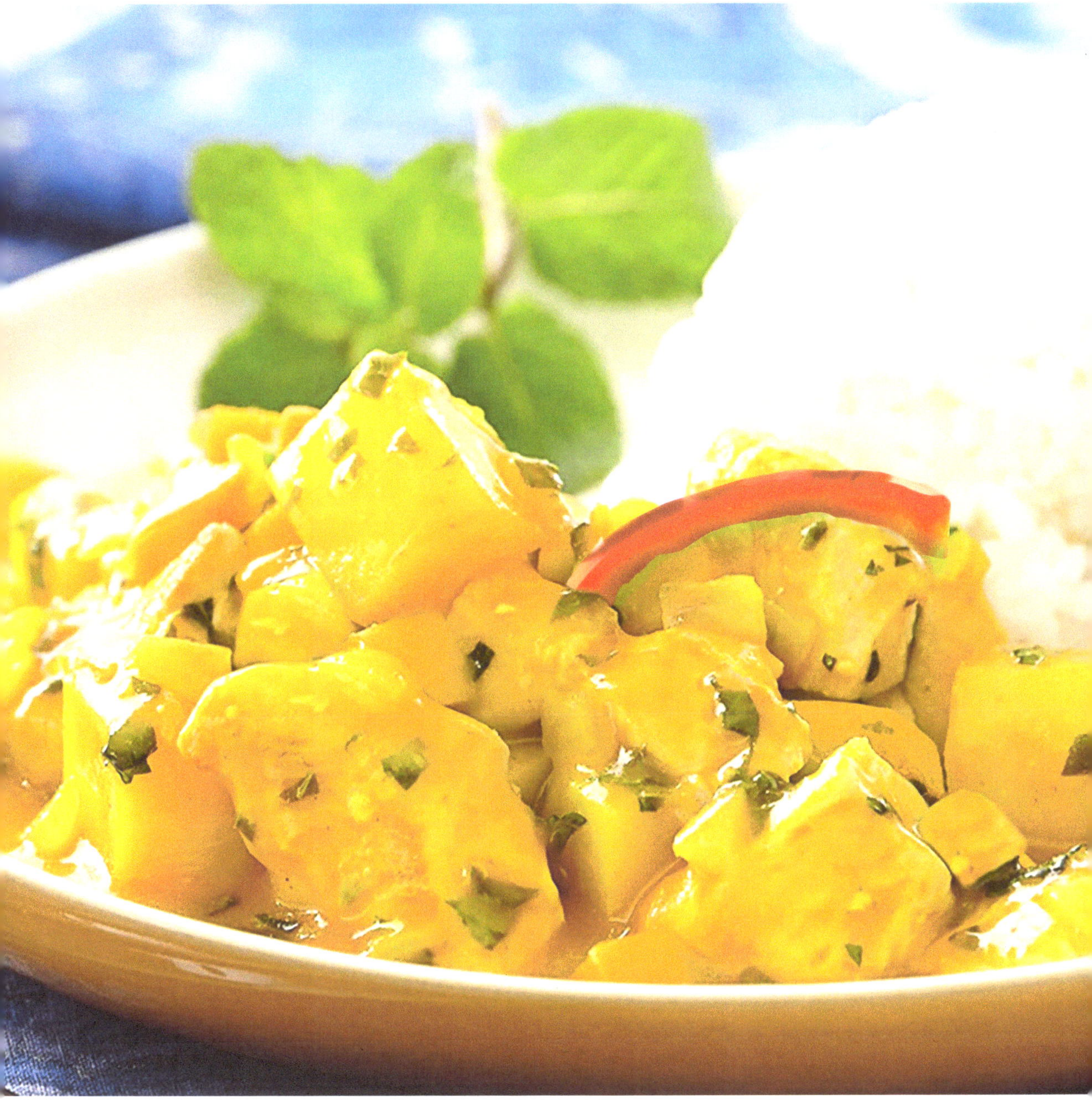

CHICKEN CILANTRO RICE

Arroz con Pollo

SPICY

80'

4-6 SERVINGS

Most Peruvians are very fond of rice. Many of our dishes are accompanied by a side of rice. In fact, we have a broad repertoire of rice dishes. Arroz con Pollo is a popular rice main dish whose green color comes from the spicy cilantro mixture. The other key ingredient is beer. This is one of those dishes that is cooked in layers, each one bringing something special to the final result—bright, earthy, and spicy.

This is a very comforting and satisfying dish. You can make it mild or spice it up according to your personal taste. It's typically served with a lemony Onion Relish that will add even more brightness to the dish. And if you're in the mood for a few more carbs, pair it with Potatoes with Huancaina Sauce, and you'll taste perfection!

Ingredients

6 skinless chicken pieces (thighs, drumsticks or/and breasts)
½ cup vegetable oil, divided
1 cup red onion finely chopped
½ cup yellow hot pepper paste
3 tablespoons minced garlic
2 cups cilantro leaves
½ cup cold water
1 cup dark beer
2 ½ cups low-sodium chicken broth
1 cup peeled and diced butternut squash
2 cups long-grain rice (basmati or jasmine)
¼ cup green peas, fresh or frozen
¼ cup carrots, small diced
½ red bell pepper, julienned
1 cup white corn kernels (if frozen, no need to defrost)
Salt and pepper to taste

Preparation

1. Dry chicken pieces with paper towels and season with salt and pepper. Heat a quarter of the oil in a Dutch oven over medium heat, and fry the chicken until golden brown on both sides. Remove from pot, and set aside.
2. In the same heavy pot, add the remaining quarter cup of oil; sauté onion for about 5 minutes until lightly golden. Add the garlic and yellow hot pepper paste and sauté for an additional 2 minutes.
3. Blend cilantro with the ½ cup of water and add the mixture to the pot. Next, add the beer, chicken broth and squash to the Dutch oven. Bring to a boil, then lower the heat, and continue to simmer until the squash is cooked.

4. Add the rice, peas, carrots and bell pepper. Bring to a boil and place the previously seared chicken on top of the rice. Reduce heat, cover and let simmer for 20 minutes.
5. Keeping the cover on the pot, remove it from the heat and let it rest for at least 10 minutes. Remove cover and fluff the ingredients with a fork. The following arc some serving tips for you to see.

Serving suggestions: Spoon a generous amount of rice into a shallow bowl, or a serving plate, and top it with a piece of chicken. Garnish with Onion Relish (see page 114, Sides & Sauces). This dish is traditionally served with Potatoes with Huancaina Sauce (see page 112 or 116, Sides & Sauces).

CHICKEN FRICASÉ

Fricasé de Pollo

LOW FAT

45'

4–6 SERVINGS

I'll be honest. This is not the best-looking dish, but once you try it, you'll be enamored with the flavors. It's not complicated to make, no uncommon ingredients are required, and yet, what a well-balanced, juicy and tender chicken this is. It's also a quick meal to prepare, and you probably already have most of the ingredients at home right now. You can enjoy it with a number of tasty, carby sides: crunchy toast, rice, sweet potatoes, pasta, or roasted potatoes. It's an easy, tasty go-to meal!

Ingredients

4–6 pieces whole boneless, skinless chicken pieces: thighs, drumstick or breasts (if using breasts, cut in half)
1 cup red onion small diced
2 tablespoons vegetable oil
½ cup Roma tomato small diced
2 tablespoons yellow hot pepper paste
2 tablespoons garlic paste, or minced and mashed garlic
1 teaspoon ground cumin
Salt and pepper to taste
1 cup chicken broth, or water
1 handful chopped parsley
1 egg, lightly scrambled

Preparation

1. Heat the oil in a large sauté pan over medium-high heat, and sear the chicken until just golden brown, but not cooked through. Remove the chicken from the pan and set aside. Do not clean the pan.
2. Add the red onion in the same pan and sauté until translucent, about 5 minutes. Then add the tomato, the yellow hot pepper paste, garlic paste, and cumin. Season with salt and pepper. Stir all together, then add the chicken.
3. Add broth, or water. Cover and bring to boil, cooking for about 10 minutes, or until the chicken is tender. Add the parsley and then the beaten egg. Stir briefly and remove the pan from the heat.

Note: This dish pairs well with White Garlicky Rice (see page 102, Sides & Sauces), or Whipped Mashed Potatoes (see page 100, Sides & Sauces).

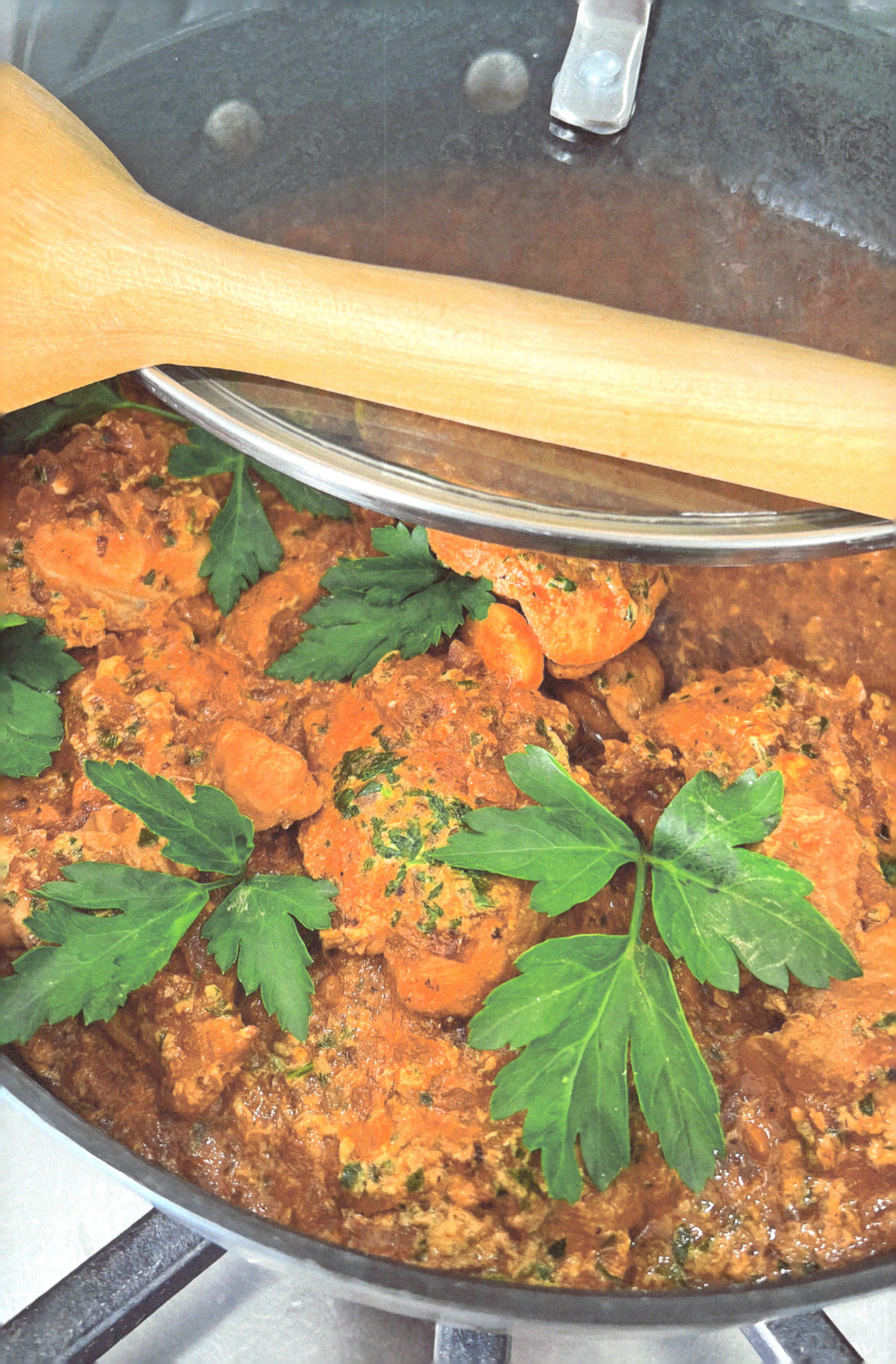

CHICKEN QUINOA MEDLEY

Guiso de Quinua con Pollo

SPICY · 50' · 8 SERVINGS

One of the reasons why I decided to include this recipe is because I grew up eating quinoa. Even as a baby, I've been told, there was quinoa in my feeding bottle. To me, its super tasty, flavorful and has a great texture; quite the opposite of what some people think or have experienced when it comes to quinoa. The secret is that quinoa takes on the flavors you season it with. If you do not season quinoa, you might start believing some of the less than glowing reviews!

But I give you my word, if you try this recipe, you'll remember my advice and come to love and enjoy this healthy, protein-packed, grain-like seed as much as I do. Now it's your turn to discover its charms!

Ingredients

4 boneless, skinless chicken breasts, cut into 1-inch pieces
¼ cup vegetable oil
1 cup red onion, diced
3 tablespoons garlic paste, or minced and mashed garlic
4–6 cups chicken broth
3–4 tablespoons Panca hot pepper paste
3 tablespoons yellow hot pepper paste
Salt and pepper to taste
1 cup pre-washed white quinoa
½ cup pre-washed red or black quinoa
1 handful finely chopped parsley (optional)
10 ounces Queso Fresco (optional)

Preparation

1. Pat the chicken dry and cut into 1-inch pieces.
2. In a large pot, or Dutch oven, heat the oil over high heat, and sauté the chicken for about 5 minutes. Remove the chicken from the pot and set aside. Keep the oil and chicken drippings in the pot.
3. In the same pot, over medium heat, sauté the onions until golden brown; add the yellow and the Panca hot pepper and garlic paste and sauté for an additional 3 minutes.
4. Return the chicken to the pot and reduce the heat to low. Season with salt and pepper. Add the quinoa and broth, and simmer over for 20 minutes.

Note: To plate, top the stew with crumbled Queso Fresco and finely chopped parsley. Serve with White Garlicky Rice (see page 102, Sides & Sauces) and Rocoto or Street Hot Pepper Sauce (see page 120, Sides & Sauces). What a perfect pairing!

Helping hand
FLUFFY QUINOA

Ingredients

½ cup quinoa
1 cup chicken or vegetable stock
½ teaspoon salt

Preparation

1. In abundant water rinse quinoa three times, then drain well.
2. Place a medium saucepan over medium heat.
3. Add drained quinoa, stock, and salt.
4. Bring to a boil then reduce heat to low, cover and simmer until the liquid is absorbed, about 13–15 minutes.
5. Check with a fork to ensure the liquid has been absorbed, and there's no more stock at the bottom of the pot.
6. Remove from heat and let it rest covered for another 5 minutes then fluff with a fork.

CHICKPEAS WITH SWISS CHARD AND SAUSAGES

Garbanzos con Acelgas y Chorizos

SPICY
60'
4–6 SERVINGS

This is a dish perfectly suited for autumn or winter. It is quick to put together and is very comforting.

One of the things I like about this dish is that you can totally omit the oil. Once you preheat your pan and start cooking the sausages, you may not need additional fat to cook the onions and garlic, which add a lot of flavor to the chard and the chickpeas.

While I most often serve it with a side of White Garlicky Rice, you can enjoy a bowl by itself. It's also a hit with my boys, who often ask me to make this for dinner.

Ingredients

1 pound mild Italian sausage, or your favorite sausage, cut into ½-inch pieces
1 cup red onion small diced
2 pounds Swiss chard, preferably rainbow chard, washed and stems separated
2 tablespoons garlic paste, or garlic, minced and mashed
1 teaspoon ground cumin
Pinch red pepper flakes (optional)
3 cans (15.5 ounces) Chickpeas, rinsed and drained
1 can (15 ounces) tomato sauce
2–3 cups of chicken broth or water
Salt and freshly ground black pepper

Preparation

1. Preheat a Dutch oven, or similar pot, over medium heat and cook the sausage on both sides. Remove the cooked sausages from the pan and set aside. Leave the rendered fat in the pan.
2. Prepare the chard by separating the stems from the leaves. Chop the stems crosswise into ½-inch length; set aside. Stack the leaves and chop coarsely. Keep the chopped stems and leaves separate.
3. Add the red onion to the Dutch oven and sauté over medium heat in the rendered fat from the sausage for about 4 minutes. Then, add the chard stems and cook, stirring occasionally, about another 4 minutes, or until the stems soften. Stir in the garlic and cook for 2 minutes. Stir the cumin, and the red pepper flakes, if using.
4. Add the tomato sauce and the chickpeas, and 2 to 3 cups of broth or water. Increase the heat and bring to a boil for about 5 minutes.
5. Reduce the heat to medium, and stir in the chopped chard leaves; cover and cook, stirring occasionally, until the chard is tender, about 5 minutes. Taste and season with salt and pepper as needed.
6. Ladle into serving bowls while hot.

Note: Serve hot in a bowl, with a side of White Garlicky Rice (see page 102, Sides & Sauces).

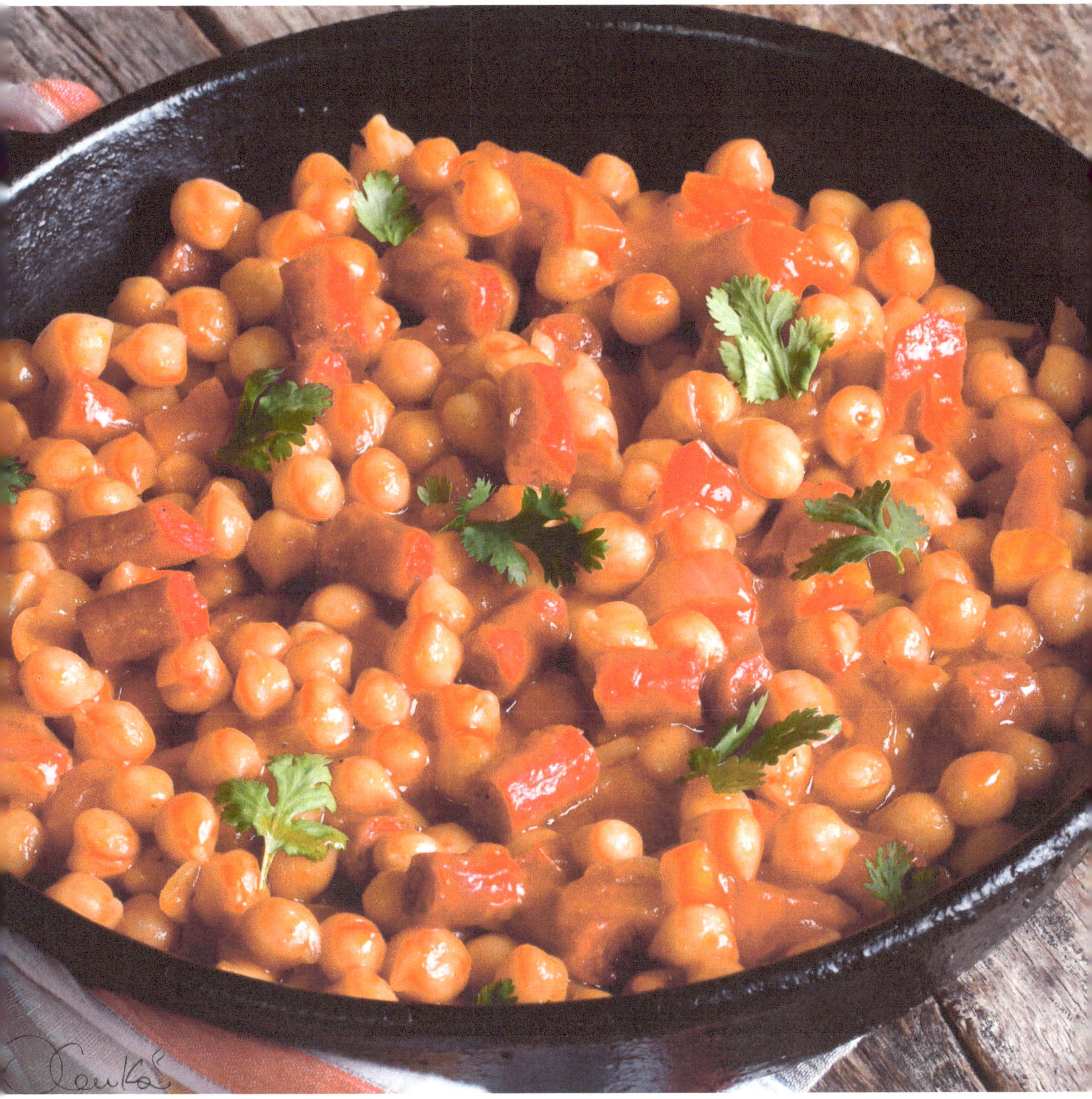

CREAMY PESTO PASTA

Tallarines Verdes

So many memories of my childhood come with this dish. I remember my Mamama boiling the slices of peeled potatoes with the pasta—in the same pot. Somehow that Genovese method gave the potatoes a special flavor. Then, she tossed the pasta with the Pesto Sauce, and the plating process was to place a few slices of the potatoes on each plate, top them with the tossed pasta, followed by an extra ladle of sauce, a drizzle of olive oil, and a final sprinkle of freshly grated Parmesan cheese. Heaven! Another way that we used to enjoy this dish was at my Auntie Cucha's house, with boiled green beans, also delicious.

    Creamy Pesto Pasta is also a great sauce to make ahead and freeze. Besides being delightful, it is packed with iron and nutrients from the fresh spinach and basil. To me, this sauce is one of the best in the world, because it is creamy, cheesy and savory, and all of the ingredients are easy to find at your local grocery store.

Ingredients

½ pound spaghetti
3 tablespoons salt

For the Pesto sauce
¼ cup olive oil
½ cup red onion, medium diced
3 whole garlic cloves, peeled
3 cups fresh basil leaves
1 cup fresh spinach leaves
½ cup evaporated milk (unsweetened)
¼ cup toasted Brazilian nuts, pine nuts or walnuts
½ pound Queso Fresco, roughly chopped
Salt and pepper

Preparation

Pesto Sauce:
1. Heat olive oil in a saucepan over medium heat. Add the diced onion and whole garlic cloves and cook, stirring, for 6 minutes or until softened. Let cool.
2. Place cooled onion mixture and remaining ingredients: basil, spinach, milk, nuts and Queso Fresco in a blender and process to a thick purée. Season with salt and pepper, then set aside.

Spaghetti:
1. Bring the water and salt for the spaghetti to a boil and follow the instructions on the package.
2. Reserve 1 cup of the pasta cooking water, then drain and return the spaghetti to the pot. Stir in the Pesto sauce, gradually adding some of the cooking pasta water to create a loose but creamy sauce to coat the pasta.
3. Serve and enjoy it warm.

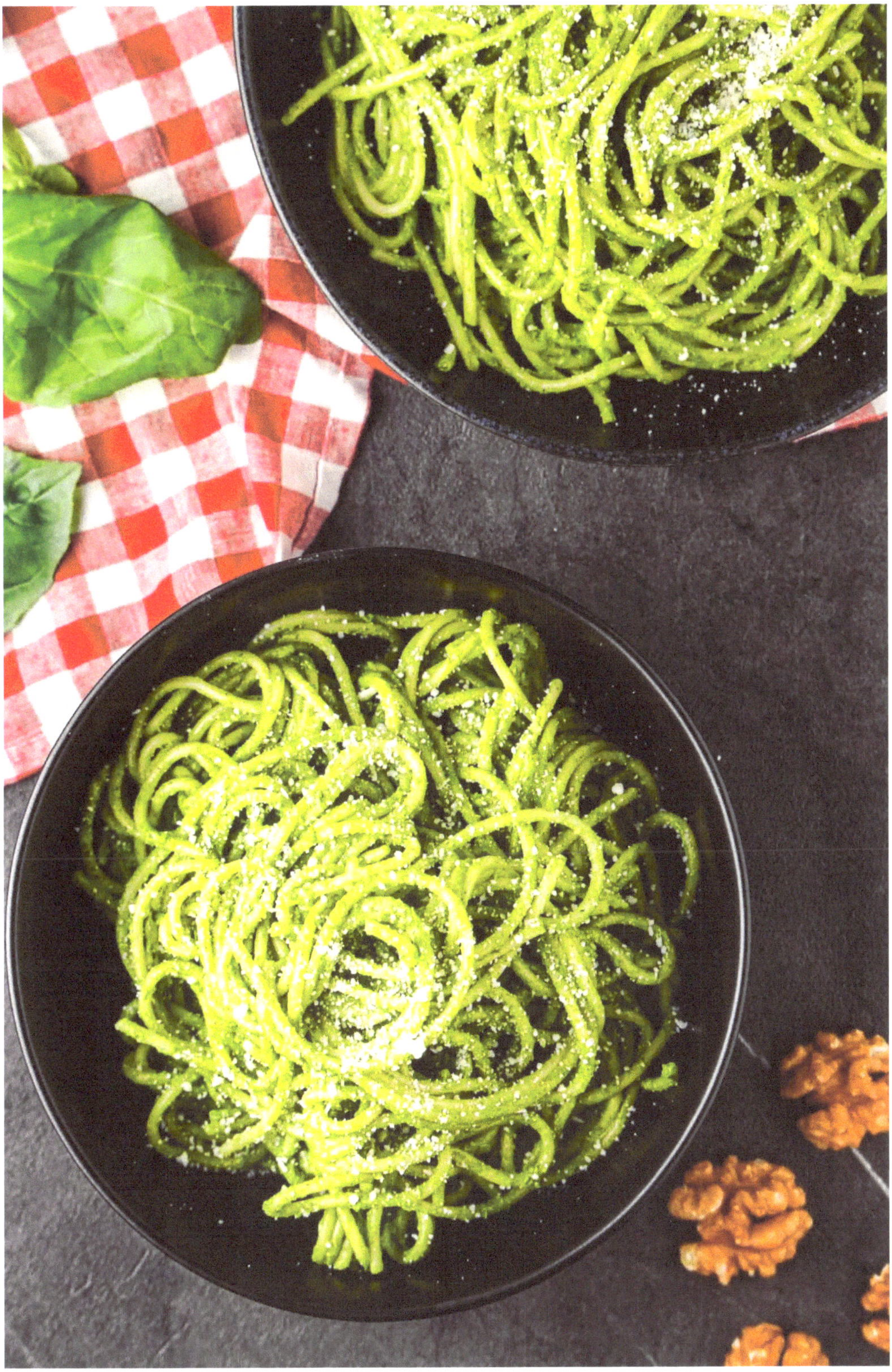

CRISPY PORK BELLY

Panceta Crocante

Crispy, salty, savory pork belly is hard to resist. So, let me share this with you if you're a fan of cracker-crisp, crunchy pork skin and tender-juicy meat. My secret is a combination of cooking methods, and the result is a totally out-of-this-world pleasurable experience!

GLUTEN FREE | 48h | 4–6 SERVINGS

Ingredients

For the dry rub (the day before)
4–5 pounds pork belly
3 tablespoons kosher salt, divided
1 tablespoon ground black pepper
1 tablespoon ground cumin

The day off
2 white onions cut in half and sliced ½-inch thick
2 large carrots cut into 1-inch rounds
2 stalks celery cut into 4-inch lengths
½ cup whole garlic cloves, peeled

Preparation

1. The day before, with the pork belly fat-side up, score with a sharp knife through the fat layer only, in a crisscross pattern. Rub 2 tablespoons of the salt onto the fat layer. Next, mix together the remaining tablespoon of salt, the pepper and cumin, and rub the mixture onto the underside of the meat.
2. Set a rack over a baking sheet. Place the pork belly on the rack fat-side up and refrigerate, uncovered, overnight or up to 24 hours.
3. Next day, remove the pork from the refrigerator and let it rest at room temperature for 45–60 minutes. Meanwhile, preheat the oven to 425 °F, with the rack set in the center position.
4. Using paper towels, pat the pork dry all over, removing as much moisture as possible.
5. Keeping the pork belly fat side up on the same rack and baking sheet, place it in the oven for 30 minutes.
6. After 30 minutes, lower the oven temperature to 350 °F, and roast for an additional hour.
7. When the pork is done, remove it from the oven. Using tongs, carefully place the pork on a cutting board.
8. Remove the rack from the baking sheet and set aside. Place the vegetables directly on the baking sheet, making a bed for the pork. Carefully, with the help of your tongs, place the pork belly fat side up on top of the vegetables.

9. Put the pork and vegetables back in the 350 °F oven for one more hour.
10. After, and if needed, increase the oven temperature to broil and let the pork belly broil for 15 minutes. After broiling, remove the pork from the oven and let it rest for about 30 minutes.

Note: Now, what you've been waiting for! Slice the pork across the grain and enjoy the crunchiest, juiciest, out-of-this-world pork belly! Discard the vegetables.

FISH A LO MACHO

Pescado a lo Macho

45'

2 SERVINGS

This recipe is a good example of the way Peruvian fishermen's wives brought out the richest flavors from the bounty of the Pacific Ocean. This dish is called *A lo Macho* because it has a variety of seafood, and will make you feel vigorous, powerful, potent (and maybe a little sweaty), due to its high content of phosphorus, calcium, and its wealth of minerals, such as iron, zinc, iodine, magnesium, selenium, and potassium. That's why you'll feel how you'll feel after you enjoy it. Got it?

This dish is composed of fried fish fillets blanketed with a creamy-spicy seafood-based sauce enhanced with Peruvian spices, and a variety of shellfish. It is typically served with a side of rice, Fried Yuccas or potatoes, and some wedges of lime to brighten it up.

One of my favorites!

Ingredients

3–4 tablespoons vegetable oil, divided
½ cup red onion finely chopped
2 tablespoons minced garlic
Shells from the peeled shrimps
1 tomato peeled, seeded, and finely chopped
1 tablespoon yellow hot pepper paste
1 tablespoon Panca hot pepper paste
½ cup white wine
1 ounce Pisco
2 firm white fish fillets (cod, sea bass, etc.), about 5–6 ounces each
4 mussels
6 medium size shrimp, peeled and deveined (shells reserved for the stock)
6 ounces squid cut in rings
6 clean clams
¼ cup heavy cream
¼ teaspoon cumin
Salt and pepper to taste
3 limes, cut in wedges
Fresh cilantro, to garnish

Preparation

1. Heat 1 tablespoon of oil in a large sauté pan over medium heat. Add the chopped onions, the minced garlic, the shrimp shells, and cook until golden and softened, about 5 minutes.
2. Add the tomato, the Panca and the yellow hot pepper pastes; stir in and let cook for a few minutes.

3. Increase the heat to medium-high; add the wine and Pisco and bring to a boil for about 2 minutes. Reduce the heat to medium, add the cream and season with a bit of salt and pepper.
4. Pour the sauce into a blender; purée until smooth. Strain the sauce back into the sauté pan and set aside.
5. In a clean skillet over a medium burner, heat the remaining 3 tablespoons of oil; season the fish with salt and pepper and fry just until golden, and almost cooked through. Set aside and keep warm in the oven, or at the lowest temperature setting.
6. Next, heat the sauté pan, set aside with the sauce, and add the seafood beginning with mussels and clams, after 5 minutes, add the shrimp and squid, keep on stove for 3 minutes. Season with cumin, salt and pepper.
7. To serve, place a warm fish filet in the center of each plate and top each fillet with half of the seafood sauce.

Note: This dish is traditionally accompanied with slices of fried potatoes or Fried Yuccas (see page 22, Appetizers), and/or White Garlicky Rice (see page 102, Sides & Sauces). Garnish with fresh cilantro and lime wedges.

FREEZE-DRIED POTATO MEDLEY

Carapulcra

CONTAINS NUTS

36h

8 SERVINGS

This dish's main ingredient is called Papa Seca. During harvest time, the Incas—always so smart—ate some of the recently harvested potatoes, but they also set some aside to freeze-dry naturally in the crisp, dry clean Andean air, to rehydrate and eat during long winters. Feeze-dried Potatoes are an ancient ingredient, and very different from freshly cooked potatoes.

Carapulcra is a medley of hearty meats and dried potatoes made with the addition of peanuts, a variety of yellow hot pepper and Panca hot pepper, warm spices and chocolate. It is a dish that takes time and patience to prepare, but every minute is worth it.

My brother-in-law and his wife once came to visit us for the holidays, and we made reservations at a very nice restaurant to welcome the New Year. We were all so happy and excited. As usual, I wanted to spoil them by cooking an authentic Peruvian dish. I made the mistake of cooking this dish to serve for lunch on New Year's Eve day—a terrible decision! My brother-in-law had three servings, and had to take a long nap. So, we couldn't have dinner that night! Therefore, I suggest enjoying this dish for lunch, with no further plans for dinner (except maybe a long walk!). Even better if it's a weekend.

Oh! And by the way, it's traditionally served with boiled Yuccas and a good side of warm White Garlicky Rice.

Ingredients

1 pound freeze dried potatoes or sundried potatoes
3 tablespoons vegetable oil
1 pound pork loin or pork belly, cut into 2-inch chunks
1 pound skinless, boneless chicken breasts or thighs, cut into 2-inch pieces
1 ½ cups red onion finely diced
¾ cup Panca hot pepper paste
¼ cup yellow hot pepper paste
2 tablespoon garlic paste, or finely minced garlic
½ teaspoon cumin powder
Spice Sachet (6 whole cloves, 1 cinnamon stick, 1 star anise)
3 cups chicken stock
¾ cup roasted peanuts, roughly chopped
½ cup Port wine
1 bar (32 grams) of Sublime Peruvian chocolate, or 1 ⅛ ounces of Mr. Goodbar roughly chopped
Salt and ground black pepper to taste

Preparation

1. The day before, to prepare the stew, roast the sundried potatoes on the stovetop over medium heat, cooking them without oil, in a large heavy-bottomed sauté pan. Cook for 5–10 minutes, turning frequently, until deep golden brown.

Transfer the dried potatoes to a large bowl, cover it with double its volume in cold water, and leave to soak overnight at room temperature.
2. The day of preparation, heat the oil in a Dutch oven over medium heat, and sear the diced chicken and pork for a few minutes on each side. Add the onion to the pot, and cook until the onions are softened. Stir in the Panca hot pepper and yellow hot pepper pastes, and minced garlic, cook for about 3 minutes. Add the cumin, salt and pepper.
3. Tie the spices (cloves, cinnamon and star anise) in cheesecloth to create a sachet, and place spice sachet in the middle of the pot.
4. Strain the water from the dried potatoes left to soak overnight, and add it to the pot along with the chicken stock; simmer for 40 minutes to 1 hour over low heat without the lid, stirring every 5 to 10 minutes.
5. After an hour or so (or when the dried potato is fully cooked), add the peanuts, Port and chocolate. Mix everything and taste. Add more salt if needed.
6. Serve hot with either boiled Yucca or fluffy White Garlicky Rice (see page 102, Sides & Sauces).

Note: These potatoes are freeze dried Peruvian potatoes from which all the moisture has been removed. Resembling small crystals, they have a very long shelf life, and can be stored at room temperature for more than a year. Available online and in some Latin markets.

FRIED RICE
Arroz Chaufa

Gluten Free • 45' • 4-6 servings

Arroz Chaufa is the Peruvian version of fried rice. The word Chaufa comes from the Chinese word Chaofan which literally translates into 'fried rice'. In Peru, there are Chinese restaurants named Chifas. At these establishments the most popular order is the Fried Rice, served in generous portions. We could say that this is one of the first dishes inspired by the Chinese-Peruvian culinary fusion.

The best way to make this Fried Rice is with leftover rice, a little meat, vegetables, soy sauce, ginger, and sesame oil. Most of the ingredients may already be in your pantry, and the rest is up to your own creativity and whatever leftovers are in your fridge!

Ingredients

2 tablespoons vegetable oil
½ cup finely sliced scallions or green onions, both white parts and green tops (separate white from the green tops; the greens will be used, to garnish)
1 tablespoon grated fresh ginger
1 tablespoon garlic paste, or minced and mashed garlic
2 cups boneless and skinless chicken thighs or breast meat, cut into ½-inch pieces
½ cup sliced Chinese sausage (available in some supermarkets and Asian markets)
1 cup snow peas, thinly sliced on the bias
1 cup soy sprouts (available supermarkets and Asian markets)
4 cups cold cooked white rice (see page 102)
4 eggs, scrambled and roughly chopped
¼ cup low-sodium soy sauce
2 tablespoons toasted sesame seeds
1 tablespoon toasted sesame oil

Preparation

1. Heat a wok or skillet over high heat. When it's very hot, add the vegetable oil and sauté the white part of the green onions, the ginger and garlic. Cook for 1 to 2 minutes.
2. Stir in the chicken pieces and cook until just cooked through.
3. Add the Chinese sausage and cook for one minute.
4. Stir in the snow peas and soy sprouts. Incorporate the rice and mix in quickly.
5. Add the chopped scrambled eggs, then season with soy sauce and sesame oil.
6. Remove the pan from the heat and scatter with the toasted sesame seeds and the green tops of the scallions. Serve immediately.

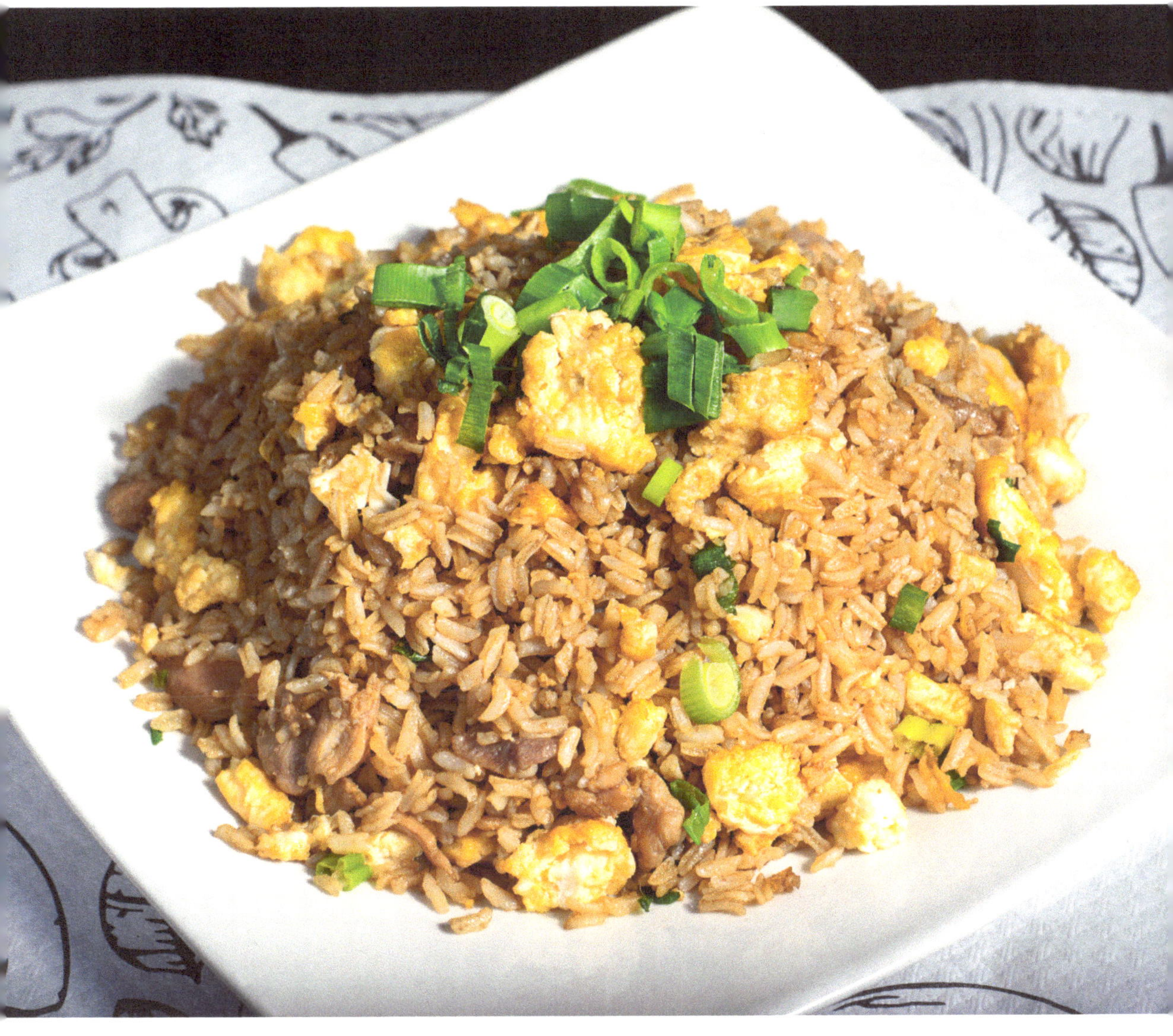

GREEN RISOTTO WITH SEAFOOD

Risotto Verde con Mariscos

SIGNATURE RECIPE

40'

4-6 SERVINGS

When I was in cooking school, I took a class named "Professional Cooking Basics". Towards the end of the season, our chef instructor told us that we needed to create a dish, which would be evaluated and would have a considerable percentage of the final grade. Well, I started spinning my wheels and remembered when I went to Punta Sal and Mancora, up in the Peruvian North coast. I had the most unbelievable Seafood Paella, or as we call it in Peru "Arroz con Mariscos". But the difference from the red ones, I've always enjoyed in Lima, was the color and flavor. This one had minced cilantro; therefore, it was on the green side. Then, the memory of a creamy, perfectly cooked, homemade risotto came to me. And I thought, "well I guess I'll pair my Italian and Peruvian roots and memories…"

So, I developed this green risotto with shrimp and scallop, but also, I incorporated Peruvian corn, yellow hot pepper, and a good amount of Parmigiano Reggiano cheese. What can I tell you? When I was done cooking my risotto, I plated it, and took it to the Chefs to be assessed. The first one tasted it and looked at me with a "poker face", and then she looked at the other chef next to her and said "Try this". The other chef did the same and asked an assistant to call another chef who was in another classroom. At this point, I was thinking two things; either they really like it or I'm in big trouble!… The third chef came, and they invited him to try it. He did, and immediately he questioned, "Who made this?" I was observing everything and sweating like crazy not knowing what was really happening, until they told me to come closer. And they said that this dish triggered all their taste buds and areas in their mouth, and it was well balanced, none of the ingredients were fighting or competing against each other.

From that day on, I cherish this recipe and remember that proud moment in my path of cooking with love.

Ingredients

6 tablespoons clarified butter
2 tablespoons olive oil
1 minced shallot
1 tablespoon garlic paste
2 tablespoons yellow hot pepper paste
1 cup Arborio rice
1 cup corn kernels (fresh or frozen)
½ cup white wine
3 cups hot fish/seafood stock, or broth
1 pound small shrimp
1 cup petite peas
½ cup Parmesan cheese
1 tablespoon lime juice
1 bunch cilantro
4-6 colossal scallops (U-10)

Preparation

1. Sauté shallots for about 2 minutes in 2 tablespoons of the clarified butter and the 2 of olive oil.
2. Time for the garlic and yellow hot pepper paste to join the party for about 1 minute.
3. Incorporate the rice, corn kernels and white wine. Stir and let cook for about 3 minutes, until the alcohol evaporates.
4. Pour in 1 ½ cups of the fish broth, and bring to a boil over high heat, stirring occasionally. Reduce heat to medium-low, and simmer, uncovered, for 10 minutes, continuing to stir. Pour in the remaining broth, increase heat to medium, and cook for about 7 more minutes, stirring constantly.
5. Add shrimp and peas. Cook, stirring constantly, until the remaining liquid is almost absorbed, and the seafood has cooked, about 2–3 minutes. When the rice is just tender *al dente*, season with Parmesan cheese until it melts.
6. Blend the cilantro with a ¼ cup of cold water.
7. Turn off the heat and add the cilantro to the pot with the lime juice.
8. Sear the scallops to place them on top when serving.

Note: Garnish with a slice of lemon.

HUANCAINA RISOTTO

Risotto a la Huancaína

VEGETARIAN

40'

4–6 SERVINGS

This comforting dish is the result of a marriage between Peruvian and Italian gastronomy. It's creamy, savory, spicy, with tons of umami. This Risotto can be served as an entrée, or as a side dish paired with multiple options such as beef or chicken Milanese, Beef Stir-Fried, seafood, and grilled or roasted vegetables.

A couple of tips that will make your Risotto a success is to use a good quality Arborio rice, and heated, flavorful broth for each addition. But the real key to this delicious dish is the Huancaina Sauce.

Gather your ingredients and get ready for your taste buds to travel between Italy and Peru!

Ingredients

¼ cup olive oil
1 shallot, minced
1 tablespoon garlic paste, or minced and mashed garlic
2 cups Arborio rice
1 cup dry white wine
5 cups heated vegetable or chicken broth or stock
½ cup grated Parmesan cheese
1 ½ cups Huancaina Sauce (see page 112 or 116, Sides & Sauces)
Green peas and freshly chopped parsley, to garnish (optional)

Preparation

1. Heat the oil in a large sauté pan, over medium heat, and sauté the shallot for about 2 minutes. Stir in the garlic paste, or minced garlic, and cook for about 1 minute. Add the Arborio rice and sauté for a couple of minutes, then add the wine. Stir and let cook for about 3 minutes, until the alcohol evaporates.
2. Begin adding the warm broth to the rice mixture pan, one ladle at a time, stirring frequently and letting the rice absorb each ladle of stock almost completely between additions. Stop adding broth once the rice is al dente and looks creamy. Do not add broth after this point, or the rice will become mushy.
3. Stir in the grated Parmesan cheese and Huancaina Sauce, starting with 1 cup, adding more if desired, to reach your preferred consistency.

Optional: Add green peas and/or top with a sprinkle of freshly chopped parsley.

Serving suggestion: This dish pairs well with Beef Milanese (see page 132, Main courses) and Beef Stir-Fried (see page 134, Main courses).

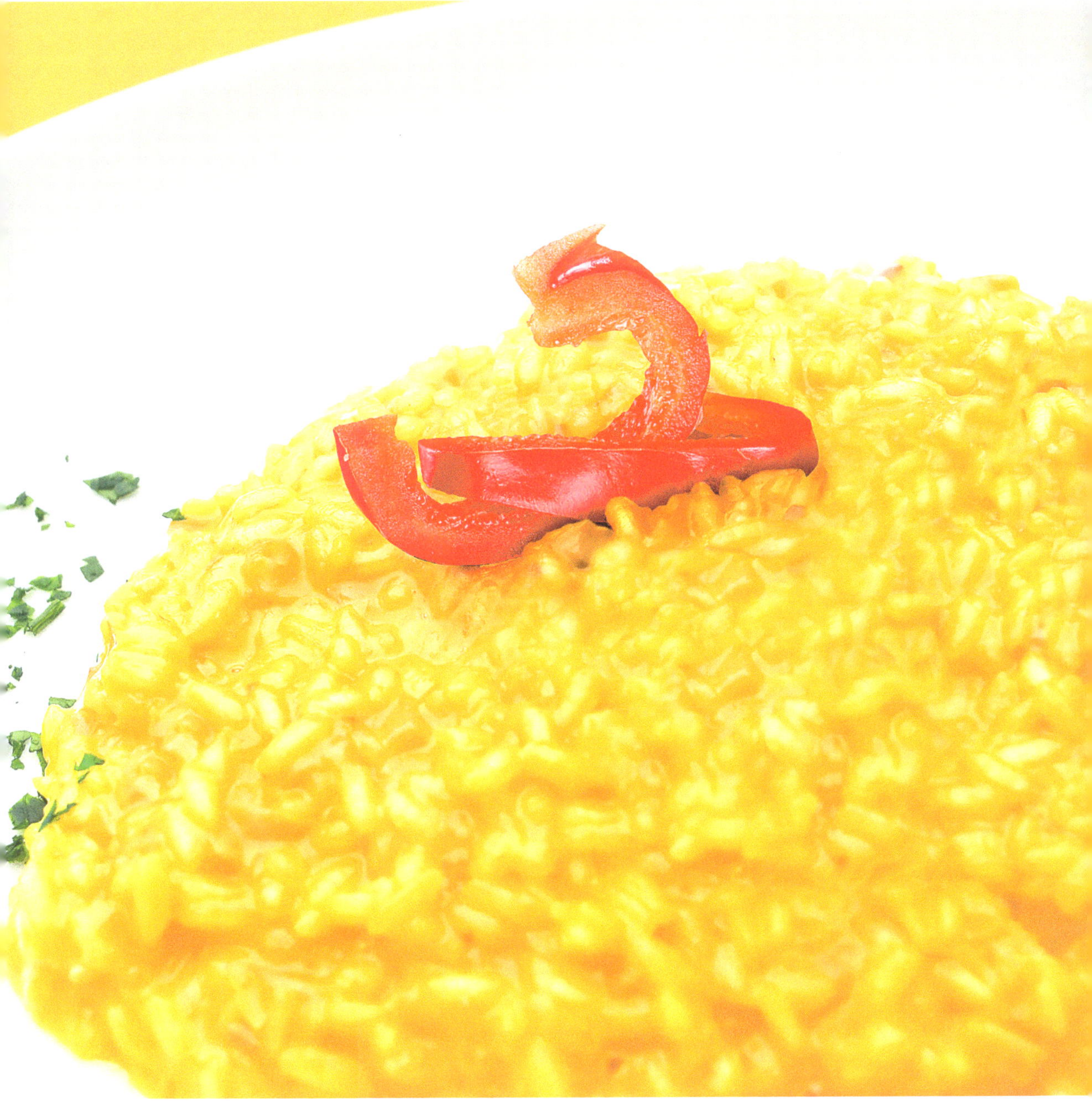

MAMAMA'S POOM CHICKEN

Pollo Pum de mi Mamama

GLUTEN FREE

40'

4 SERVINGS

My Mamama had a few quick but awesome meals in her cooking arsenal. And one of them was this. It is a flash style meal, done in 20 minutes. The name after this recipe has a story that makes me smile every time. I remember when asking my Mamama for it, and she said: "Oh! It's simple, look, Cholita, Poom! You grab your pot, Poom! add some oil, Poom!, seared the chicken, Poom! Add your other ingredients, and Poom! Your dinner is ready!" I laughed...

Some time ago, I had literally only 20 minutes to cook. I thought, what should I make? I had rice and boiled potatoes... hmmm. Then I remembered! I knew just what to make: My Mamama's Poom Chicken! My children were excited about eating it, and my husband asked why I'd never made it before. I told him with a sassy look: "I had a trick up my sleeve". So it was a good thing I had so little time to cook, and Poom!

Ingredients

2 tablespoons peanut oil, or vegetable oil
1 pound chicken tenders, legs or thighs patted dry with paper towels
1 tablespoon minced fresh ginger
1 tablespoon minced garlic
1 red bell pepper, diced
2 tablespoons light soy sauce
2 tablespoons rice vinegar
¼ teaspoon Chinese five spice powder
1 can (12 fluid ounces) Cola
1 teaspoon cornstarch stirred into 3 tablespoons cold water, to make a slurry
1 tablespoon toasted sesame oil
1 tablespoon combined white and black toasted sesame seeds
½ cup finely chopped green onions or scallions (green part only), to garnish

Preparation

1. Heat oil in a deep nonstick skillet over medium-high heat. When heated, add chicken and cook until the underside is golden brown, 3 to 4 minutes. Flip the tenders and fry until golden. Remove the pan from the heat and transfer the chicken to a plate. Set aside. Keep the chicken cooking oil in the pan.
2. In the same skillet, over medium heat, add the ginger and garlic and stir several times until fragrant. Add the diced bell pepper, soy sauce, rice vinegar, five-spice powder, and Cola, and stir to combine. Carefully add chicken and stir to coat with the sauce.

3. Bring to a boil, then immediately turn the heat to low, and simmer for 15 minutes.
4. Gently stir in the cornstarch slurry, and mix until the sauce has slightly thickened. Just before serving, stir in toasted sesame oil.
5. Serve warm and garnish with green onions and sesame seeds.

Note: Serve with White Garlicky Rice (see page 102, Sides & Sauces), Fried Rice (see page 156, Main Courses), or your favorite vegetables.

MAMAMA'S SPANISH EGGS

Huevos a la Española de mi Mamama

VEGETARIAN

25'

2-4 SERVINGS

Well, according to my grandparents we had an aunt, from my Mamama's side, who didn't know how to cook (much). Actually, the one thing that she knew how to make was Huevos a la Española. It is such an effortless dish, with essentially four ingredients, that could actually be served for breakfast, lunch, or dinner.

And even for the ones that think "cooking is not my thing" this recipe will be a good ace under your sleeve.

Ingredients

2 tablespoons olive oil
1–2 tablespoons minced garlic
Salt and pepper to taste
1 teaspoon dried oregano
2 cups tomato purée*
4 large eggs
A handful of fresh flat-leaf parsley, finely chopped

*If making purée using fresh tomatoes, peel and seed four medium-size tomatoes and process in a blender or food processor. Alternatively, you can also purée canned whole or chopped tomatoes.

Preparation

1. Heat a medium-large saucepan over medium heat. Add the oil and sauté the garlic until light golden. Season with salt, pepper, and the oregano, then stir in the tomato sauce and let cook for 5–10 minutes, until slightly thickened.
2. With the back of a spoon, make four wells in the sauce. Crack an egg into each well in. Cover the pan with a lid and let the eggs cook for about 3–5 minutes, or until they reach preferred doneness.
3. Serve immediately and top with the chopped parsley.

Serving suggestion: This quick and versatile dish can be served for breakfast with crusty bread or toast, or an easy lunch or dinner served with fried potatoes, White Garlicky Rice (see page 102, Sides & Sauces), pasta or your favorite vegetables.

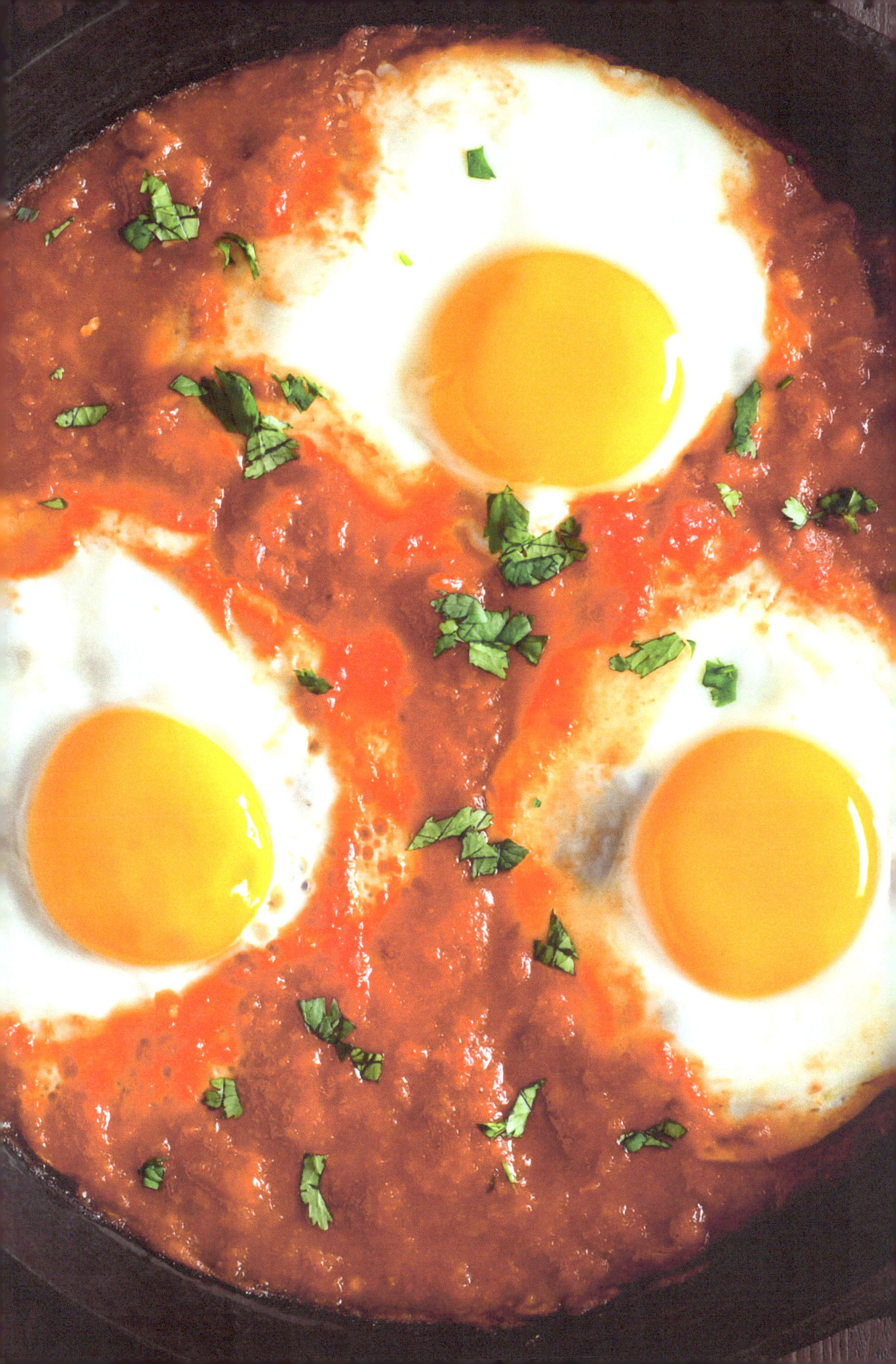

MARINATED FISH ESCABECHE

Escabeche de Pescado

4h • 6 SERVINGS

I remember being at the kitchen table at my Mamama's and Tata's house. On it were several enameled metal trays, white serving dishes with blue edges, filled with this beautiful, deep dark, and shiny, red color sauce over thick slices of pickled onions, thin slices of yellow pepper, Botija olives, chunks of Queso Fresco, rounds of hard-boiled egg, and fresh sprigs of parsley completely blanketing the fried fish fillets underneath—a hidden treasure!

The trick to this magnificent dish was to let it rest overnight to allow the fish to absorb the deliciousness of the onion and pepper juices. Oh, my! The following day, it was served for lunch, topped with slices of sweet potatoes. Believe me, the contrast of the savory-tangy-sweet and crunchy onions were to die for! This dish is supposed to be eaten cold or at room temperature, but if you prefer you can warm it up.

To me, a good Escabeche is a pleasure that lives on in my mental and taste memory. Try it!

One of my favorites!

Ingredients

3 cups water
½ cup vinegar
3 peppercorns
1 ½ tablespoons salt
2 big red onions cut in thick 1-inch slices
2 pounds Sea bass fillets cut in 3 x 2 inches
1 tablespoon salt
¼ teaspoon ground pepper
Pinch of cumin (for the fish)
½ cup flour
3 yellow hot peppers, julienned
3 tablespoons vegetable oil
½ cup Panca hot pepper paste
¼ cup garlic paste
½ cup chopped parsley
1 teaspoon salt
1 teaspoon oregano
1 teaspoon cumin (for the sauté)
¼ teaspoon black pepper

Garnish
Lettuce, hard boiled egg halves or wedges, Queso Fresco, black olives, yellow hot pepper, fresh parsley

Preparation

1. Bring to a boil water, vinegar, peppercorns and salt in a pot. Cook onion slices for 3 minutes, and reserve in the refrigerator. Also reserve the water-vinegar liquid for later.
2. Season the fish with salt, pepper, cumin, and dust the pieces with flour.

3. Pan fry, or deep fry the fish. Reserve in a deep platter.
4. Make sauté with oil, Panca hot pepper paste, garlic paste, oregano, cumin, pepper and salt.
5. When the sauté is ready add the reserved water-vinegar liquid until it boils all together.
6. Lower the temperature and add the cooked onions and the julienned yellow hot pepper, just until warm.
7. Pour all this onion mixture liquid over the fried fish, and let the fish marinade a few hours or overnight.
8. Before serving, garnish with lettuce, hard boiled eggs, olives, Queso Fresco, yellow hot pepper, and parsley.

Note: It could be served with a side of rice, sweet potatoes, fried Yuccas or potatoes, and some wedges of lime to brighten it up.

OLLUCO MEDLEY
Ajiaco de Ollucos

SPICY

40'

4 SERVINGS

This, by far is my favorite one! There are different medleys, some made with slipper gourd (caigua), others just with potatoes.

My Mamama used to make the one with Ollucos, and topped it with either a fried fish fillet, or fried egg, and some Onion Relish.

The creaminess, that the potatoes, milk, and cheese bring, and the spiciness of the yellow hot pepper and the black mint make this dish super comforting. If you are familiar with Peruvian gastronomy, you might be thinking if we also serve it with a side of rice, and the answer is YES! It's so good...

I've also served it with other proteins and by itself. You have to try it and let me know what you think. It will be a pleasant surprise to your palate!

Ingredients

3 tablespoons vegetable oil
1 cup red onion small diced
1 tablespoon garlic paste
2 tablespoons yellow hot pepper paste
¼ teaspoon ground cumin
1 pound Yukon Gold potatoes, peeled and medium diced
1 cup fava beans
½ pound Ollucos*
2 mint sprigs**
2 black mint sprigs
1 ½ cups of vegetable broth
Salt and pepper to taste
½ cup evaporated milk (unsweetened), or half and half
1 cup Queso Fresco, medium diced

Preparation

1. Preheat over medium heat a heavy bottom pot, add oil and sauté onions for 6 minutes.
2. Add garlic paste, and yellow hot pepper paste for 2 to 3 minutes.
3. Add cumin, potatoes, fava beans, Ollucos, ½ of the sprigs of mint and black mint, and vegetable broth.
4. Add salt and pepper and stir. Cover with a lid, and cook for approximately 6 minutes or until potatoes are soft enough to pierce with a fork.
5. Add milk and cheese with the rest of sprigs of mint and black mint. Simmer for a couple of minutes.

Serving suggestion: This dish can be served with fried, poached eggs, and fresh minced black mint, or with Onion Relish (see page 114, Sides & Sauces).

* Ollucos can be found canned, frozen or fresh.
** Black mint can be used as a paste.
(See Glossary, Ollucos and Black Mint)

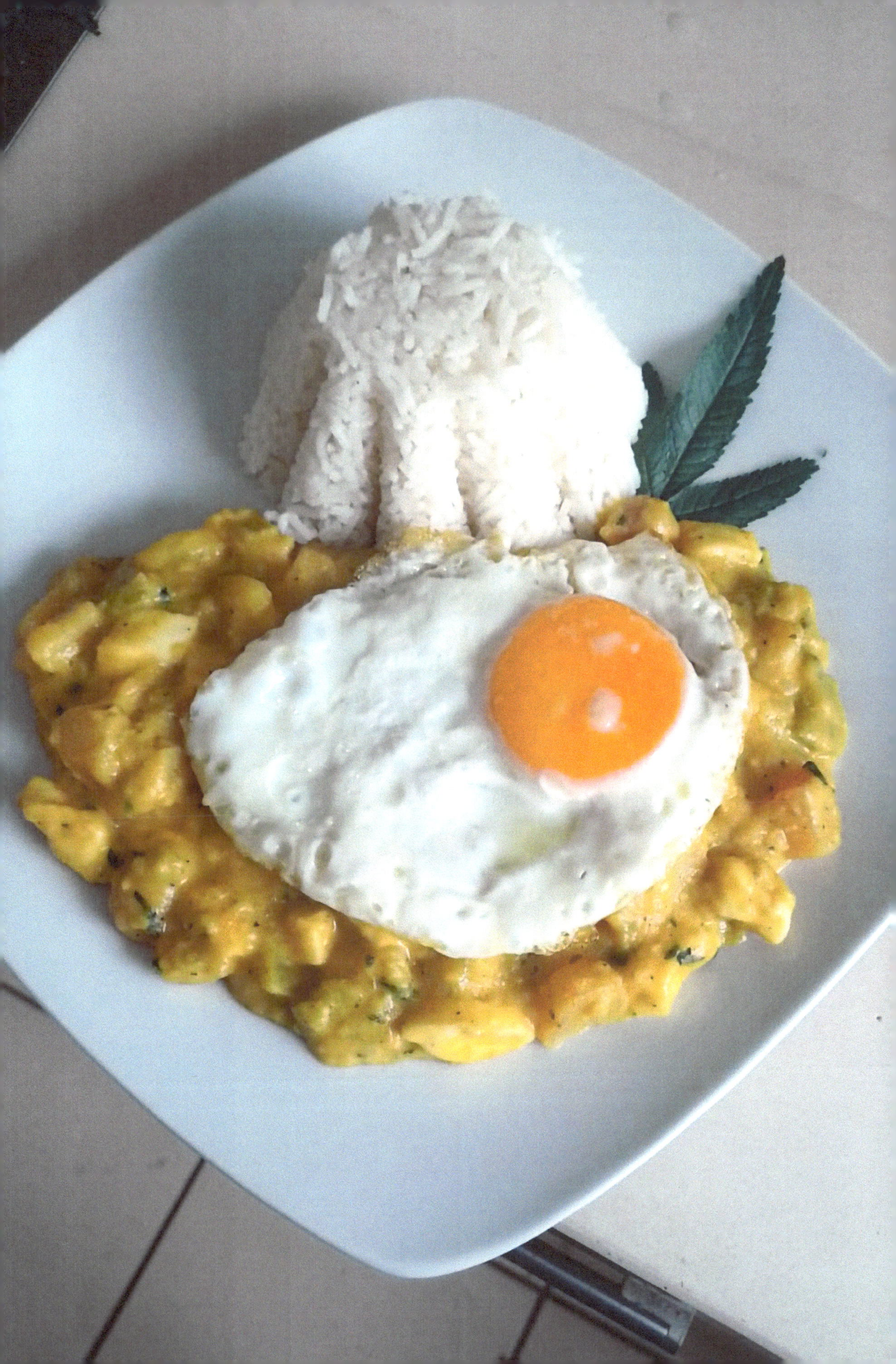

PICADILLO STUFFED POTATOES
Papas Rellenas

The day that my Mamama and nana Mery would make Papas Rellenas was a full-on kitchen production. Expectation would build as the hours went by, and the mounting desire to eat them was insane.

While the Picadillo was simmering, the potatoes were passed through the ricer to make them super smooth, until they were the perfect consistency to be stuffed and shaped. Frying them was very exciting for me, and a lot of work, but oh, boy—when they were ready to be served at lunchtime with a fresh Onion Relish (see page 114), and yes, a side of rice—ay ma-ma!

The thin, crispy outer layer, the creamy potato inside hiding the savory and flavorful Picadillo—yum! These are flavors and textures you won't want to miss, so I hope you'll try this recipe at least once. But odds are that once you've had it, you'll get hooked on this dish, and will serve it and pass the recipe on to your loved ones.

A tip: Try to recruit some family members or friends to help make a Picadillo Stuffed Potatoes production line, and have some fun!

Ingredients

For the Potato Dough
3 pounds Yukon Gold potatoes (about 6 medium, unpeeled)
½ teaspoon salt, or to taste
¼ teaspoon pepper, or to taste
1 cup flour, plus some more for dusting

For the Picadillo
¼ cup vegetable oil
2 cups red onion small diced
3 garlic cloves, minced
¼ cup yellow hot pepper paste
¼ cup Panca hot pepper paste
2 tablespoons tomato paste
½ teaspoon ground cumin
1 teaspoon dried oregano
1 pound ground beef
½ cup red wine, or beef broth
½ cup black olives, sliced
½ cup raisins (optional)
Salt and pepper to taste
2 hard-boiled eggs, roughly chopped
2 tablespoons chopped fresh parsley

Preparation

1. Boil the potatoes in a large pot of salted water, until they can be easily pierced with a fork, about 20–25 minutes. While the potatoes are boiling, make the Picadillo.

Picadillo
1. In a large skillet, with the oil over medium heat, cook the onions, garlic, yellow hot pepper, Panca hot pepper and tomato paste, until soft and fragrant. Add the cumin and oregano and cook 2 minutes more, stirring.
2. Add the ground beef and cook until browned. Add the red wine or beef broth, and simmer 10 to 15 minutes more, or until most of the liquid has evaporated. Stir in the olives and raisins (if using) in the beef mixture, season with salt and pepper to taste. Remove the Picadillo from the heat and set aside to cool.

Potato Dough
" When the potatoes are cooked, drain them in a colander. When warm enough to handle, peel the potatoes and then mash thoroughly, or pass them through a potato ricer. Season the mashed potatoes with salt and pepper to taste. Set aside.

Assembling and Frying the Picadillo Stuffed Potatoes
1. Using floured hands, scoop about ½ cup of mashed potatoes in one hand and make a well in the center. Fill the well with 1 to 2 tablespoons of the Picadillo, and a piece of hard-boiled egg.
2. Then, mold the potatoes around the beef, adding more mashed potato if necessary, to fully enclose the filling. Shape into an oblong with slightly pointed ends, about the size of a medium potato. Coat each Picadillo Stuffed Potato generously with flour. Repeat with the rest of the mashed potato dough in each one.
3. In a deep skillet or deep-fat fryer, heat 2 inches of oil to 360 °F.
4. Fry the Picadillo Stuffed Potatoes in batches until they are golden brown. Drain them on a rack, or a plate lined with paper towels.
5. Keep them warm in a 200 °F oven, until ready to serve.

PICADILLO STUFFED RICE

Arroz Tapado

GLUTEN FREE

35'

4-6 SERVINGS

If you're curious as to what is an everyday dish that Peruvians eat at home, you're on the right page! Arroz Tapado is the perfect go-to main course to enjoy with friends and family. Every household adds its own touch to this dish. For example, my Mamama used to stuff it with Bolognese sauce topped with Parmesan cheese, and she always made sure to serve it with warm thin slices of fried sweet potatoes. As bold as it sounds, it was delicious.

My version is more traditional, and if you're in the mood for a fried egg on top, please don't hold back. The egg yolk combined with the rice and the stuffing is absolutely delicious.

Ingredients

4–6 cups hot freshly-cooked rice (Garden Rice, see page 84, Sides & Sauces, or White Garlicky Rice, see page 102, Sides & Sauces)
¼ cup vegetable oil
1 red onion, chopped
3 garlic cloves, chopped
2 large tomatoes, chopped
1 pound ground beef
½ cup low-sodium beef broth, to moisten the ground beef (optional)
2 tablespoons soy sauce
½ cup raisins (optional)
½ cup black olives, pitted and sliced
Salt, pepper
2 chopped hard-boiled eggs
2 tablespoons chopped parsley

Preparation

1. Heat the oil in a sauté pan over medium-high heat, and sauté the onion and garlic. When the onion is soft and translucent, add the tomatoes, and stir for a few minutes.
2. Lower the heat to medium-low, add the soy sauce and the ground beef, breaking up the beef with a wooden spoon; cook for 15 minutes, stirring occasionally. If the mixture looks dry, add beef broth to moisten, as needed.
3. Add the raisins (if using), and cook for an additional 5 minutes to allow them to plump. If not, add the sliced olives and season with salt and pepper. Next, add the chopped hard-boiled eggs and parsley, and combine. Turn off the heat and set aside.

Assemble

1. Fluff the cooked rice. Then, using a ramekin as a mold, place a layer of rice in the bottom, pressing and smoothing it down into the ramekin with the back of a spoon. Top the rice base with a layer of the ground beef mixture. Cover the beef mixture with a final layer rice, pressing down gently.

2. To serve, invert a plate over the ramekin, then turn both upside-down. Remove the ramekin and you will have a nicely formed Picadillo Stuffed Rice!
3. Repeat the molding process for the remaining servings. Garnish with some picadillo and parsley.

Note: This dish is served topped with a fried egg and fried bananas in its Picadillo Stuffed Rice *a lo Pobre* version.

PORK AND PEANUT QUINOA MEDLEY

Guiso de Quinua con Cerdo y Maní

CONTAINS NUTS

45'

6 SERVINGS

One of the reasons why I decided to offer this recipe is because I grew up eating quinoa, even as a baby. To me, it is tasty and flavorful as well as being nutritious and a great source of plant protein. I'm aware that some people find quinoa bland, but it's important to know that quinoa will take on the taste of your seasonings. If you do not season your quinoa, it will not be as appealing as you might hope.

I give you my word, if you try this recipe, you'll remember my advice and come to love and enjoy quinoa as much as I do. Your turn to learn to love it!

Ingredients

2 tablespoons vegetable oil
1 pound pork tenderloins, cut into 1-inch cubes
1 cup red onion, small diced
1 pound white quinoa (washed thoroughly, unless its precooked, see page 145)
3 tablespoon Panca hot pepper paste
3 tablespoon yellow hot pepper paste
3 tablespoons garlic paste, or minced and mashed garlic
4–5 cups chicken broth
Salt and pepper to taste
1 cup roasted and salted peanuts, roughly chopped
Queso Fresco, cut into ¼-inch dices
Chopped parsley, to garnish

Preparation

1. Preheat a Dutch oven over high heat, add the oil and sear the pork chunks, cooking in batches to avoid crowding the meat. Remove the pork when seared on all sides, and set aside.
2. Using the same pot, reduce the heat to medium, and add the chopped onion; sauté for about 5 minutes, or until soft and golden.
3. Add the yellow hot pepper, Panca hot pepper, and garlic pastes, and cook for about 2 minutes. Return the pork chunks and any juices to the pot. Add the chicken broth and quinoa and bring to a boil; lower the heat and simmer with the lid on, stirring occasionally, for 20 minutes.
4. Add salt and pepper, incorporate the peanuts and serve.
5. To plate, top with crumbled Queso Fresco and chopped parsley.

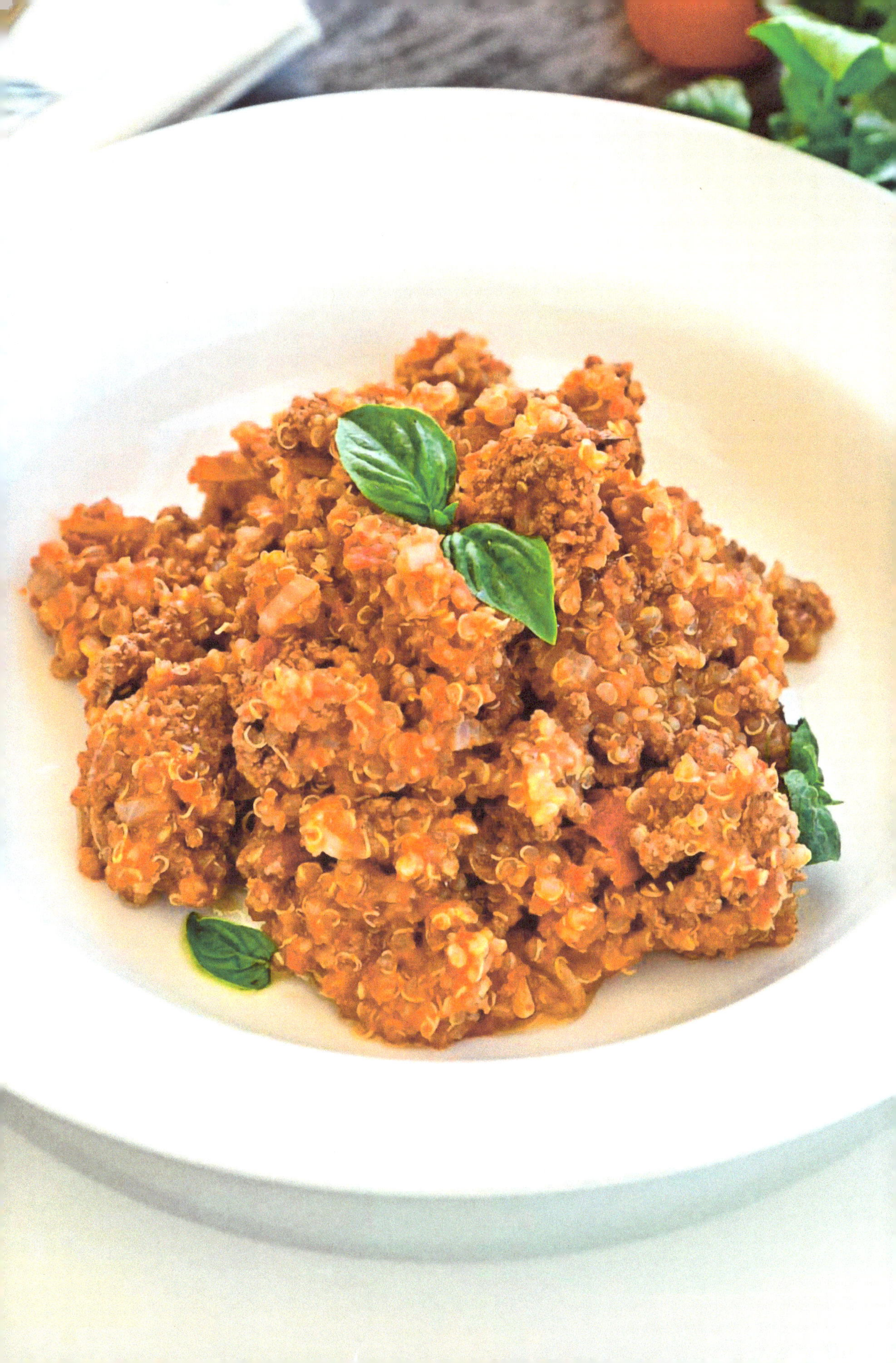

ROASTED TURKEY

Pavo al Horno

The star of the holiday table—the turkey! It may seem like a bit challenging, but believe me, it is much easier to make than it appears on the page. In the following recipe I share how to make the brine, the rub, and how to cook it to achieve a juicy bird with that golden color that everyone loves!

Ingredients

For the Brining
1-gallon cold water, divided
1 cup kosher salt
½ cup granulated, or brown sugar
Aromatic options: rosemary, bay leaf, peppercorns, cloves, juniper berries, allspice berries, orange peels, lemon peels, etc.

For the Turkey Rubbing
1 turkey, 10–12 pounds
3 tablespoons kosher salt
¼ cup fresh lime juice
10 garlic cloves
¼ cup Panca hot pepper paste, or red pepper paste
3 tablespoons Mirasol hot pepper paste, or yellow hot pepper paste
⅓ cup soy sauce
½ cup red wine vinegar
1 teaspoon dried oregano
1 tablespoon ground cumin
¼ cup olive oil

1 lime, halved
3 fresh sage leaves
3 fresh thyme sprigs
2 bay leaves
2 carrots, peeled and roughly chopped
2 celery stalks, roughly chopped
1 medium onion, roughly chopped

Preparation

Brining (2 days before cooking)
1. Combine in a large pot, ½-gallon (8 cups) of water, salt, sugar, aromatics of your preference, and place over medium-high heat. Bring to a boil, lower heat and simmer for 5 minutes, stirring to dissolve salt and sugar.
2. Remove the pot from the heat and allow cooling. Stir in the remaining ½-gallon of cold water and allow to cool completely.
3. Pour the brine into a container just large enough to hold turkey comfortably (a 4–5 gallon vessel should hold the brine and a 10 to 12 pound turkey).
4. Immerge the turkey in the brining liquid; if needed, add more water or ice, to thoroughly cover the turkey; if it floats, place a heavy plate over the turkey to keep it submerged.
5. Chill the turkey in the brining liquid overnight.

Turkey Rubbing (1 day before cooking)
1. Remove the turkey from brine, rinse the turkey under cold water inside and outside. Pat dry with paper towels inside and outside and discard the brine.
2. After drying the turkey, rub it inside and out with the salt and lime juice, carefully lifting up the skin without tearing, rubbing the lime and salt mixture underneath.
3. In a blender, place the garlic, Panca and Mirasol hot pepper paste, soy sauce, vinegar, oregano, cumin and olive oil, then mix for 30 seconds.
4. Rub the turkey with the mixture, inside and out.
5. Place the lime halves, sage, thyme and bay leaves in the turkey cavity. Tuck the wings under and tie the legs with kitchen string.
6. Let the turkey rest in the refrigerator, uncovered, for 24 hours.

Cooking day
1. Remove the turkey from the refrigerator and allow to sit at room temperature for about 1 hour.
2. Preheating the oven to 350 °F.
3. In a large heavy roasting pan, place the chopped carrots, celery and onions. Sit the turkey breast-side up on top the bed of vegetables.
4. Put the roasting pan in the oven, and let the turkey roast for 1 hour, then cover loosely with aluminum foil and roast for an additional hour.
5. Uncover the turkey and roast for another 30–45 minutes, or until the inserted thermometer in the thickest part of the turkey registers 165 °F.
6. When the turkey is done, remove the pan from the oven and place the turkey on a platter. Cover loosely with aluminum foil and let it rest for about 15–20 minutes before carving and serving.

SEAFOOD CAU-CAU

Cau-Cau con Mariscos

SEAFOOD | **30'** | **4 SERVINGS**

There are many variations of Cau-Cau, which may be made with chicken or seafood instead of tripe, which was used in the traditional version. But one of the distinctive, irreplaceable ingredients is fresh mint. Its clean, sharp aroma and flavor enhances the dish and makes it unique.

In Peru, Cau-Cau is traditionally served with a side of fluffy White Garlicky Rice, which absorbs the sauce and helps you savor the flavors even more. A good squeeze of fresh lime juice will broaden the flavors and add brightness to this outstanding dish.

Ingredients

2 tablespoons vegetable oil
2 cups red or yellow onions finely diced
2 tablespoons minced garlic
¼ cup yellow hot pepper paste, or to taste
¼ teaspoon ground cumin
1 teaspoon turmeric powder
Salt and pepper to taste
3 cups seafood stock, or clam juice
1 pound red potatoes medium diced
8 ounces mussels in the shell
12 clams in their shells
½ pound medium shrimp
6 ounces large sea scallops
½ pound calamari, cut into ½ inch rings
1 tablespoon lime juice
¼ cup mint finely chopped

Preparation

1. Heat the oil in a saucepan over medium heat. Sauté the onion and garlic until medium brown; add the yellow hot pepper paste, cumin, turmeric, salt, and pepper. Cook for 5 minutes.
2. Add the stock and the diced potatoes. Bring to a boil and let the potatoes cook just halfway, about 7 minutes.
3. Add the seafood in the following order: First, mussels and clams, cooking for about 3–5 minutes. Next, add the shrimp, and cook for 1 minute, then the scallops and calamari, cooking for one more minute. Remove the pan from the heat and stir in the lime juice and mint. Taste for seasoning.

Serving suggestion: Serve with White Garlicky Rice (see page 102, Sides & Sauces). If you're a chilli lover, serve with additional Yellow Hot Pepper Paste (see page 124, Sides & Sauces).

Note: To prepare the mussels and the clams, wash them thoroughly before cooking. It is very important to discard any shell that hasn't opened after cooking.

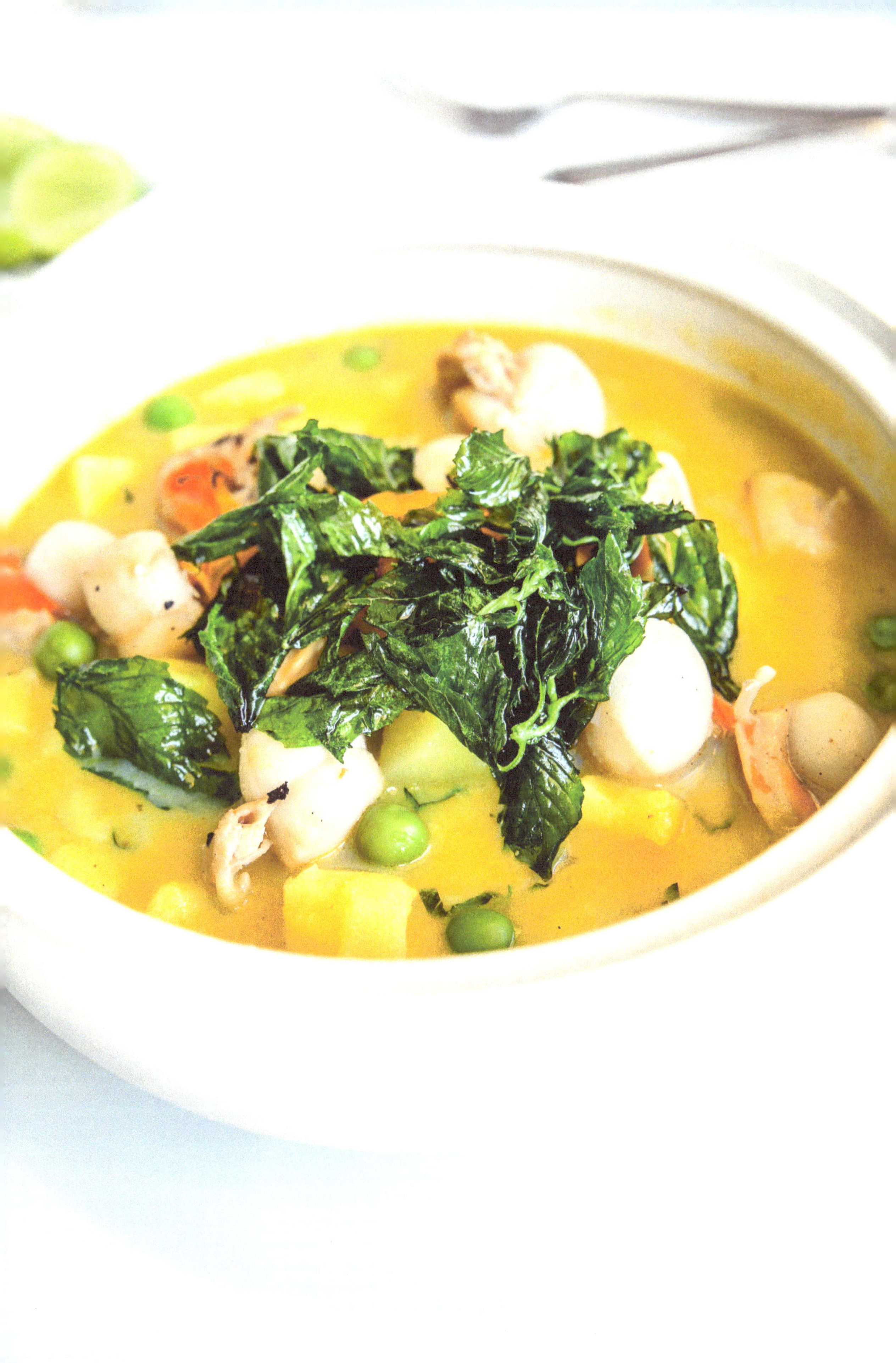

SEAFOOD RICE

Arroz con Mariscos

35'

4-6 SERVINGS

Arroz con Mariscos is made with one of the most-consumed grains that we have in Peru: rice! Peruvians' relationship with rice can be referred to using a similar endearment that Julia Child shared with her husband: "You are the butter to my bread and the breath to my life." What she said! But about rice!

This dish is best eaten inmediately to enjoy the tender seafood at peak perfection. Otherwise, if reheated, the seafood suffers the indignity of becoming tough and chewy.

Like other dishes from my beloved Peru, this one is the outcome of a tango of gastronomic cultures, resulting in a scrumptious, aphrodisiacal, sexy, umami-packed, super good looking, good-tasting dish. It pairs great with a Chilcano de Pisco, a cold beer or a light, crisp white wine. *Salud*!

Ingredients

3 tablespoons vegetable oil
½ cup red onion finely diced
3 garlic cloves, minced
1 tomato, peeled, seeded and chopped, or
1 tablespoon tomato paste
1–2 tablespoons yellow hot pepper, chopped
½ teaspoon dried oregano
1 bay leaf
¼ cup Panca hot pepper paste
¼ cup white wine
¼ cup fish stock
3 cups cooked white rice (see page 102)
10 cleaned mussels
10 cleaned clams
12 medium size shrimp, peeled and deveined
8 ounces squid, cut in ½-inch rings
⅓ cup roasted red bell pepper, roughly chopped
½ cup cooked green peas
½ cup grated Parmesan cheese
1 tablespoon cilantro leaves, chopped
Salt and pepper to taste
1 fresh lime

Preparation

1. Heat the oil in a large sauté pan over high heat, and cook the onion, stirring for 3 minutes.
2. Lower the heat to medium, add the minced garlic and continue cooking 2 more minutes.
3. Add the chopped tomato (or tomato paste), yellow hot pepper, dried oregano, bay leaf, and Panca hot pepper. Cook for 5 minutes.
4. Add the white wine, bring to a boil and let it reduce by half. Add the fish stock and the pre-cooked rice.

5. Next, add the seafood in the following order: mussels and clams first, cooking them 4 minutes; add the shrimp and cook 2 minutes; finally, add the squid and cook for 1 minute. Immediately remove the pan from the heat and discard the bay leaf.
6. Quickly and gently incorporate the chopped bell pepper, the peas, the Parmesan cheese, cilantro leaves, salt and pepper.
7. Squeeze fresh lime juice over the rice and serve immediately.

Note: This dish is typically garnished with Onion Relish (see page 114, Sides & Sauces). The exciting finale? Serve with a refreshing Pisco Sour (see page 292, Cocktails & Drinks) or Chilcano de Pisco (see page 276, Cocktails & Drinks)!

STEAMED FISH

Sudado de Pescado

45'

4 SERVINGS

I don't have many memories of my father, but one that pops vividly to my mind is a vision of him, tall, eating a huge bowl of Sudado de Pescado.

I recall the fragrance and the look of the dish, and the way my father would eat it with a pleasurable groan. A good squeeze of lime was always in order, and a lot of yellow hot pepper. My father's face would turn red from the heat of the peppers, and a few tears even fell from his big green eyes.

So, you may have guessed that this could be a dish to wake up the dead, making it an effective remedy for a *resaca* (hangover). Just enjoy and embrace it, let it flush out the demons and you'll notice the benefits!

The word in Spanish *sudado* translates to 'sweaty', so this dish could be called Sweaty Fish, but that's not a very appealing name, right? Shall we say the fish is perspiring in a savory sauna? The whole point is that the fish is cooked or steamed on a bed of vegetables, with white wine and beer. And believe me, it will warm the coldest heart, or at least warm your body. Try it and you'll see.

Ingredients

2 tablespoons vegetable oil
1 cup red onion finely diced
2 tablespoons garlic paste, or minced and mashed garlic
¼ cup yellow hot pepper paste
2 tablespoon ginger (optional)
1 cup white wine
1 cup Chicha de Jora or ½ cup beer
1 ½ cups fish stock
Pinch of ground cumin
1 ½ cups fresh Roma tomatoes in thick julienne, divided
2 medium red onions, cut lengthwise into ½-inch thick julienne strips, divided
½ cup green onions, cut into 2-inch lengths, divided
¼ cup fresh yellow hot pepper, sliced lengthwise into ¼ inch thick slices, divided
10 fresh cilantro sprigs, divided
1 ½ pounds red snapper, halibut, cod, or other firm white fish fillets
Salt and pepper to taste
1 or 2 Limo hot pepper, cut crosswise into thin rounds
1 lime

Preparation

1. Heat the oil in a large high-sided skillet over medium heat. Sauté the diced onions and garlic for about 5 minutes. Stir in the yellow hot pepper

paste and the ginger (if using) and cook for 3 minutes. Add the wine and the Chicha de Jora, or beer, and cook until reduced slightly, about 3 to 5 minutes.
2. Stir the fish stock in the skillet with a pinch of cumin. Place ½ of the tomatoes, ½ of the raw onions, ½ of the green onions, ½ of the fresh yellow hot pepper, and ½ of the cilantro sprigs atop the stock mixture. Do not stir the vegetables — they will become the "bed" for the fish fillets.
3. Season the fish fillets with salt and pepper; gently place the fillets on top of the bed of vegetables and aromatics. Top with the rest of the tomatoes, onions, green onion, fresh yellow hot pepper, and cilantro sprigs. Cover and reduce the heat. Simmer for about 5 minutes, or until the fish is cooked, depending on the thickness of the fillets.
4. When the fish is cooked, immediately remove the pan from the heat; add the Limo hot pepper and a few squeezes of lime juice.
5. Serve immediately in bowls with a good amount of the broth.

Note: In Peru we eat this dish with a generous side of White Garlicky Rice (see page 102, Sides & Sauces), or boiled Yucca.

SHRIMP FRIED RICE
Arroz Chaufa con Camarones

SEAFOOD

35'

2-3 SERVINGS

If you're a shrimp lover, this is a quick, time-friendly dish that will help you get lunch or dinner on the table in about 30 minutes, or so, and all in one skillet.

Pretty much anything can go into fried rice—usually a combination of leftover rice (when making fried rice, never use freshly cooked rice!), garlic, ginger, green onions, sesame oil, soy sauce, some finely chopped veggies, beaten eggs, and shrimp, or the protein of your choice.

One suggestion for making this dish is not to cook the shrimps all the way through initially. The reason is that you'll later add them back into the fried rice, where they will finish cooking. That way you're making sure to have tender and juicy shrimps. Yum!

Ingredients

2 tablespoons vegetable oil, divided
2 eggs
¼ cup scallions finely sliced (both parts, white and green, separated)
1 tablespoon garlic paste, or minced and mashed garlic
½ tablespoon ginger paste, or fresh ginger, grated or finely chopped
1 cup whole medium-size raw shrimp, peeled and deveined
2 cups cooked white or brown rice
½ cup cooked black quinoa (Helping hand, see page 145)
3 tablespoons soy sauce
1 tablespoon oyster sauce
1 tablespoon toasted sesame oil
2 tablespoons toasted sesame seeds (combined white and black)

Preparation

1. Heat a wok or sauté pan over medium heat, and add 1 tablespoon of the vegetable oil. Whisk the eggs, add to the pan and scramble quickly; remove the eggs from the pan and set aside.
2. Using the same pan, increase the heat to medium-high and add the remaining tablespoon of vegetable oil. Stir-fry the white slices of the scallions, garlic, ginger, and shrimp; cook just until the shrimp begins to turn pink.
3. Stir in the rice, the quinoa, the soy sauce, the oyster sauce and 1 tablespoon of sesame oil. Quickly stir in the scrambled eggs and immediately remove the pan from the heat.
4. Plate the servings and top with the toasted sesame seeds and the green parts of the scallions. Serve immediately.

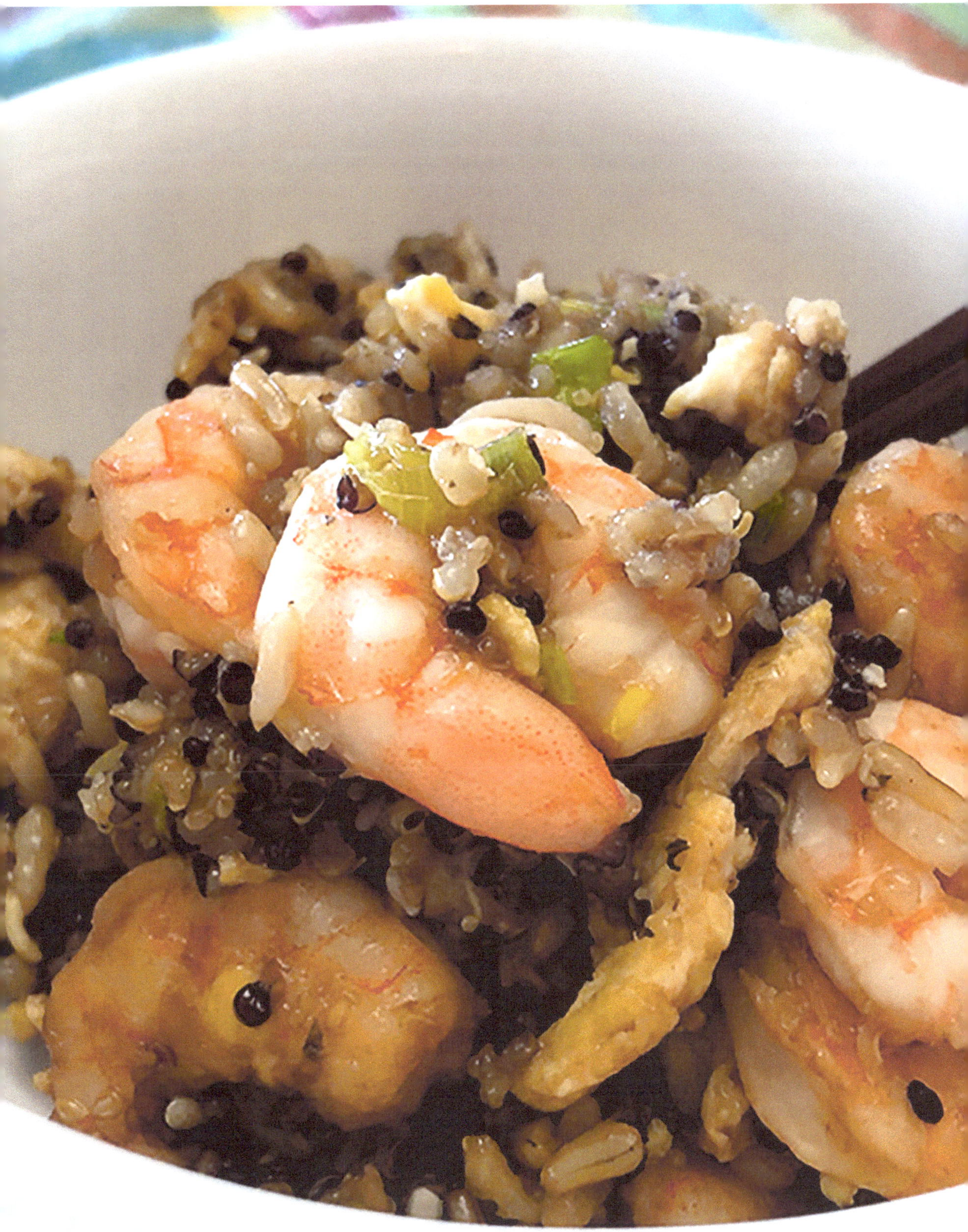

SPICY BEEF STEW

Picante de Carne

GLUTEN FREE

45'

4–6 SERVINGS

There's something about this dish that makes it so satisfying! Maybe it's because the mixture of ingredients make it nutritious and light, with a unique spicy richness thanks to the yellow and Panca hot peppers, which hug all the components, imparting their exquisite essence. You can make it super spicy, medium, or mild—it's up to you. This recipe has a medium to mild spiciness, so feel free to adjust it to your liking.

This is an ideal stew to serve with rice, because it will absorb the irresistible sauce. And the neutral starchiness of rice perfectly balances the hot pepper. However, this delicious Picante de Carne will surely win your affections.

Ingredients

¼ cup vegetable oil, divided
1 ½ pounds filet mignon or sirloin steak, cut into 1-inch pieces
2 cups finely diced red onion
2 tablespoon yellow hot pepper paste
3 tablespoon Panca hot pepper paste
1 tablespoon garlic paste, or minced and mashed garlic
1 teaspoon ground cumin
2–3 cups unsalted beef stock
2 cups medium diced Russet or Red potato
½ cup medium diced carrot
½ cup frozen corn kernels
½ cup green peas, fresh or frozen
Salt and ground black pepper to taste
Fresh chopped parsley, to garnish

Preparation

1. Preheat a heavy-bottomed pot on medium-high heat, and coat the bottom of the pot with some oil. Add the steak and sear for about 3–4 minutes. Remove the steak from the pot and set aside.
2. In the same pot, put additional oil if needed; when the oil is hot, add the onions and sauté until golden brown. Incorporate the yellow and the Panca hot pepper pastes, and sauté for 3 minutes, until fragrant. Add the garlic and the cumin and sauté for 1 minute. Season with salt and pepper.
3. Return the steak to the pan, combining with the onion and hot peppers mixture. Pour the stock. Add the potatoes, carrots, and corn and bring the stew to a simmer; cover and cook for 8 minutes, or until the potatoes, carrots and corn are cooked. Add the peas and cook another 3 to 5 minutes.
4. Serve topped with a sprinkle of chopped parsley.

COOKS!

SPICY CREAMY CHICKEN MEDLEY

Ají de Gallina

SPICY

60'

6–8 SERVINGS

This satisfying dish—with a sauce based on Yellow Hot Pepper Paste—is a tradition in any Peruvian household, and for me, brings fond memories. Enhanced with walnuts or pecans, Parmesan cheese, milk and shredded chicken. Learning to make a delicious Spicy Creamy Chicken Medley recipe is one of the first steps in discovering a bit more about the rich flavors of Peruvian cuisine.

Admittedly, this dish probably wins the carbohydrate prize! It includes our own Peruvian version of roux, made with milk and bread. In addition, it is also served with potatoes and a generous portion of rice. It is a comforting caress to the belly.

Ingredients

4 Yukon Gold potatoes
4–6 slices soft white bread
¾ cup evaporated milk (unsweetened)
2 pounds cooked chicken breast
2–4 cups chicken stock
⅓ cup vegetable oil, plus 3 tablespoons
3–4 whole yellow hot peppers, stems removed
1 tablespoon Panca hot pepper paste
1 large red onion small diced
2 tablespoons garlic, minced or paste
1 cup chopped walnuts
1 cup chopped pecans
¾ cup grated Parmesan cheese
3–4 hard-boiled eggs
10 black Botija or Kalamata olives, pitted and halved
½ cup fresh minced parsley
Salt (if needed)

Preparation

1. Cook the potatoes in salted water until tender when pierced with a fork. Let cool, then peel, and cut into 1-inch slices, and set aside.
2. Shred the cooled chicken into bite-size pieces.
3. Place the bread slices in a small bowl, and pour the evaporated milk over it to soak. Set aside.
4. In a blender, process the yellow hot peppers with the ⅓ cup of the vegetable oil until smooth. Pour paste into a separate bowl, and set aside. (No need to rinse the blender, it will be used again in step 6).
5. In a pot, large enough to hold later the chicken and the chicken stock, preheat the 3 oil tablespoons over medium heat, and cook the onions until soft and golden. Incorporate the hot pepper pastes (Panca and yellow) and the garlic; sauté for one minute, then remove the pan from the heat.

6. Next, add the soaked bread and milk to the blender; purée until smooth. Return the pan with the onion mixture to a burner set to low heat, and gently stir the bread purée.
7. Now add 2 cups of chicken stock to the pan. Bring to a low simmer, then stir in the chicken. Add more chicken stock if the sauce becomes too thick.
8. Add the nuts, and Parmesan cheese. Taste and add more salt if necessary.

Note: To serve, place a few potato slices on each plate, and top with the chicken medley. Garnish with halves or wedges of hard-boiled egg, black olives, and minced parsley.

This dish is traditionally served with a side of White Garlicky Rice (see page 102, Sides & Sauces). For spiciness to your likeness, add more Yellow Hot Pepper Paste (see page 124, Sides & Sauces).

SPICY CREAMY TUNA MEDLEY

Ají de Atún

SEAFOOD

30'

4 SERVINGS

Not long ago, I was home in the middle of some projects, and I totally lost track of time. Suddenly, it was almost time for dinner, and I had nothing prepared. So, I got into action! First thing, lets set a kettle with boiling water, next, open the pantry and check what's in hand. Quickly my eyes landed on some canned tuna, and the inspiration for dinner was there. Finally, I gathered my ingredients, and in no time, we had a super flavorful, nutritious, and warm meal.

This is one of those dishes that you can make in 20 minutes, and done. The origin of this dish comes from the inspiration of the traditional Spicy Creamy Chicken Medley. It is typically served with a side of rice, hard-boiled egg, olives, and some slices of potatoes (because we love carbs!).

This dish was in semi-regular rotation at my Mamama's, and I hope you'll incorporate it at home because it is delicious, and we love it!

Ingredients

4 slices wonder bread
¾ cup evaporated milk (unsweetened)
3–4 yellow hot peppers, stems removed
⅓ cup vegetable oil, plus 3 tablespoons
1 large red onion small diced
1 tablespoon Panca hot pepper paste
2 tablespoons garlic, minced or paste
2–3 cans of tuna (3 ounces each)
1 cup fish stock (or more if necessary)
¾ cup grated parmesan cheese

To serve
2 Yukon Gold potatoes, boiled and sliced
3–4 hard-boiled eggs
10 black olives (Botija or Kalamata), pitted and halved
½ cup fresh minced parsley

Preparation

1. Place the bread slices in a small bowl and pour the evaporated milk over it to soak. Set aside.
2. In a blender, process the yellow hot pepper with ⅓ cup of vegetable oil until smooth. Pour into a separate bowl and set aside. No need to rinse the blender; it will be used again for step 4.
3. In a pot large enough to later hold the tuna and fish stock, preheat the 3 tablespoons of oil over medium heat and cook the onions until soft and golden. Incorporate the yellow hot pepper paste set aside, the Panca hot pepper paste and the garlic; sauté for 1 minute, then remove the pan from the heat.

4. Next, add the soaked bread and milk to the blender, purée until smooth.
5. Return the pan with the onion mixture to a burner set to low heat and gently stir in the bread purée. Add the cup of fish stock to the pan. Bring to a low simmer. Drain the tuna and stir in the pan. Add the parmesan cheese. Taste and add more salt if necessary. Add more fish stock if the sauce becomes too thick.
6. To serve, place a few potato slices on each plate, and top with the Spicy Creamy Tuna Medley. Garnish with slices of hard-boiled egg, black olives, and fresh parsley.

Note: This dish is traditionally served with a side of White Garlicky Rice (see page 102, Sides & Sauces).

SPICY SEAFOOD STEW

Picante de Mariscos

Just thinking of the incredible flavors of Peruvian seafood makes me want to dig a hole and go straight to the coast of Peru! This is "THE dish!" It is well known for wining people's hearts every time.

Whenever I go back to Peru, one of the first dishes that I look for in a *Cevichería* or *Picantería* is this one. These two types of restaurants specialize in cooking seafood using many different preparations. Their ambience, vibe, the fragrance of fresh seafood, the look in the diners' eyes, the servers, the cooks—everything and everyone has a special swing, and that's what makes these restaurants so special.

Spicy Seafood Stew isn't too spicy, and the flavor is so scrumptious you'll probably want to lick your plate!

Ingredients

4 tablespoons vegetable oil
2 red onions finely chopped
12 garlic cloves finely chopped
1 tomato, skinned, seeded, and chopped
Salt and pepper to taste
Pinch of cumin
8 tablespoons yellow hot pepper paste
1 tablespoon Pisco
1 tablespoon white wine
½ cup evaporated milk (unsweetened)
4 slices white sandwich bread
1 sprig fresh oregano
1 cup vegetable broth or stock
16 large shrimps, peeled and deveined
4 jumbo shrimps, peeled and deveined
¼ cup (3 ounces) cooked octopus
½ pound calamari, cut into ½-inch rings
8 medium size scallops, cleaned
1 ½ ounces ground pecans or walnuts

To serve

4 Yukon Gold potatoes, boiled and sliced
4 hard-boiled eggs
Salt and pepper
Lemon or lime, juice and wedges
Curly parsley

Preparation

1. Preheat a large sauté pan over medium heat; pour the oil and sauté the onion until golden brown, add the garlic and tomato, and sauté for another 3 minutes, season with salt and pepper. Then mix in the cumin and yellow hot pepper paste, and cook over low heat for another 3 minutes, until fragrant. Add the Pisco and wine and allow the alcohol to evaporate about 2 minutes.

2. Meanwhile, in a blender, blend the evaporated milk and bread slices together.
3. Pour the bread mixture to the sauté pan along with the oregano sprig. Increase the burner heat to medium-high, gradually adding the fish or vegetable stock. Cook until thickened and creamy, about 4 minutes.
4. Add the shrimp and octopus, and cook for 1 minute. Add the squid, scallops and ground nuts. Cook for another 2 minutes until the scallops and squid are just cooked. Taste and adjust the seasoning.

Serving suggestion: Divide the potato slices and hard-boiled eggs between large shallow bowls and ladle over the stew. Add a squeeze of lemon or lime, and garnish with wedges and a few sprigs of parsley.

SPICY SHRIMP STEW

Picante de Camarones

SEAFOOD

45'

4 SERVINGS

This dish is delicious, and brings me mixed feelings. I once participated in a cooking show and cooked this dish from beginning to end in 30 minutes. It was superb, and the judges told me that the sauce was killer. But unfortunately, my shrimp were undercooked, and I got disqualified. I just had to accept it. But something that really shocked me was seeing the reaction of some of the judges when I placed a whole, beautiful, magnificent, colossal shrimp on top of my dish. It was so stunning! But they found it scary, saying that they felt a creature was staring at them, and they couldn't eat it. I didn't believe what I was hearing! After all, they were chefs! I think I turned purple… Those who know me well would tell you that, I don't have to speak to let you know how I feel or what I think, even though my husband tells me on occasions not to look too intense, or, as he puts it: "Do not make faces!" Sometimes it's almost impossible to moderate my expressions, but I try. And happily, my face is usually preoccupied with smiling and laughing!

Anyway, I had to get this loss out of my system, so as soon as I got back home, I created a pop-up dinner, where I cooked Spicy Shrimp Stew for everyone. It was perfect, if I do say to myself! And I felt so vindicated! I hope you'll feel proud yourself, too, when you make this stew.

I'm grateful for the learning opportunities mistakes allow, and the lessons they teach. They've taught me to stand up, shake it off, rethink, and improve. And I never lose sight of my essence in the kitchen: "Cooking with Love." So, don't let the occasional kitchen hiccup set you down—just keep on cooking!

Ingredients

4 tablespoons vegetable oil
2 red onions finely chopped
12 garlic cloves finely chopped
1 tomato, skinned, seeded, and chopped
Salt and pepper to taste
Pinch of cumin
8 tablespoons yellow hot pepper paste
1 tablespoon Pisco
1 tablespoon white wine
½ cup evaporated milk (unsweetened)
4 slices white sandwich bread
1 sprig fresh oregano
1 cup vegetable or fish broth
16 large shrimps, cleaned and peeled
4 jumbo shrimps, cleaned and peeled
1 ½ ounces ground pecans or walnuts

To serve

4 Yukon Gold potatoes, boiled and sliced
4 hard-boiled eggs
curly parsley, to garnish

Preparation

1. Heat the oil in a pan over low heat and sauté the onion until translucent, about 5–7 minutes. Add garlic and tomato for 3 minutes, until softened. Season with salt and pepper. Add the cumin and yellow hot pepper paste, and cook over low heat for 3 minutes until fragrant. Add the Pisco and wine and allow the alcohol to evaporate—about 2 minutes.
2. Meanwhile, blend the evaporated milk and bread slices together in a mixer, and add the mixture to the pan, along with the sprig of oregano. Cook over medium heat, gradually adding the broth, for 4 minutes, until thickened and creamy.
3. Add the shrimps, and cook for 2 minutes or until cooked to your preference. Add the ground nuts. Taste and adjust the seasoning.

Serving suggestion: Divide the potato slices and hard-boiled eggs among large shallow bowls and ladle over the stew. Serve hot.

TOP-ROUND BEEF
Asado

When I was a kid, my Mamama had the tradition of asking us what we wanted for our Birthday lunch. My answer was always "*Asado con puré*, please Mamama!" And every time it was heavenly… the most tender and juicy Top-Round Beef. I remember vividly how she used to plate it; first a portion of garlicky fluffy rice with corn kernels, then a good side of silky Creamy Mashed Potatoes, then the slices of Top-Round Beef, and to finish, gently with a spoon she used to make sort of like a nest in the center of the mashed potatoes and pour there the most amazing Top-Round Beef sauce… It was indeed a moment of ecstasy!

Ingredients

2 pounds top-round beef
2 tablespoons garlic paste
1 tablespoon salt
2 teaspoons ground black pepper
1 teaspoon ground cumin
1 tablespoon extra-virgin olive oil
4 carrots cut in long quarters
2 tablespoons vegetable oil
1 cup small diced red onion
1 cup tomato sauce
1 cup red wine
4 cups hot beef broth
2 dashes Worcestershire sauce
2 tablespoons potato starch (optional)

Preparation

1. In a bowl, mix garlic, salt, pepper, cumin, and olive oil until it looks like an even paste. Reserve.
2. With a thin knife make horizontal incisions in your beef. Introduce some of the paste in the incisions and one piece of carrot per hole. Spread the rest of the paste evenly around the beef. Reserve.
3. In a good thick pot, preheat oil in high temperature and sear the beef. Incorporate the onion and slightly sauté it for about 2 minutes, then add the tomato sauce, the wine, and bring it to a boil until the alcohol evaporates, about 3 minutes. Add about ⅓ cup of the broth and Worcestershire sauce. Cover pot with the lit.
4. After 20 minutes turn the beef and add another ⅓ cup of broth. Repeat this procedure for about 2 hours. Or until the beef is fork tender.
5. When done, take beef out, slice it, and put it back into the pot with the juice.

Note: If you prefer a slightly thicken sauce, dissolve potato starch with 2 tablespoons of cold water and whisk into the sauce.

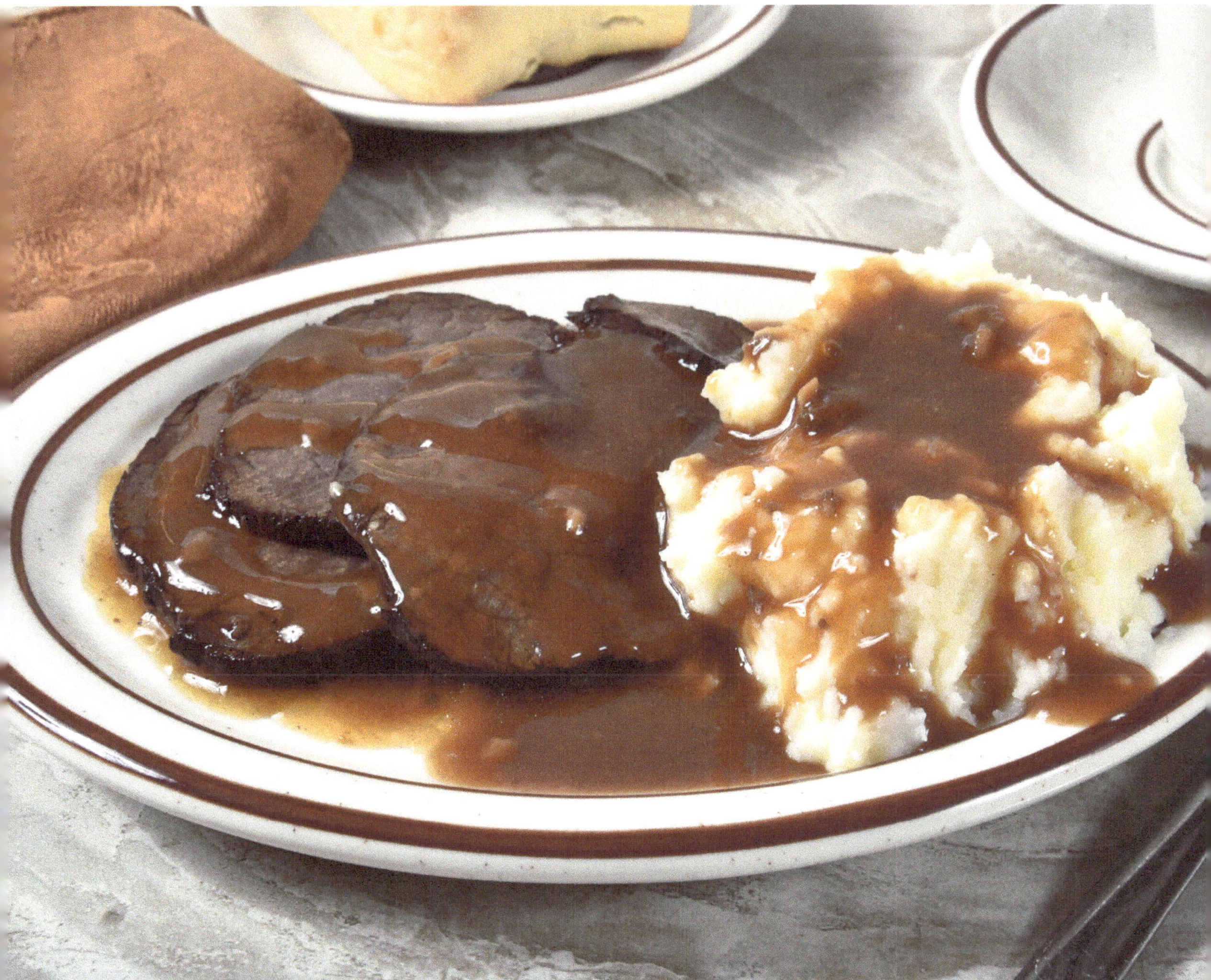

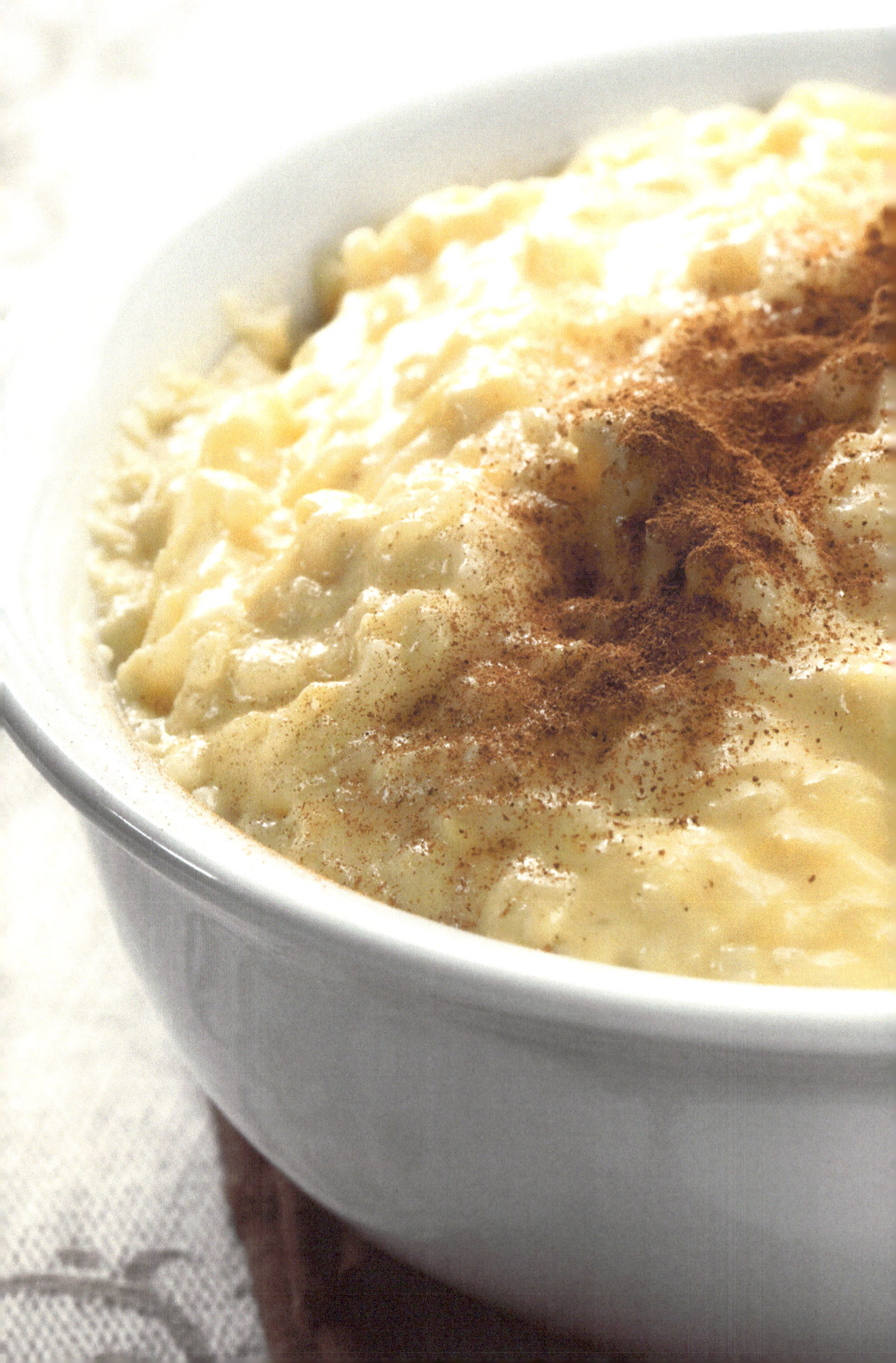

Desserts

APPLE FRITTERS WITH CHANCACA SYRUP

Torrejas de Manzana con Miel de Chancaca

DAIRY

35'

12-15 FRITTERS

Traditionally, every 19th of March, Saint Joseph's Day, was celebrated at home in Lima, because of my Italian heritage. And it was a perfect reason to get together and enjoy each other's company. Thus, my Mamama made some delicious apple fritters and we enjoyed them so much!

My Mamama forbade us to enter the kitchen while she was preparing the fritters because no person who came in went by without a fritter in hand. It was inevitable!

The best part was when it was the time to eat them with a good drizzle of Chancaca Syrup… Unforgettable!

Ingredients

2 cups sweet-tart apples (3–5, depending on size; Gravensteins, Honeycrisps or Granny Smiths)
1 cup all-purpose flour
1 tablespoon sugar
1 teaspoon baking powder
¼ teaspoon salt
2 large eggs, room-temperature
½ cup whole milk
1 teaspoon vanilla extract
Neutral oil for frying

Preparation

1. Peel, core and cut the apples into medium dices.
2. In a large skillet, preheat enough oil to a depth of ½ inch.
3. While the oil is heating, in a small bowl, whisk together the flour, sugar, baking powder and salt. Set aside.
4. In a larger bowl, beat the eggs with a fork, and add the milk and vanilla. Gently stir the dry ingredients into the egg mixture until just combined. Do not overmix. Fold in the apples.
5. Drop several individual spoonfuls of the batter into the hot oil and fry until golden brown on both sides, about 4–6 minutes total, depending on the size.
6. Transfer the cooked fritters to a wire rack to drain any excess oil. Repeat with the remaining batter.

Note: These fritters can be dressed up and enjoyed in many ways. In my family, the tradition is to enjoy them with Chancaca Syrup (see page 218, Desserts). Other options include drizzling with your favorite syrup, caramel sauce, or sweetened condensed milk. Or a simple dusting powdered sugar or cinnamon sugar. Serve alone or with vanilla ice-cream.

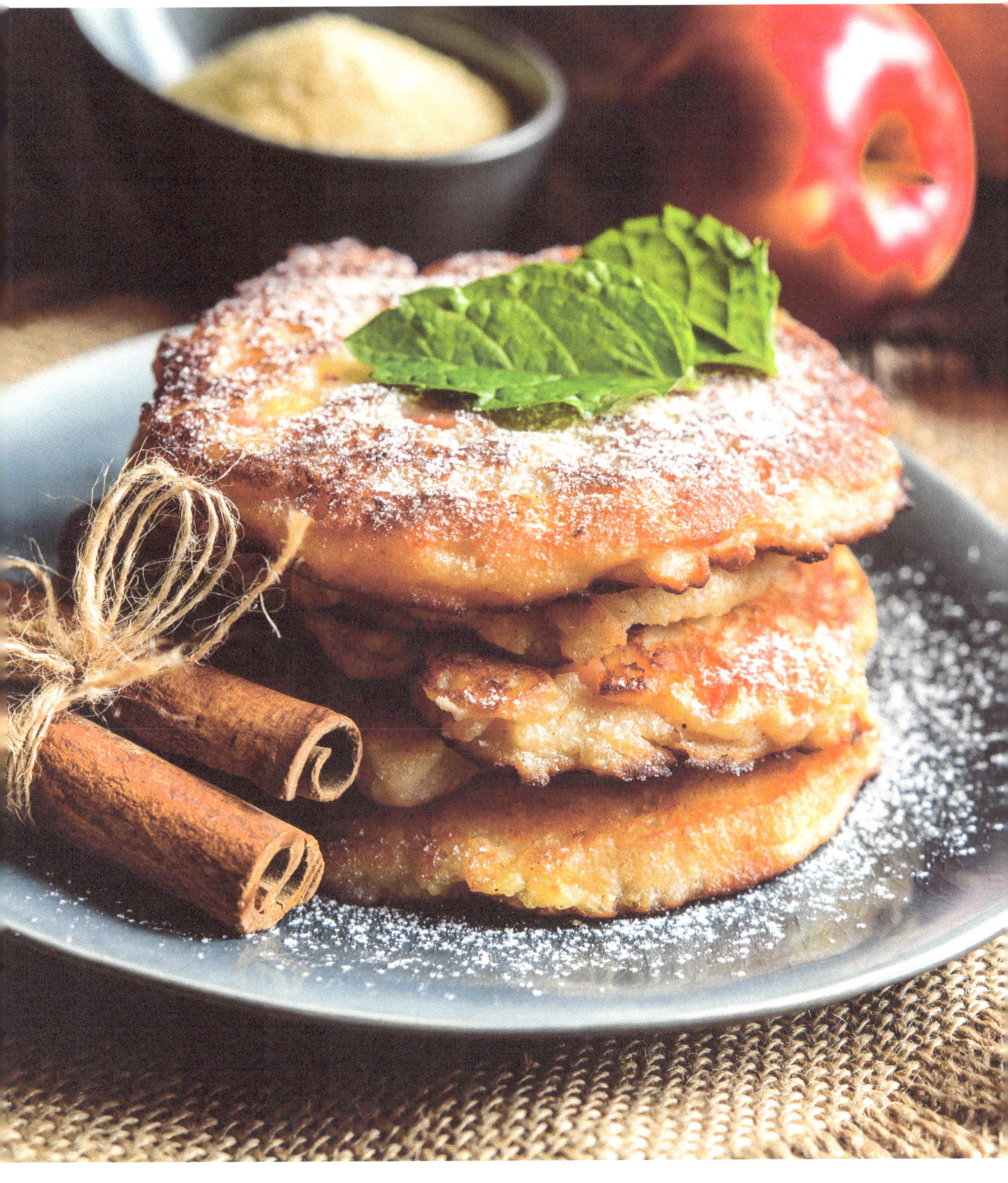

APPLE OATMEAL BREAD

Queque de Manzana y Avena

Packed with fresh apples, either grated or diced, this lightly sweet bread is a quick treat ideal for breakfast, teatime, lunch boxes and after-school. Warm it up and top it with a scoop of vanilla ice cream, and you have a (somewhat) healthy dessert or midnight snack. You won't even notice that it's heart-healthy and full of fiber, but you'll get the benefits nonetheless. It can be made in very little time; just combine your dry ingredients with the wet, add the apples and pop it in the oven. Delicious!

Ingredients

2 cups all-purpose flour
1 cup quick-cooking rolled oats
2 teaspoons baking powder
½ teaspoon baking soda
½ teaspoon salt
1 tablespoon ground cinnamon
⅛ teaspoon nutmeg
⅛ ground cloves (optional)
½ cup granulated sugar
½ cup light brown sugar
½ cup unsweetened applesauce, or apple-pear sauce
2 large eggs, room-temperature
2 tablespoons neutral oil, or melted butter
1 ¼ cups room-temperature milk (whole or low-fat)
2 teaspoons vanilla extract
2 medium apples, shredded

Preparation

1. Preheat the oven to 350 °F. Grease and flour a 9 x 5 inch loaf pan and set aside.
2. In a large bowl, whisk together the flour, oats, baking powder, baking soda, salt and spices (cinnamon, nutmeg and cloves, if using), until well combined.
3. In a medium bowl, add the sugars, the applesauce, the eggs, and the oil; using a whisk or an electric hand mixer, beat together just until the sugar is well incorporated and free of lumps. Add the milk and the vanilla and mix until well combined. Set aside.
4. Shred the apples (doing so just before adding them to the batter will keep the apples from turning brown).
5. Add the wet ingredients mixture to the dry ingredients, and stir just until all the flour is incorporated. Do not overmix. Now fold in the apples.
6. Pour the batter into the prepared loaf pan. Bake for 1 hour, or until a cake tester, or bamboo skewer, inserted into the center of the bread comes out clean, or with just a few crumbs, but no raw batter. Cool in the pan for 10 minutes, then remove the bread from the pan and place on a wire rack, to cool completely.

Note: This bread is nutritious and delicious, whether enjoyed with your morning coffee or as an afternoon snack with tea. It also makes a perfect after-school treat for kids.

APPLE PIE
Pie de Manzana

DAIRY

90'

10 SERVINGS

As it is in the US, Apple Pie is a classic in Peru, either plain or *à la mode*. This recipe is not overly sweet, and the tender dough will make you go for seconds. My Mamama had this recipe in one of her handwritten cookbooks, and she taught me how to make it, step by step. She once asked me to make it for her doctor as a thank-you, and I did. She was so proud of the result, and I imagine that her doctor enjoyed it. Who doesn't like Apple Pie? Every time I make it, my Mamama is with me in my heart.

Ingredients

For the Crust
2 ¼ cups all-purpose flour, spooned into measuring cup and leveled with a knife
1 tablespoon sugar
½ teaspoon salt
1 cup cold unsalted butter cut into small cubes
7 tablespoons ice cold water
Additional flour to dust the working surface
1 tablespoon milk, to brush the crust top before baking
Coarse turbinado sugar, or sanding sugar to sprinkle the crust (optional)

For the Filling
3 ½ pounds baking apples (Gala, Granny Smith, Gravenstein, Honeycrisp, or else), peeled, cored, sliced ¼-inch thick
½ cup granulated sugar
½ cup packed dark brown sugar
1 teaspoon lemon zest, plus 1 tablespoon lemon juice from 1 lemon
1 teaspoon vanilla extract
¼ cup all-purpose flour
1 teaspoon ground cinnamon
¼ teaspoon ground nutmeg
Heaping ¼ teaspoon salt

Preparation

Crust
1. In the bowl of a food processor fitted with the steel blade, place the flour, sugar and salt. (The dough can also be made by hand in a large bowl using a pastry cutter or the fingers to cut in the butter. If using your fingers, work quickly to avoid warming the butter.)

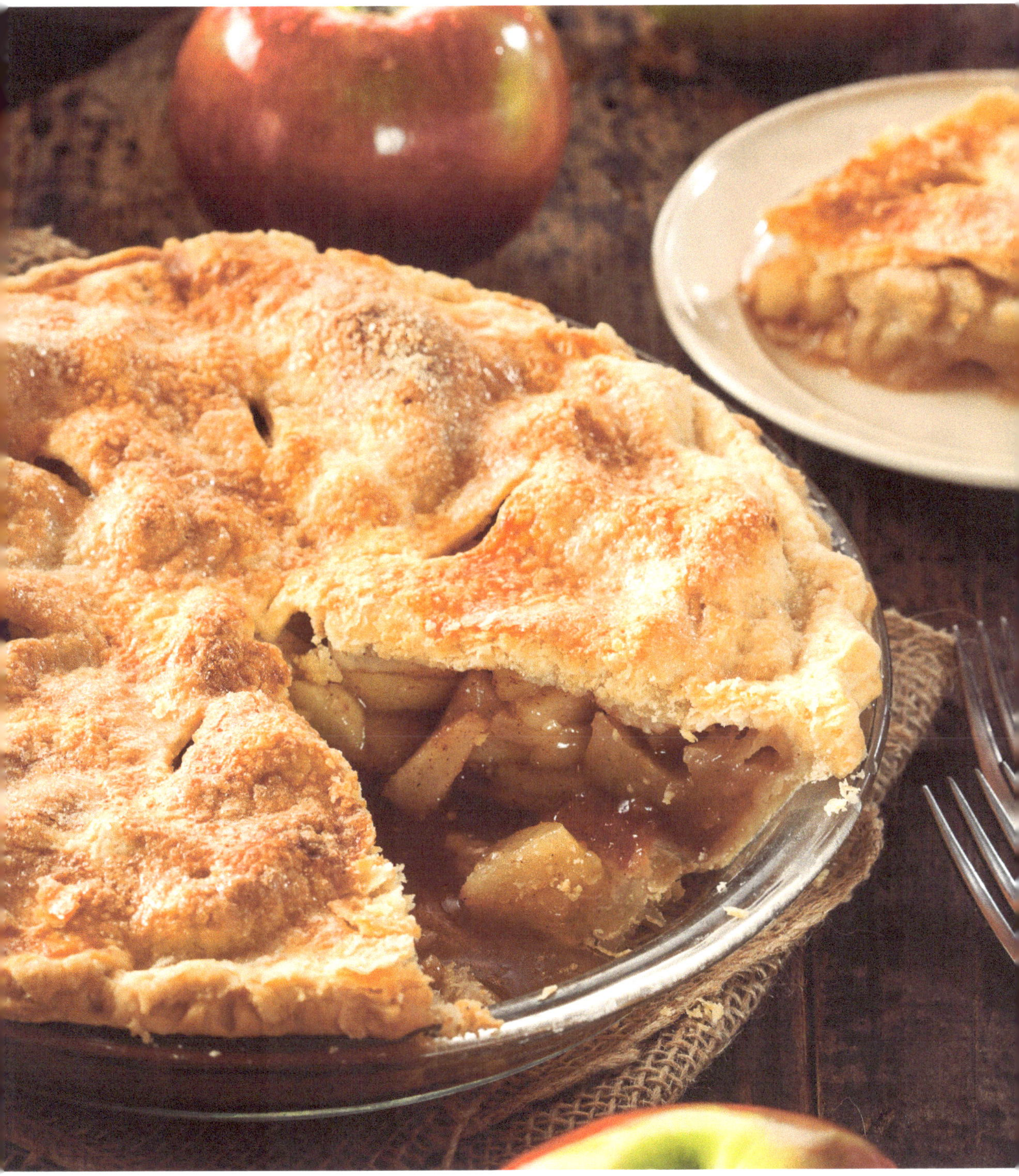

2. Pulse to combine the dry ingredients. Add the cubes of cold butter and pulse about 10 times, until the largest butter pieces are the size of small peas. Add the ice-cold water and pulse just until the dough comes together. Do not allow it to fully form into a ball, or the pastry will be tough.
3. Transfer the dough to a lightly floured work surface (it's OK if it's still slightly crumbly) and form it into a ball. Cut the ball in half and shape each half into a thick round disk. Wrap one of the disks in plastic and place in the refrigerator. (To make the pastry ahead, you may also wrap and refrigerate both disks for 2–3 days.)
4. Lightly flour a rolling pin and your work surface. Roll the un-chilled disk into a 12-inch round and transfer it to a deep-dish pie plate by loosely wrapping the rolled dough around your rolling pin, then lowering it onto the pie plate. Ease the pastry into the pie plate, being careful not to pull or stretch the dough. Gently press it into the bottom and sides of the pan. Trim off the excess dough, leaving just enough to extend about ½-inch over the rim of the pie plate. Chill the pastry (plate and all) while you make the filling.

Filling
1. Place the peeled, cored, sliced apples in a large bowl and immediately toss with the lemon juice.
2. Lightly toss the apples with the granulated sugar and brown sugar, the lemon zest and the vanilla. Sprinkle the apples with the ¼ cup of flour, cinnamon, nutmeg and salt; stir to combine.

Assemble the Pie
1. Remove the pastry-lined pie plate and the remaining disk of dough from the refrigerator. Allow to sit briefly (15–20 minutes) at room temperature, which will make the dough easier to handle. Roll the disk of dough into a 12-inch round.
2. By this time, the apples should have released some of their juices. Stir the apple mixture to make sure everything is well combined, then pour the apples and their juices into the bottom pie crust.
3. As soon as the filling has been transferred to the pastry-lined pie plate, use your finger or a pastry brush to apply a thin film of water to the rim of the bottom crust (this will create a good seal when the top and bottom crust are crimped together). Immediately place the top crust over the bottom crust and trim off any excess dough, leaving one inch extending over the rim of the plate. Fold the edges of the top crust over the bottom crust and press together to seal. Crimp between your thumb and forefinger, or gently press together with the tines of a fork.
4. Chill the pie for 30 minutes before baking.
5. While the pie is chilling, position the oven rack in the lower third of the oven, and preheat to 400 °F.

6. Remove the pie from the refrigerator and brush the top crust with the milk (to help with browning, and to make the sugar crystals stick). Cut a few slits in the top crust to act as vents, allowing steam to escape and to prevent the juices in the fruit from overflowing. Sprinkle the crust with the turbinado or sanding sugar, if desired.
7. Bake the pie at 400 °F for 20 minutes, then reduce the temperature to 350 °F. Continue baking the pie for 40–50 minutes more, until the filling is bubbly. Check on the pie halfway through the baking time and tent it loosely with foil as needed, to prevent the crust from over-browning.
8. Let the pie cool at room temperature for at least 2 hours before serving, to allow the filling to set.
9. The pie may be stored at room temperature up to one day, or in the refrigerator, covered with plastic wrap, up to 5 days. The pie may also be frozen—wrapped tightly in an inner layer of plastic and an outer layer of aluminum foil, up to 3 months.

BAKED CREAM CARAMEL CUSTARD

Crema Volteada

GLUTEN FREE

2h

8 SERVINGS

This Peruvian dessert is a favorite in many households, and in mine as well. I feel that we should always try to add something sweet to our lives. And this easy recipe is a sweet-bomb that undoubtedly will elevate the happy quotient in your life. It requires only a few ingredients, and just a bowl, a mold and an oven. The most exciting part is when it's done and must be flipped over, which is how it got its name, Crema Volteada (flipped cream). After flipping, the caramel oozes all over. And then when you try a bite, it melts in your mouth. It's impossible not to love it!

Ingredients

For the Caramel
1 cup sugar
½ cup water

For the Custard
1 can (14 ounces) sweetened condensed milk
1 can (12 ounces) evaporated milk (unsweetened)
⅔ cup whole milk
⅓ cup white sugar
2 teaspoons vanilla extract
4 large egg yolks
2 large eggs

Preparation

Caramel
1. Place the sugar and the water in a heavy skillet, or heavy-bottomed saucepan, over medium heat and let it boil—carefully swirling the pan occasionally—until it reaches a medium amber color.
2. Pour the caramel into a 9-inch round baking dish or mold, swirling the pan to be sure the caramel fully covers the bottom of the pan. Set aside and allow the caramel to cool completely.

Custard
1. Preheat the oven to 350 °F.
2. In a bowl, gently whisk the milks with the sugar and vanilla, until the sugar if fully dissolved. Next, incorporate the eggs, egg yolks and vanilla, being careful to avoid creating too many bubbles.
3. Using a fine mesh strainer, run the custard through about 7 times, then pour the strained custard over the cooled caramel in the pan or mold.
4. Create a bain-marie by placing the custard pan or mold in a larger pan, adding enough water to the larger pan to come halfway up the side of the custard pan.

5. Bake at 350 °F for 60–90 minutes, until the center is still somewhat jiggly when the pan is gently shaken.
6. Remove the custard pan to a cooling rack and allow to cool. Cover and refrigerate overnight.
7. To un-mold, run a knife around the inside edge of the pan. Invert a rimmed serving dish or platter over the custard pan and turn, both, upside down. Some of the caramel will pool around the base of the custard.

BANANA BREAD

Queque de Plátano

Overripe bananas? No problem! Let's make a *Quequito*! I'm a firm believer that the best Banana Bread comes from mushy, brown bananas! Their sweetness and depth of flavor make the best banana bread. And the secret to this recipe's great flavor? Butter! This bread is tender and moist and delicious just as-is, but go ahead and add nuts, raisins, or chocolate chips if you feel the need to zhuzh it up!

CONTAINS NUTS

90′

1 LOAF

Ingredients

2 cups all-purpose flour
1 teaspoon baking soda
¼ teaspoon salt
½ cup butter, room temperature
½ cup brown sugar
2 large eggs, room-temperature
1 teaspoon vanilla
2 ⅓ cups mashed overripe bananas
½ cup toasted pecans or walnuts, finely chopped (optional)

Preparation

1. Preheat the oven to 350 °F. Lightly grease a 9 x 5-inch loaf pan or spray with cooking spray.
2. In a large bowl, combine the flour, baking soda and salt.
3. In a separate bowl, cream together the butter and the sugars, by hand or using an electric mixer. Stir in the eggs, one at a time; add the vanilla and mashed bananas and mix until well blended.
4. Stir the banana mixture into the flour bowl, mixing just to moisten. Briefly stir in the nuts, if using. Do not overbeat. Pour the batter into the prepared loaf pan.
5. Bake in preheated oven for 60 to 65 minutes, until a toothpick inserted into center of the loaf comes out clean. Let the bread cool in the pan for 10 minutes, then turn out onto a wire rack to cool completely.

Note: The taste of Banana Bread keeps well and improves over the next day or so, if it lasts that long!

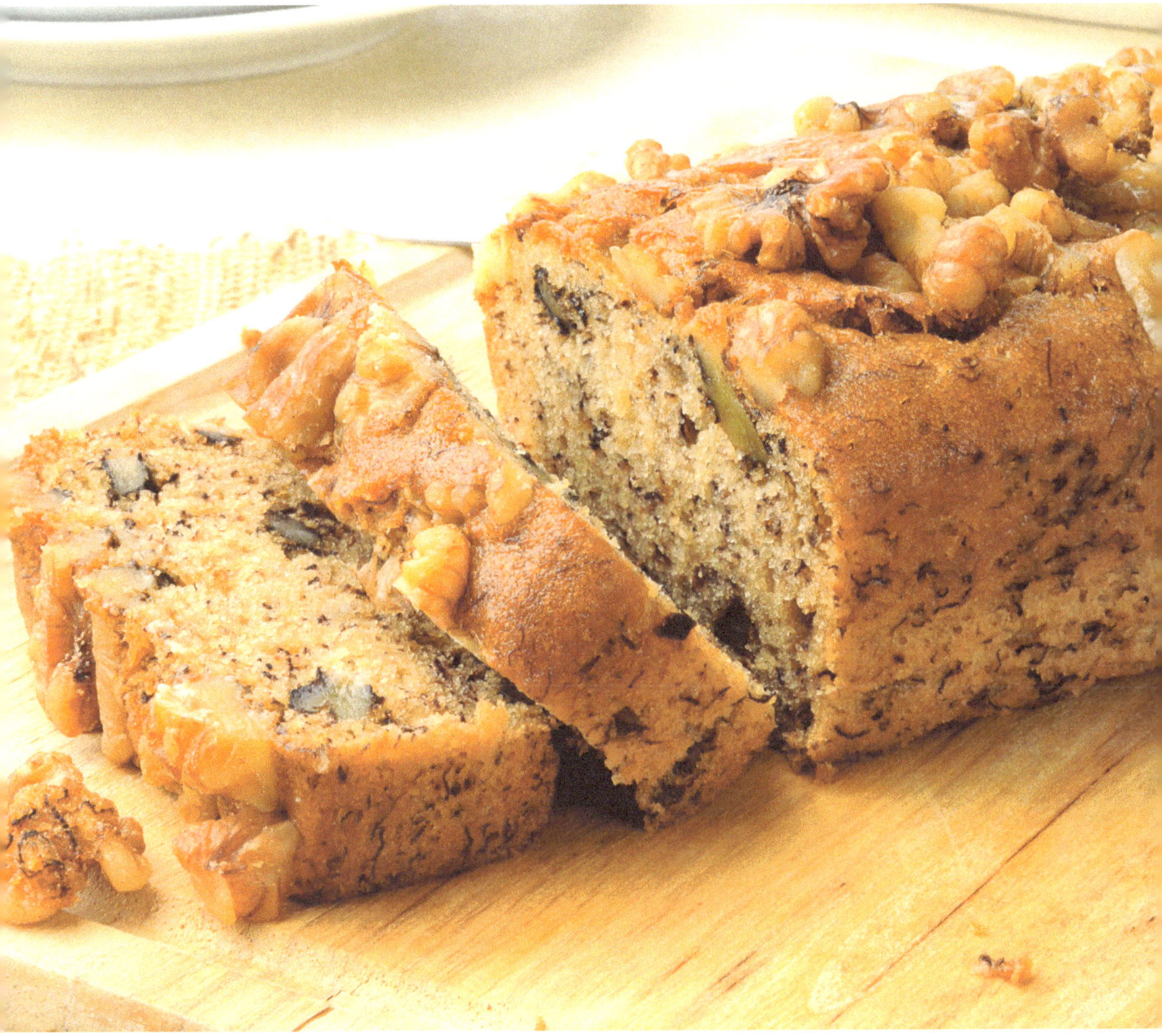

BAVAROIS

Bavarois de Durazno

Wow! Years and years since I had my last piece of Bavarois. We had a non-blood-related auntie who used to sell them in La Punta, where I grew up. It was a delight when we could enjoy it... Her classic ones were prunes and one that was made out of peppermint and chocolate sauce... Yummy! This is such an airy, light, fluffy, elegant dessert. Best of all you can add your favorite fruits, spices, coffee, chocolate, liqueur, or none if you prefer. To me, the best part of the bavarois is the garnish of Crème Anglaise, it is super! The combination is exactly as I remember when I was a kid.

To be honest, I haven't found Bavarois in the US, and moreover, I believe, in Peru, it is a dessert that is not as popular as it used to be when I was a kid. Best of all is that it basically requires two or three ingredients, and you can have a great dessert for a group of people that will be forever impressed with the flavors and the presentation. You are welcome!

Ingredients

For the Caramel
1 cup sugar
¼ cup water

For the Bavarois
7 egg whites
½ teaspoon cream of tartar
½ cup sugar
1 cup medium diced canned peaches (drained)

For the Crème Anglaise
¾ cup whole milk
¼ cup sugar
3 egg yolks
1 teaspoon vanilla extract

Preparation

Caramel
1. Place a pan over low to medium heat, and add sugar and water.
2. Melt sugar and water until it becomes light golden-brown color. DO NOT STIR. Just swirl sugar in the pan.
3. Pour the caramel and spread it evenly into the round pan. Additionally, butter the inside wall of the pan over the caramel. Set aside.

Bavarois
1. Pre-heat oven at 350 °F.
2. Beat the egg whites with cream of tartar until soft peaks form. Gradually add sugar until stiff and shiny.
3. Gently fold peaches with the help of a spatula.
4. Transfer meringue into the caramelized and butter pan. Distribute evenly inside the pan, making sure that there are no air pockets.

5. Place the pan in a bigger pan filled with 1-inch hot water, bain-marie method, put in the preheated oven.
6. Bake for 25–30 minutes, or until top turns golden brown. Let cool the Bavarois and refrigerate for at least 4 hours.
7. Unmold in a platter. It will loosen itself from the sides of the pan.

Crème Anglaise
1. Meanwhile the bavarois is cooling, prepare the Crème Anglaise.
2. In a heavy bottom saucepan, add the milk, sugar, egg yolks, and vanilla.
3. Wisk constantly over medium heat until it gets thick, about 5 to 7 minutes.
4. Transfer to a bowl. Cover with plastic wrap and refrigerate the Crème Anglaise.
5. To serve the Bavarois, slice pieces and drizzle with Crème Anglaise.

BUTTER COOKIES
Galletitas de Mantequilla

DAIRY

3h

40 COOKIES

Some time ago, my boys asked me to make cookies in the shape of stars and various figures. I had never made rolled, cut-out cookies before, so I ended up making butter cookies. While we were mixing the dough, I shared memories with my children about teatime with my Mamama: every afternoon we sat down for tea and ate delicious Danish butter cookies. Fond memories...

The cookies my boys and I made were delicious! They helped with the cookie-cutters, placing the cut-outs as carefully as possible on the baking trays (though eating some of the raw dough was inevitable). The most important thing is that we always love our time together in the kitchen, but they enjoyed their cookies just as much. They're super easy to make, and I'm sure you (and any little helpers) will love them!

Ingredients

8 ounces unsalted butter room-temperature (but not too soft)
¾ cup granulated sugar
¼ teaspoon salt
1 ½ teaspoons pure vanilla extract
1 large egg yolk
2 cups all-purpose flour

Preparation

1. In a mixer, or by hand, beat the butter, sugar, salt, and vanilla together until smooth and creamy. Add the egg yolk and mix until well incorporated, scraping down the sides of the bowl at least once. Then add the flour and mix just until combined. Scrape onto a lightly floured board, and knead a few times, just until the dough smooths out.
2. Turn the dough onto a sheet of plastic wrap and roll into a 2-inch diameter log. Twist the ends of the plastic wrap to seal, and refrigerate the dough for several hours before baking. May also be refrigerated up to 72 hours, or frozen for up to 3 months.
3. Before baking, preheat the oven to 325 °F.
4. Line your baking sheets with baking parchment paper.
5. Slice the dough about ⅛ inch thick and place the slices on the baking sheets about an inch apart (they won't spread very much, but they need space for air to circulate around each cookie).

6. Bake until JUST beginning to turn golden around the edges, about 16–18 minutes.
7. Allow to cool briefly on the baking sheets, then transfer to a wire rack to cool completely. The cookies will keep for 3 to 5 days stored in an airtight container at room temperature.

CARAMEL COOKIES
Alfajores

DAIRY

90'

50 SERVINGS

Let me tell you that growing up in Peru, this was a very popular treat. Most of my memories come from gatherings, such as baptisms, first communions, birthday parties, teatimes. One thing is certain; any event was, and now-a-days is the perfect one to indulge yourself. Let's see; alfajores have a unique combination of textures and flavors; from pillowy, crumbly, soft, and sweet. They could be described as shortbread cookies stuffed with Manjarblanco, or as some friends named them Peruvian cookies.

This is one of the sweet inheritances that we got from Spain, who acquired their *alfajor* habit from the Moors. Regardless of the name, Caramel Cookies are absolutely delicious! My kids love them, and I don't know of anybody that doesn't fall in love with this sweet and soft temptation. Easy to make with few ingredients, any excuse is the perfect one to indulge yourself and especially when it's made with lots of love!

Ingredients

For the dough
1 ½ cups all-purpose flour
½ cup Confectioners' sugar
½ cup cornstarch
8 oz. unsalted butter, room temperature

For the Manjarblanco
See recipe on page 232

Preparation

1. In a food processor place all the ingredients and run it for about 2 minutes.
2. Transfer the dough to a clean working surface and knead it for 1 minute. Wrap it in plastic, and let it rest for at least 30 minutes in the refrigerator.
3. Remove your dough from the refrigerator and with your hands make it pliable like a "playdough", forming a thick disc.
4. Lightly dust your clean working surface with flour.
5. With the help of a rolling pin stretch your dough to ⅛-inch of thickness.
6. Use a cookie cutter of 1-inch diameter and start transferring your cut discs into a clean cookie sheet. No parchment, nor silicon pad is required.
7. Bake at 350 °F for 8–10 minutes. Just until the edges start to turn golden.
8. Allow cookies to cool completely before touching them.
9. With the help of a pastry bag fill them like a sandwich with Manjarblanco.

10. When your Caramel Cookies are all filled, dust them with sifted Confectioners' sugar and enjoy!

Note: You can make the discs in a variety of shapes such as stars, hearts and flowers.

CHANCACA SYRUP

Miel de Chancaca

Chancaca syrup is a sweet sugarcane-based sauce flavored with warm spices and fig leaves. It's often served with Picarones, a creole dessert similar to a doughnut or a beignet popular in Peru. Using a generous amount of this distinct syrup, you can dip or drizzle the Picarones. Yum!

But at my grandparents' house, when we celebrated Saint Joseph's Day every year on the 19th of March, it was my Mamama's tradition to make delicious Apple Fritters, which we enjoyed with this same syrup. It is absolutely delicious!

Ingredients

1 pound Chancaca or Panela (unrefined sugar, raw cane sugar, available at supermarkets, Latin markets and online)
4 cups water
1 tart apple, quartered (no need to peel or core)
4 fresh whole fig leaves (available online)
2 star anise
1 cinnamon stick
1 teaspoon whole cloves

Preparation

1. In a heavy-bottom pot, bring all ingredients to a full boil. Lower the heat to medium, and continue to cook at a gentle boil for 30 minutes.
2. Strain into a glass container and let cool.
3. The syrup will keep in the refrigerator for up to a month.

Note: This syrup is great drizzled over Picarones (a typical Peruvian creole dessert), plain Greek yogurt, on Apple Fritters (see page 200, Desserts), bananas, and poached pears.

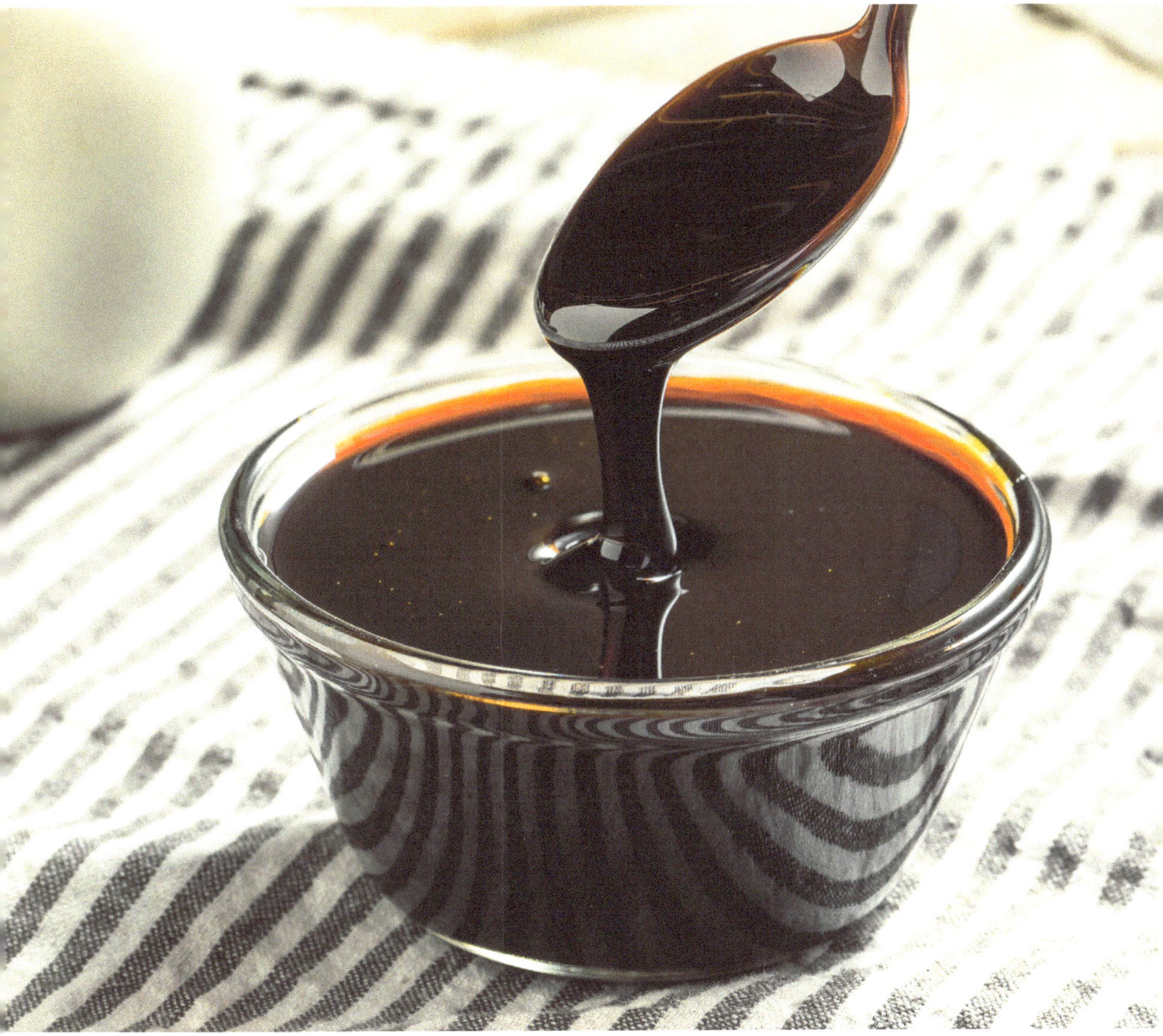

CHOCOLATE CAKE WITH STRAWBERRIES AND CREAM

Torta de Chocolate con Fresas y Crema

This recipe is a miracle! The result is a super moist, light, and fluffy cake. It is easy to make, and I give you my word: you will look like the king or queen of the kitchen, even if you believe you cannot bake. I dare you to prove yourself. Just do it!...

Grab a bowl and a whisk, or even a fork. No need to use an electric mixer. If you have children, let them help you. You'll have a good time and lots of laughs, and maybe even end up with a decent cake! Cooking with children can be a challenge, and more so when it calls for chocolate! So, what if an egg ends up on the floor and flour takes flight. After all, happy chocolate faces, sticky little chocolate hands and a plopped egg or two can easily be dealt with using a bit of soap and water, and communal cooking with kids is well worth the effort!

Ingredients

1 ¾ cups all-purpose flour
1 ½ cups sugar
¾ cup Dutch-process cocoa powder
2 teaspoons baking soda
1 teaspoon baking powder
1 teaspoon salt
2 large eggs, at room temperature
1 cup strong brewed coffee (or prepared instant coffee*), at room temperature
1 cup buttermilk**, room temperature
½ cup vegetable or other neutral oil
1 teaspoon vanilla
2 tablespoon Confectioners' sugar, for dusting the finished cake

For the Filling
1 pound fresh strawberries, hulled and roughly chopped
1 cup whipping cream
1 tablespoons Confectioners' sugar
8–10 additional whole strawberries, to decorate

Preparation

1. Butter two 9-inch round cake pans and place a round of parchment in the bottom of each. Butter the parchment as well and dust the interior of the pans with cocoa powder. Knock out any excess cocoa powder and set the prepared pans aside.
2. Preheat the oven to 350 °F.
3. In a large bowl, whisk together the dry ingredients: flour, sugar, cocoa, baking soda, baking powder and salt. Set aside.
4. In a separate bowl, or large liquid-measuring cup, combine the eggs, coffee, buttermilk, oil and vanilla; mix with manual egg beater, or an electric mixer on medium speed for 2 minutes (batter will be thin).

5. Pour the batter into the prepared pans and bake on the middle rack at 350 °F for 45–50 minutes, or until a cake tester inserted in the center comes out clean.
6. Cool the cakes in their pans for 10 minutes, then release the cakes from the pans and place on a wire rack to cool completely.

Filling
1. In a medium bowl, use an electric mixer to whip the cream into firm peaks. Gently fold in the strawberries.
2. Place the bottom cake layer on a serving plate; spoon all the cream on top and spread to cover the layer evenly.
3. Place the top cake layer over the cream, and use a sieve to lightly dust it with Confectioners' sugar.
4. Place the additional strawberries in a pyramid on top.

Note: This cake is best enjoyed the day it's made, but will keep for 2–3 days in the refrigerator.

*To use instant coffee, dissolve 2 teaspoons in 1 cup boiled water; allow to cool to room temperature.
**To create your own buttermilk, add 1 tablespoon white vinegar or lemon juice and enough milk (whole or low-fat) to equal 1 cup.

CINNAMON LAYERED CAKE

Encanelado

DAIRY

70′

8–10 SERVINGS

As its name implies, cinnamon is the star ingredient of this soft, spongy, sweet and moist dessert, originally introduced by European nuns living in convents in Peru.

Imagine a thin layer of delicate sponge cake moistened with a Pisco-infused syrup, then spread with a generous layer of Manjarblanco (or thick caramel, or Dulce de Leche), and topped with another layer of this sponge cake, then dusted with cinnamon and powdered sugar. It is absolutely divine! In Peru there are some *dulcerías* (pastry shops) that specialize in this classic, traditional old fashioned dessert, and they are the best. This recipe will get the hearts of all you share it with.

Ingredients

For the Cake
1 ½ cups all-purpose flour
1 teaspoon baking powder
7 large eggs (separate whites and yolks)
1 cup granulated sugar
2–3 tablespoons cinnamon
2–3 tablespoons Confectioners' sugar

For the Syrup
1 cup granulated sugar
1 cup water
1 shot (2–3 ounces) of Pisco

For the Manjarblanco
See recipe on page 232

Preparation

Cake
1. Preheat the oven to 350 °F. Grease and line a 14 x 9 x 2-inch rimmed baking sheet with parchment paper, then grease the parchment paper as well. Set aside.
2. In a bowl, sift together flour and baking powder. Set aside.
3. Using an electric mixer, whip the egg whites at medium-high speed until soft peaks have formed; beat in the egg yolks one at a time, making sure they are well incorporated before the next addition. When all the eggs have been incorporated, gradually add the sugar until all is well combined.
4. Using a spatula, fold in the previously sifted flour mixture. Pour the batter into the prepared pan, evening out the batter with the spatula. Bake for 25 minutes or until a toothpick inserted in the center comes out clean.
5. Remove the cake from the oven and let it cool in the pan for 10 minutes. Carefully flip the cake out of the pan and onto a cooling rack to cool completely.

Syrup
1. In the meantime, make the syrup by combining the cup of water and the cup of sugar in a small pot; bring to a boil for 10 minutes, then briefly stir in the Pisco, and remove from the heat. Set aside to cool.

Assemble
1. Once the cake has cooled completely, cut in half to create two 7 x 9 x 2 layers. Place one of the cake layers on a serving plate and brush the surface evenly with half of the syrup. Top with the Manjarblanco. Place the other half of the cake on top and brush with the remaining syrup.
2. Just before serving, dust the Cinnamon Layered cake with cinnamon and Confectioners' sugar.

Note: The Cinnamon Layered Cake may be stored, covered, up to one day at room temperature. To keep longer, cover and refrigerate up to 3 days.

COCONUT FLAN

Flan de Coco

This flan is definitely for coconut lovers. If you like coconut, this combination is dessert dynamite. The creamy, sweet, smooth custard is a twist on the classic Latin dessert. It is luscious and not only beautiful, but very simple to make and a great treat for just about any occasion.

Ingredients

For the Caramel
1 cup sugar
½ cup water

For the Custard
14 ounce or 1 ¾ cups sweetened condensed milk
1 ½ cups coconut milk
6 eggs, lightly beaten
1 cup shredded unsweetened coconut

Preparation

Caramel
1. In a small, heavy-bottomed saucepan, bring the sugar and water to a boil over medium heat. Allow to boil, undisturbed, until it becomes a medium amber caramel color.
2. Pour the caramel in a 5-inch by 10-inch baking dish or mold, and let it cool completely.

Custard
1. With a rack in the center position, preheat the oven to 350 °F.
2. Whisk together the sweetened condensed milk and the coconut milk.
3. Incorporate the eggs and coconut, mixing gently to avoid creating too many bubbles.
4. Poor the mixture over the cooled caramel in the pan or mold.
5. Bake covered with aluminum foil for 45 minutes or until the center slightly jiggles.
6. When the flan has baked, remove to a cooling rack, uncover the pan and allow the custard to cool to room temperature. Cover the cooled flan and refrigerate overnight in its pan.
7. To unmold the chilled flan, run a sharp knife around the edge of the pan to loosen the custard. Place a serving plate with a raised rim over the pan, and invert both serving plate and pan.

8. Lift the pan from the flan, which will now be presented upside down on the serving plate with the caramel.

CREPES

Crepes

DAIRY

2h

12 CREPES

When we were kids, whenever my beloved cousin Claudia and I had the opportunity, we used to prepare crepes with caramel or Manjarblanco, which we both loved so much.

I especially like this recipe because the crepes are so thin and soft. You can fill them with anything you desire as marmalade, chocolate-hazelnut spread, or even ice cream, and I assure you, it will be a heavenly experience… Delectable!

Ingredients

1 ½ cups milk (preferably 2 %)
1 cup all-purpose flour (use scoop-and-level measuring method)
3 large eggs
2 teaspoons granulated sugar
¼ teaspoons salt
3 tablespoons unsalted butter melted (plus additional butter, for pan)
½ teaspoon vanilla extract
Confectioners' sugar, for dusting (optional)

Optional fillings
Manjarblanco (see page 232, Desserts), caramel sauce, or chocolate-hazelnut spread, melted chocolate…

Preparation

1. In a blender, add milk, flour, eggs, sugar, salt, melted butter and vanilla. Blend at low speed until well combined, about 10 seconds.
2. Using a spatula, scrape the sides and bottom of the blender. If there is any unincorporated flour, blend a few seconds longer.
3. Cover and chill the batter for 1 hour, or overnight.
4. Remove the batter from the refrigerator several minutes before making the crepes.
5. Heat a 10-inch, non-stick skillet over medium heat.
6. Gently stir the batter to blend separated layers.
7. Lightly butter the skillet. When the butter is melted, pour a scant ¼ cup batter into pan. Immediately lift the pan from the burner, tilting and swirling in a circular motion until the batter evenly coats the pan.
8. Cook until light golden brown on bottom. Then, using an offset spatula, lift an edge of the crepe, grab the edge with your fingertips and flip to cook the other side. Cook until golden brown spots appear on bottom.
9. Transfer the crepe to a wire rack. Lower the burner temperature if needed, and heat ¼ teaspoon additional butter—just enough to create a light film—and repeat the cooking procedure until all the batter has been used.

Note: Dust crepes with powdered sugar and roll or fold into fourths, or top up with desired fillings, then fold or roll. Complete with another dusting of Confectioners' sugar.

FLUFFY BANANA-OATMEAL PANCAKES

Panqueques de Plátano y Avena

Some time ago, I decided that I would devise a delicious and nutritious version of pancakes for my family. These pancakes are truly fluffy, and you can make them so easily in a blender. If for any reason you have some leftover pancakes, you can freeze them, layer them between sheets of waxed paper, and they'll be ready to pop in the toaster to enjoy whenever you like!

Ingredients

1 cup milk or non-dairy milk
2 large ripe bananas
2 large eggs
2 teaspoons pure vanilla extract
2 cups old fashioned or quick-cooking rolled oats (for gluten-free oats, check GF certification on packaging)
2 teaspoons baking powder
1 teaspoon ground cinnamon
½ teaspoon salt

Preparation

1. In a blender, place the wet ingredients first, milk, bananas, eggs, and vanilla; followed by the dry ingredients: oats, baking powder, cinnamon, and salt.
2. Blend about 1 to 2 minutes, until the oats are finely ground, and there are no visible chunks of banana.
3. Let the batter sit for 15 to 30 minutes to allow the oats to hydrate. (You may cook the pancakes right away, but they will be fluffier if the batter is allowed to sit).
4. Heat a nonstick griddle or large nonstick pan over medium heat. For each pancake, ladle ¼ cup batter onto the hot griddle, and cook about 2 to 3 minutes per side.

Note: These pancakes can be served hot, with the traditional additions of butter and maple or Chancaca Syrup (see page 218, Desserts). Or, enjoyed warm or cold, with whipped cream, fruit and berries, peanut butter, chocolate-hazelnut spread, etc.
Any leftover pancakes can be frozen and reheated directly from the freezer in a toaster (for a crispier texture) or a microwave (for a soft texture).

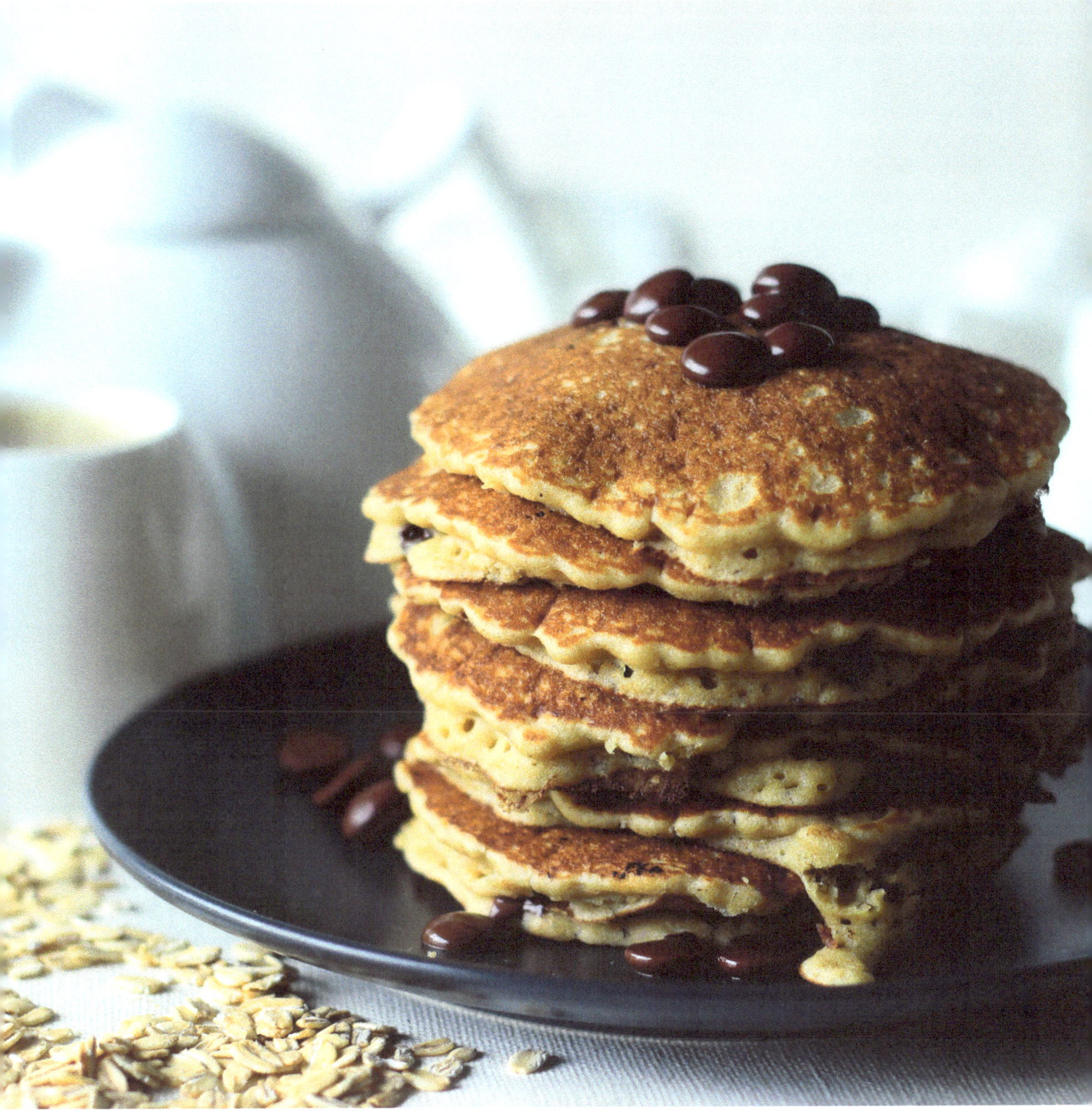

GLORIOUS GO-TO BROWNIES
Gloriosos Brownies

CONTAINS NUTS

1h

12 BARS

I have to make a confession: I'd never made brownies before. Yes, exactly as you are reading it. I don't know why. I usually bought them. And when I was working on this book, my dear friend Pamela, suggested I work on a 'to-die-recipe'; and I accepted the challenge. I made them during the evening, and I had the first piece the following morning with my coffee, and... Oh my! I couldn't believe it. Let me tell you, I can't wait for you to try them. I'm pretty sure this will be one of your family favorites.

This recipe will be perfect with my Lucuma Mousse (see page 240, Desserts). It's not too sweet, and the texture is perfect, with a nice, glossy top crust. Yum, yum, and yum again!

Wish I could share these with you!

Ingredients

6 ounces bittersweet chocolate
¾ cup (1 ½ sticks) unsalted butter
1 ⅓ cups granulated sugar
3 large eggs at room temperature, lightly beaten
1 ½ teaspoons vanilla extract
1 cup all-purpose flour
⅛ teaspoon salt
1 cup toasted pecans or walnuts, finely chopped (optional)

Preparation

1. Position a rack in the lower third of the oven.
2. Preheat oven to 325 °F. Butter a 9 x 9-inch baking pan and set aside. (The high butter content of the brownies allows them to release easily from the pan, but if desired, you can butter the pan and then line it with a sheet of parchment paper as well.)
3. Finely chop the chocolate, and cut the butter into 1 teaspoon pieces. Combine the chocolate and butter in a microwave-safe bowl and melt at low power for 30–45 seconds. Take the chocolate-butter out and stir it, then return the bowl to the microwave, continuing to heat at low power in 15-second increments, checking and stirring in between each 15 second burst, until the preparation is almost, but not quite melted. Remove the bowl from the microwave and stir until all the chocolate-butter is melted.
4. Allow to the chocolate-butter mixture to cool slightly. Stir in the sugar until dissolved. Add the beaten eggs in 3 additions, incorporating

thoroughly after each addition, then stir in the vanilla. Add the flour and salt, stirring well until the mixture is smooth and glossy. Fold in the toasted walnuts, if using.
5. Transfer the batter to the prepared pan, and spread it evenly.
6. Bake for 30–35 minutes, or until a cake tester, or toothpick, inserted in the center comes out with a few crumbs attached, but no wet batter.
7. Set the pan on a wire rack and allow the brownies to cool in the pan.

Note: These brownies are the perfect match for your favorite hot or cold drink, such as coffee, tea, or milk. Your kids will also enjoy them in their lunchboxes, at home, or on-the-go.

HOMEMADE CARAMEL MANJARBLANCO

Manjarblanco Casero

GLUTEN FREE

1h

1 ½–2 CUPS

There are different versions of caramel around the world such as Blancmange and Dulce de Leche, to mention a few.

Manjarblanco is a creamy sweet spread that is commonly used in different Peruvian desserts. Once you learn to make it, there's not another chance to get a processed one.

You can use it as a filling in your cakes, with Crepes, Alfajores, Encanelado, Volador, even on a piece of toast, or with some fruit. Even though it's purely milk and sugar, once you'll try it, you will totally get what I am saying. Unbelievable!

Ingredients

1 ½ cups evaporated milk (unsweetened)
1 ½ cups sweetened condensed milk
¼ cup brown sugar

Preparation

1. Pour condensed milk, evaporated milk, and brown sugar into a heavy bottom saucepan over medium-low heat.
2. Stir constantly with a spatula, until filling approaches the consistency of thick caramel, 20–30 minutes. Don't stop stirring, or the milk will stick to the bottom and burn.
3. Remove from heat, mixture will firm up as it cools to room temperature, about 30 minutes.

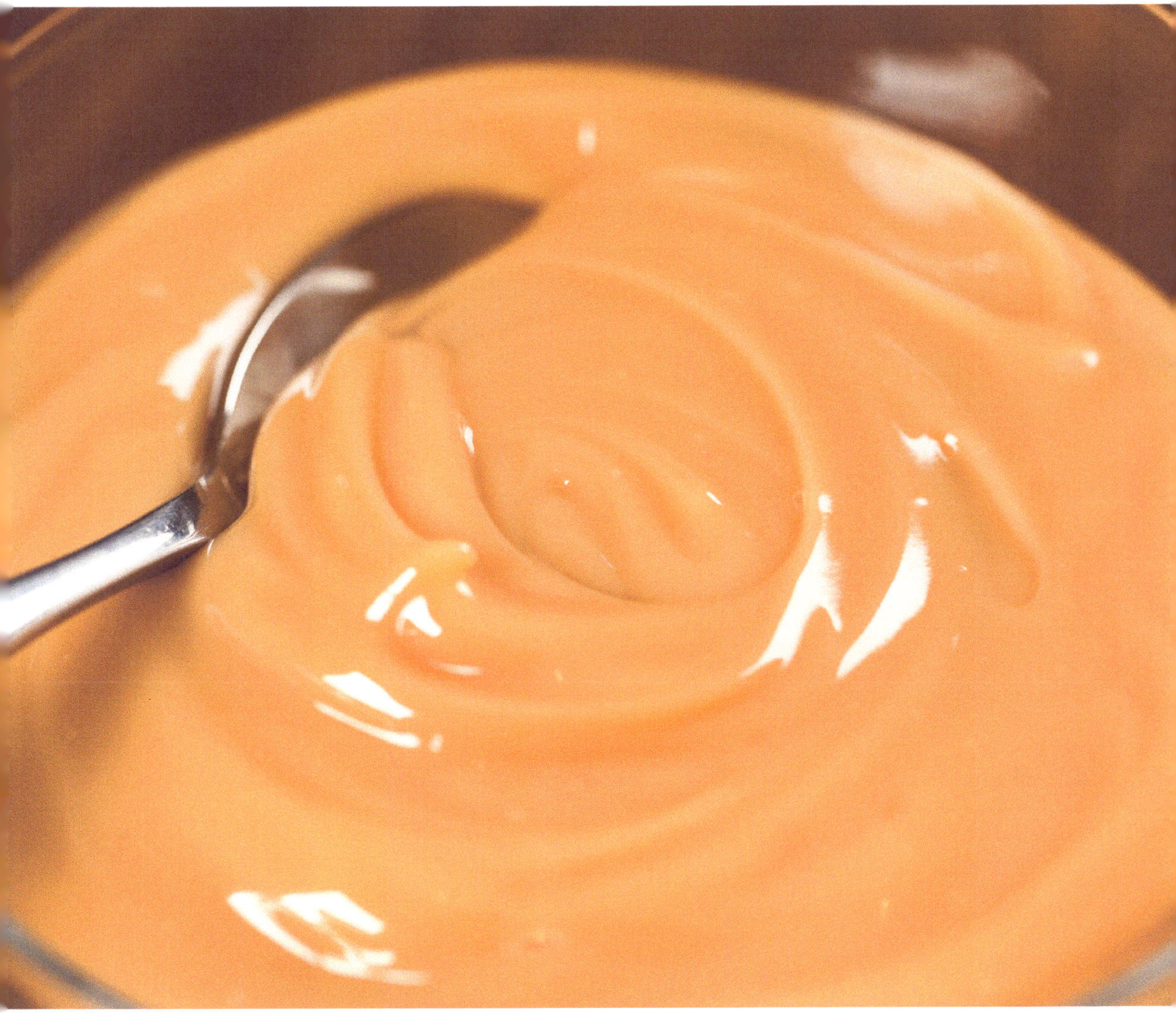

KEY LIME PIE

Pie de Limón

DAIRY

4h

8-10 SERVINGS

What can I tell you, my friends? When life gives you key limes, you make Key Lime Pie!

With this recipe you'll create a tart, sweet, easy and classic dessert that will be devoured by your loved ones. It's simple to make, and if you're a lime lover as I am, you'll be thankful for every single creamy, zesty bite.

Ingredients

<u>For the Crust</u>
2 cups Graham cracker crumbs (about 14 full crackers)
⅓ cup light brown sugar
Pinch of salt
½ cup unsalted butter, melted

<u>For the Lime Filling</u>
4 teaspoons key lime zest finely grated
4 egg yolks
1 can (14 ounces) sweetened condensed milk
½ cup freshly squeezed key lime juice

<u>For the Topping</u>
1 ½ cups heavy cream (well chilled)
3 tablespoons Confectioners' sugar
Additional lime zest or lime slices, to garnish

Preparation

<u>Crust and Lime Filling</u>
1. Preheat oven to 350 °F.
2. In a medium bowl, stir together the Graham cracker crumbs, brown sugar, and salt, being careful to break down any lumps of brown sugar. Pour the melted butter over the Graham cracker mixture and toss to combine with a fork until evenly moistened.
3. Press the crust mixture evenly into the bottom of a 9-inch pie plate, and up the sides, packing it firmly using the back of a measuring cup.
4. Bake the crust for 10 minutes at 350 °F; transfer to a wire rack to cool thoroughly before filling.
5. Meanwhile, make the filling in a medium bowl, whisk together the lime zest and egg yolks for 2 minutes. Whisk in the sweetened condensed milk, making sure the egg yolks are fully incorporated with no visible streaks of yellow. Next, whisk in the lime juice.
6. Pour the filling into the cooled crust.
7. Bake the pie at 350 °F preheated oven for 15-17 minutes, until the center of the filling is set, but still jiggles a bit when gently shaken.
8. Place the pie on a wire rack to cool room temperature, then refrigerate until well chilled, at least 3 hours.

9. After chilling, a piece of plastic wrap sprayed with non-stick cooking spray may be applied directly to the surface of the pie, which can remain refrigerated for up to 24 hours.

Topping
1. Using an electric mixer, whip the cream on medium speed until soft peaks form. Add the Confectioners' sugar, 1 tablespoon at a time, while continuing to whip the cream until stiff peaks form.
2. For decorative effect, pipe the whipped cream over the filling or spoon it over the pie and smooth with the back of the spoon. Garnish with lime slices or a sprinkling of fine lime zest.

Note: Cover any leftover pie (but don't expect to have any!) with plastic wrap and refrigerate for up to 3 days.

LIME BLUEBERRY BUNDT CAKE

Queque de Limón y Arándanos

DAIRY

90'

8-10 SERVINGS

When I was growing up in Lima, there were no blueberries to be had. It wasn't until I started traveling to the US on business in 1998 that I discovered the unique flavor of blueberries. And I was hooked for life. No wonder the Smurfs are always so happy! This is a moist, very lime-y cake, loaded with blueberries. It is perfect for any occasion, and enjoying this cake will definitely be an occasion. And of course, if you share it, even better!

Ingredients

2 ¼ cups flour (plus more for dusting the Bundt pan, and 1 tablespoon for dusting the berries)
¾ teaspoon salt
¾ teaspoon baking soda
¾ cup unsalted butter, room temperature
1 cup granulated sugar
4 eggs, room temperature
1 ½ cups milk (whole, or 2 %)
3 tablespoons lime zest
½ cup lime juice, freshly squeezed
1 ½ cups blueberries (preferably frozen)
Confectioners' sugar

Preparation

1. Preheat the oven to 350 °F.
2. Butter and flour a 10-inch Bundt pan. Tap out the excess flour and set aside.
3. In a medium size bowl, whisk together the flour, salt, and baking soda until well combined.
4. In a large bowl, beat butter and sugar at medium-high speed until light and fluffy, about 4–6 minutes. Add the eggs, one a time, beating well after each addition.
5. Reduce the mixer speed to low and alternate adding the flour mixture and the milk in 2 to 3 additions, starting and ending with the flour. Mix briefly after each addition, but only just until combined.
6. Using a spatula, stir in the lime juice and zest until just combined.
7. Gently toss the frozen blueberries with the tablespoon of reserved flour, then lightly fold the berries into the batter.
8. Transfer the batter to the prepared Bundt pan and bake for 60–65 minutes, until a cake tester or bamboo skewer inserted in center comes out clean.

9. Remove the cake from the oven and set the pan on a wire rack, allowing the cake to cool in the pan for 10 minutes.
10. Unmold the cake and place it on the rack to cool completely. Dust with Confectioners' sugar just before serving (optional).

LIME CHARLOTTE

Carlota de Limón

DAIRY

3h

8 SERVINGS

The flavors and image of this dessert have been instilled in my memory since I was a child. My Mamama used to make this version I am sharing with you now, but I also remember her making one with coffee. It is a time-consuming process, and requires patience. But the result is a fantastic, fresh, citrusy, creamy treat that even those who believe they can't make a decent dessert will surprise themselves with. Once they've tried it, kids and grown-ups alike will salivate at just hearing the name Lime Charlotte, and will likely ask you to make it every time there's a gathering.

Ingredients

1 can (14 ounce) sweetened condensed milk
1 can (12 ounce) evaporated milk (unsweetened)
¾ cup freshly squeezed lime juice
4 tablespoons lime zest, divided
36 Maria cookies or vanilla wafers, crackers or biscuits

Preparation

1. In a blender, combine the condensed milk, the evaporated milk and the lime juice, and blend for 2–3 minutes. Stir in 1 tablespoon of the lime zest.
2. In a 9 x 9-inches glass or ceramic pan, pour a thin layer of the lime cream. Then, place on top a single layer of cookies. Repeat the process, creating 3–4 layers, ending with the lime cream.
3. Sprinkle the top with lime zest. Cover and refrigerate for at least 2 hours before serving.

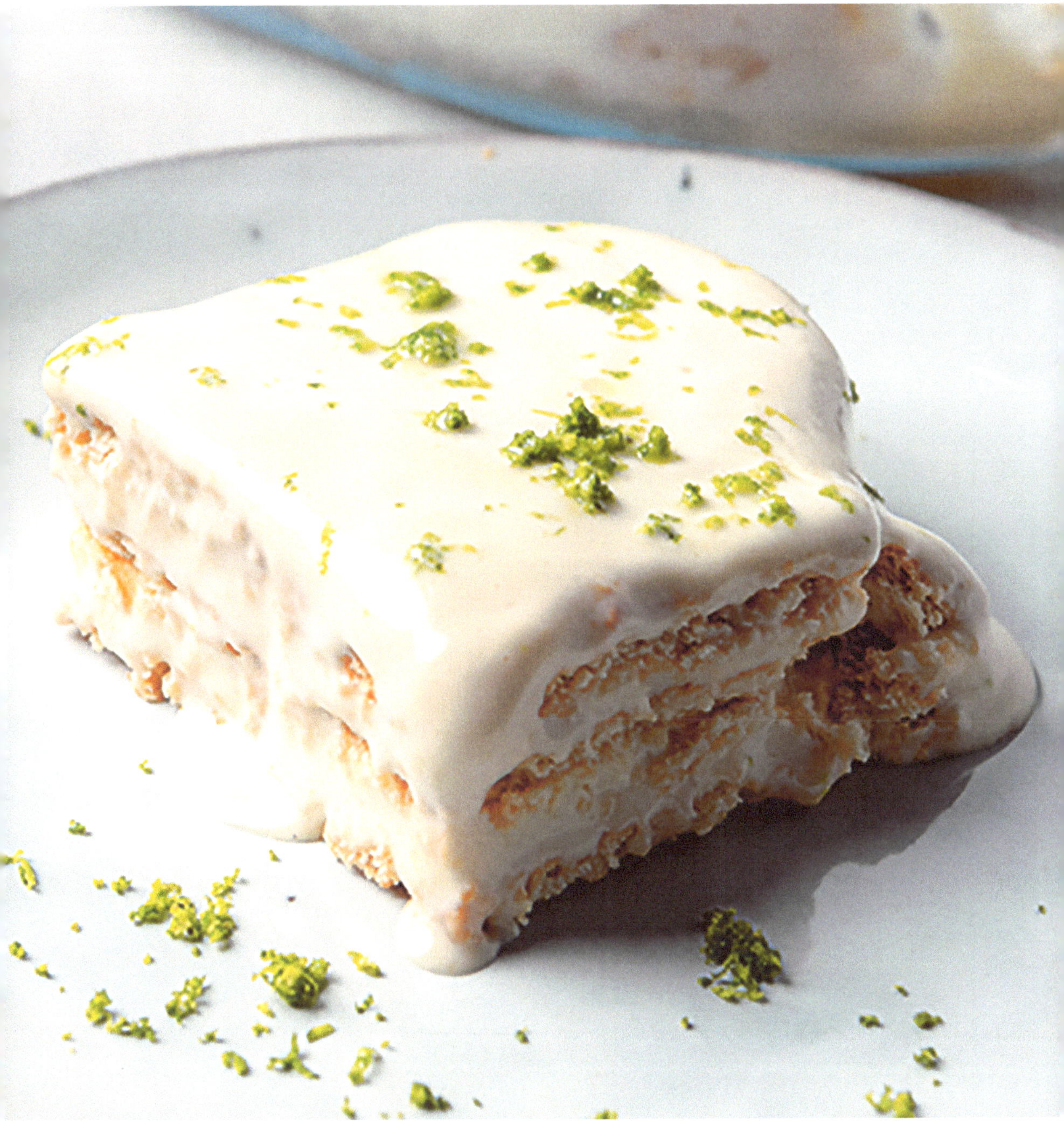

LUCUMA MOUSSE WITH BROWNIES

Mousse de Lúcuma con Brownies

DAIRY

90'

6-8 SERVINGS

When I first moved to the US, I couldn't find lucuma anywhere, so my husband took me to a market in San Francisco where they sell frozen lucuma pulp. That same day I started to play with various ingredients. I made Lucuma Mousse with Manjarblanco and whipped cream, and I felt like I was in Peru for a few minutes…

Yummy food is always better when shared, so at one of my pop-up dinner events, I introduced it to my friends and guests. We filled cannolis with my Lucuma Mousse, and Oh! Everyone asked me, "What is this filling? It's delicious!"

Lucuma is not just a delicious fruit, it is also a superfood with many nutrients and super creamy. It's the main ingredient in many delicious desserts. With a unique flavor that's a marriage of maple or caramel combined with pumpkin and sweet potato, it's well worth the search. You can find it in the frozen food section at some Latin markets, or online.

Ingredients

<u>For the Lucuma Mousse</u>
¾ cup heavy cream, well chilled
2 cups lucuma pulp, previously defrosted
½–¾ cup thick Manjarblanco (see page 232, Desserts)

<u>For the brownies</u>
See recipe on page 230

Preparation

<u>Lucuma Mousse</u>

1. Using an electric mixer, whip the cold heavy cream until it forms stiff peaks. Chill until ready to assemble the mousse.
2. In a separate bowl, use a spatula to combine the defrosted lucuma pulp and Manjarblanco.
3. Fold the whipped cream into the lucuma mixture.
4. Using a glass dish, line the bottom with brownie bars, or, if using individual serving glasses, crumble in chunks of brownies and lightly press to create a bottom layer. Pour the Lucuma Mousse over the brownie layer and chill in the refrigerator for at least 2 hours.
5. To garnish, crumble brownies over the top, or add shavings of chocolate.

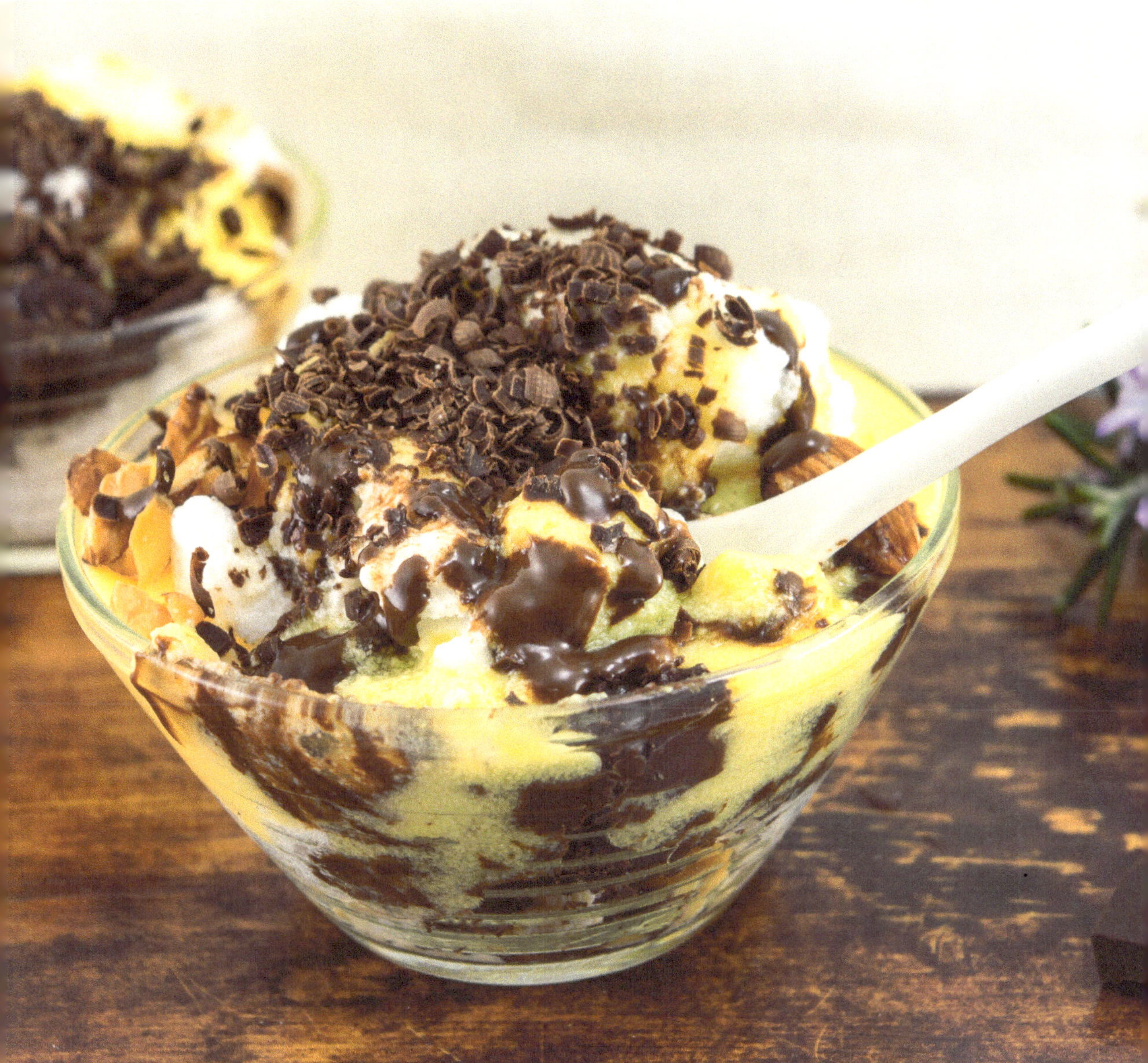

MAMAMA'S RICE PUDDING

Arroz con Leche de mi Mamama

GLUTEN FREE

1h

4-6 SERVINGS

Arroz con Leche is another traditional dessert in Peru, and it is my children's favorite. They love it and I love making it the way my Mamama taught me. The aroma of the cinnamon, cloves, and orange zest is an enticing perfume that floats around the house and gives away the "surprise" dessert. My Mamama's secret: orange peel! And to finish it, a good shot of Port!

One day, while Giacomo, one of my twins, was eating rice pudding, he told me: "This rice pudding is perfect for cold days because now my belly is warm." I melted with love. I hope you'll make this for someone you love.

Ingredients

4 cloves
1 cinnamon stick
2 long strips of orange peel
2 ½ cups water
½ cup white short grain rice
1 ¼ cups whole milk
1 ¼ cup sweetened condensed milk
1 egg yolk
4 tablespoons Port wine
Ground cinnamon for dusting

Preparation

1. Make a spice sachet by placing the cloves, cinnamon stick and orange peel in cheesecloth tied with kitchen string.
2. In a 3-quart saucepan, bring the 2 ½ water cups to a boil; stir rice and salt into the boiling water and add the spice sachet. Reduce the heat to medium or medium-low and let cook for 20 minutes, stirring occasionally.
3. Add the whole milk and cook over medium-low heat, stirring constantly, until thick and creamy, about 15–20 minutes.
4. Add the condensed milk and continue to cook, stirring for 10 more minutes.
5. In a small bowl, beat together the egg yolk with the port. Add about ¼ cup of the pudding and stir together.
6. Take the pan off the heat, and stir in the tempered egg mixture until well combined.
7. Transfer the pudding into a bowl to cool slightly, placing a sheet of parchment paper directly onto the surface of the pudding to prevent a skin forming. If serving cold, refrigerate.

8. Serve warm, cold or at room temperature in individual dessert glasses or bowls, topped with a dusting of cinnamon.

Note: In Peru, Rice Pudding is also sometimes topped with raisins and/or shredded coconut and uses Pisco instead of my Mamama's Port.

MARBLED CAKE

Queque Mármol

One of the first desserts I learned to make was this Marbled cake. My Mamama liked it so much that it became a regular staple at my grandparents' house in Peru. Now, my husband and my boys ask me for it often. What I like about this cake is that it has vanilla and chocolate, so you can please both cravings.

Ingredients

1 ½ cups all-purpose flour
1 ½ teaspoons baking powder
¼ teaspoon salt
3 egg whites
3 egg yolks
½ cup vegetable oil
¾ cup sugar plus 2 tablespoons
1 ½ teaspoons vanilla
⅓ cup milk
2 tablespoons unsweetened cocoa powder (preferably, Dutch process), sifted through a fine sieve

Preparation

1. Preheat oven to 350 °F. Grease a 9 x 5 x 3-inches loaf pan or a 7 ½ x 3-inches Bundt cake pan, and set aside.
2. Sift the flour, baking powder and salt onto a sheet of waxed paper. Set aside.
3. Separate the eggs, putting the egg whites into a medium bowl, and the yolks in a large bowl.
4. Using an electric hand mixer, beat the egg whites on high speed until they form firm peaks. Set aside.
5. In the egg yolks bowl, add the oil, sugar and vanilla. Beat on high speed for about a minute, until thickened.
6. Reduce the beater speed to low, and slowly add the milk and beat until just incorporated. Next add the flour mixture, beating just until combined.
7. Using a spatula, gently fold the egg whites into the batter. (Reserve the egg white bowl to mix the chocolate marbling batter.) Set the batter aside while you mix the chocolate layer.
8. Scoop out about ⅔ cup of the batter, and place it in the reserved egg white bowl. Fold the sifted cocoa powder and 2 tablespoons sugar into the ⅔ cup of batter.
9. Spoon alternating layers of the vanilla and chocolate batters into your prepared pan. Then,

holding a small knife vertically, swirl it from side to side through the batter, 3 or 4 times, to create a marbled effect.
10. Bake at 350 °F for 45 minutes or until a cake tester inserted in the center comes out clean. Cool in the pan on a wire rack for 10–15 minutes, then remove the cake, place it back on the wire rack and allow to cool completely.
11. Will keep 3–5 days at room temperature, tightly wrapped.

OLD FASHIONED PUDDING

Mazamorra de Cochino

DAIRY

45'

6-8 SERVINGS

Like many creole Peruvian desserts, the Mazamorra de Cochino is made in a pot with a wooden spoon. The key is to stir, and stir, and let the talk begin...

One of my childhood memories is when the pudding was already cooled down and it was served in these cute bowls at my Mamama's house, and the final touch was a couple of dashes of evaporated milk. It was amazing!

Doing a little bit of research, I've learned that the name Mazamorra de Cochino, or pork pudding, comes from the fact that this pudding requires pork lard, and it works perfectly fine. However, my version is with butter.

If you are a pudding lover, this recipe will conquer your heart!

Ingredients

3 cups + 2 ¼ cups of water, separated
1 teaspoon anis seeds
10 cloves
2 cinnamon sticks
1 pound Chancaca (piloncillo or panela)
1 cup flour
1 can evaporated milk (unsweetened)
2 teaspoons vanilla
4 tablespoons brown sugar (according to taste)
2 tablespoons butter
½ cup raisins (optional)

Preparation

1. In a heavy bottom pot over high heat, place 3 cups of water, anis seeds, cloves, cinnamon sticks, and Chancaca. Bring to a boil for 15 minutes. Lower the temperature.
2. Dissolve flour with 2 ¼ cup of water, temper the flour with some Chancaca liquid.
3. With the help of a sifter, pour the flour mix in the Chancaca liquid moving constantly for about 20 minutes. If using raisins, this is the time to incorporate them.
4. Add evaporated milk, combine and add butter and vanilla and combine well.

Serving suggestion: Serve the Old Fashioned Pudding hot in cups, garnish with ground cinnamon, coconut flakes, and/or raisins.

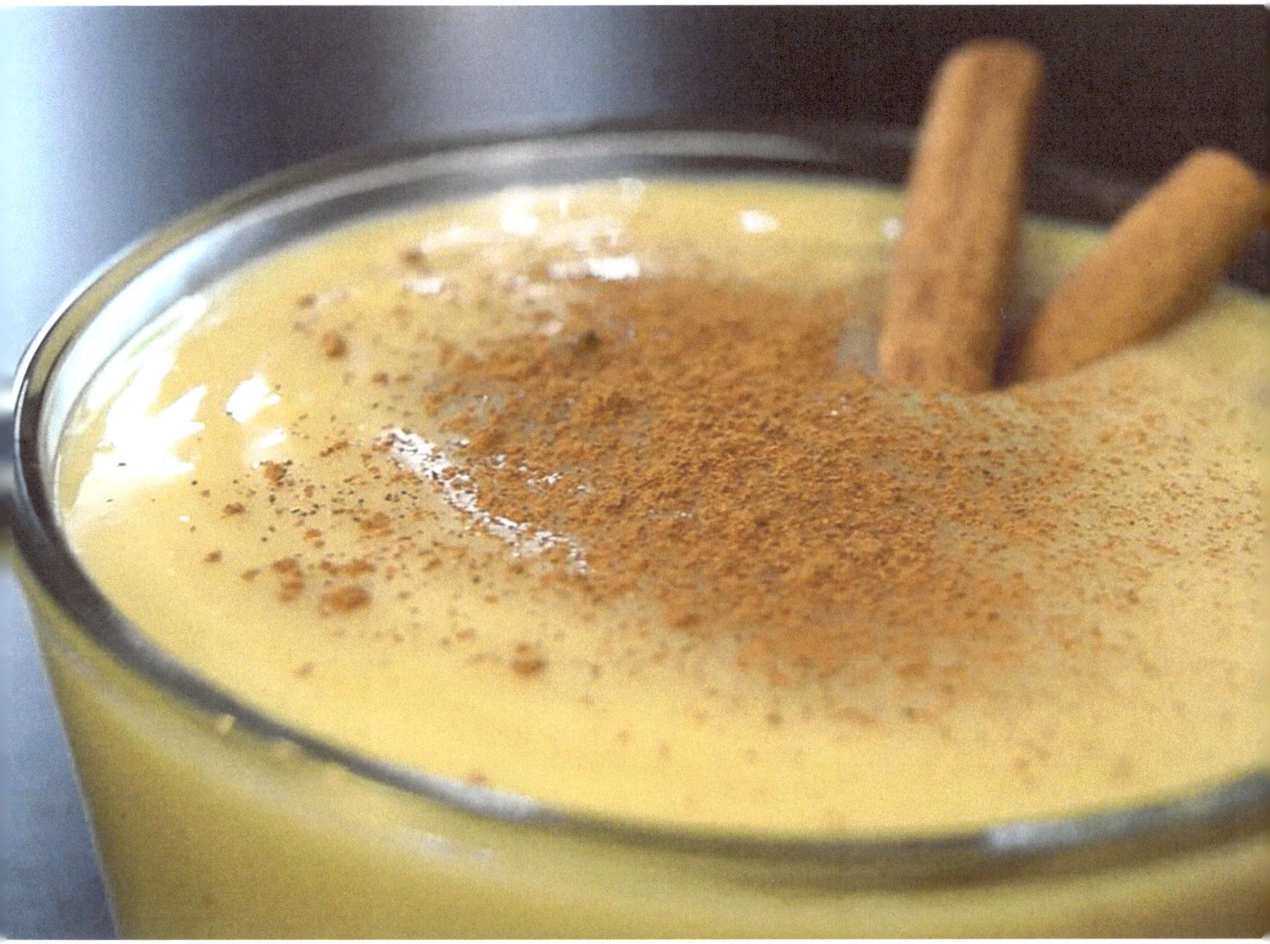

ORANGE BUNDT CAKE

Queque de Naranja

Un quequito de naranja! This classic Orange Bundt Cake can be found in many coffee shops, bakeries, restaurants and even kiosks around Peru. It is so easy to make that there's no reason to buy one at a store. Ideal for breakfast, a snack or dessert, its strong orange flavor will please your palate and perfume your house as well!

DAIRY

90'

8 SERVINGS

Ingredients

2 ½ cups all-purpose flour
1 ½ cups granulated sugar
1 teaspoon baking powder
½ teaspoon baking soda
¾ teaspoon salt
4 large eggs
½ cup sour cream
¾ cup freshly squeezed orange juice
4 tablespoons grated orange zest (from 4 oranges)
1 teaspoon vanilla
1 cup unsalted butter, softened

For the Glaze (optional)
2 cups confectioners' sugar
¼ cup orange juice, freshly squeezed
1 teaspoon lime juice, freshly squeezed
2 teaspoons orange liqueur (Grand Marnier or Cointreau)

Preparation

1. Preheat the oven to 350 °F. Butter and flour a 10-cup Bundt pan, or spray with cooking spray.
2. In a large bowl, whisk together the flour, sugar, baking powder, baking soda and salt. Set aside.
3. Put the eggs in a medium bowl, and using an electric mixer, whip up until smooth. Add the sour cream, orange juice, orange zest and vanilla, and mix until well combined. Blend in the softened butter. At this point, the mixture will appear curdled, but do not worry!
4. Add the wet ingredients to the flour mixture set aside, and beat at the lowest speed until just combined. Do not overmix.
5. Transfer the cake batter to the Bundt pan, and smooth the surface. Bake at 350 °F for 55 minutes, or until a cake tester inserted near the center comes out clean.
6. Cool the cake in the pan for 20 minutes and then invert the cake onto a wire rack; remove the pan and allow the cake to cool completely.

Glaze (optional)
1. In a medium bowl, combine all the glaze ingredients. Mixture should be runny. If too stiff, add more orange juice, if too loose, add a bit more confectioners' sugar.

2. Drizzle the glaze over the cooled cake, allowing it to drip down the sides. Let the glaze set before serving.

Note: This cake is perfect for breakfast, snacks, teatime, or to share with friends and family.

PASSION FRUIT CAKE

Queque de Maracuyá

It is said that passion fruit was named by the 17th century Spanish Catholic missionaries in the Amazon region of Brazil. They called it Flor Passionis (passionflower) or *flor de las cinco llagas* (flower of the five wounds), after its purple flower, which they believed resembled the five wounds of Christ. But regardless of the name, and that Peruvian passion fruit is yellow, not purple, its flavor and aroma are incredible. And here is a delicious coffee cake featuring this intense and uniquely tropical fruit. You probably won't be seeing this extraordinary cake at a community bake sale!

Ingredients

1 cup all-purpose flour
1 cup cake flour*
2 teaspoons baking powder
½ teaspoon salt
1 cup Greek yogurt
¾ cup granulated sugar
3 extra-large eggs
½ cup vegetable oil
½ cup passion fruit pulp (available frozen at most Latin markets)

For the White Chocolate Glaze

7 ounces white chocolate, chopped
¼ cup passion fruit pulp and seeds
1 tablespoon warm water

*You may use 2 cups of all-purpose flour instead of 1 cup each of all-purpose flour and cake flour, but the resulting cake texture will be just a bit denser.

Preparation

1. Preheat the oven to 350 °F. Grease a 9 x 5-inch loaf pan.
2. In a large bowl, sift together the flours, baking powder and salt; set aside.
3. Using an electric mixer, combine in other bowl the yogurt, sugar, eggs, vegetable oil and passion fruit pulp; blend at medium speed until well combined.
4. Pour the wet mixture into the dry ingredients set aside, and mix at the lowest speed, just until combined.
5. Transfer the batter to the prepared loaf pan and bake at 350 °F for 45–60 minutes, until a cake tester inserted in the center comes out clean.
6. Remove the cake from the oven and allow to cool completely before releasing the cake from the pan.

White Chocolate Glaze

1. To make the glaze, combine the white chocolate, passion fruit pulp and seeds and the warm water in a bowl, set over a pan of simmering water; allow the white chocolate to melt, stirring to combine with the passion fruit and water. If you

find the drizzle is too thick, add a little passion fruit pulp or water to reach the desired consistency.
2. While the glaze is still warm, drizzle it over the cooled cake and allow to set slightly before slicing and serving.

Note: If the cake is browning too quickly during baking, cover it loosely with a piece of aluminum foil halfway through baking.

PASSION FRUIT MOUSSE
Mousse de Maracuyá

Passion fruit, which is called *maracuyá* in Spanish, is a super aromatic tropical fruit. I grew up enjoying plenty of it. Mainly as a refreshment, but also as ice-cream. When you try this recipe, you'll enjoy its tangy, creamy, sweet deliciousness! You can prepare Passion Fruit Mousse up to 2 days in advance. If you can't find the fresh fruit, you can use frozen pulp. It works great!

Ingredients

For the Base
1 cup Graham cracker crumbs
2 tablespoons (¼ stick) unsalted butter, melted

For the Mousse
⅔ cup pure passion fruit pulp (without seeds)
1 can sweetened condensed milk
¾ cup heavy cream

For the passion fruit Gelatin
1 ½ teaspoons plain gelatin powder
2 tablespoons cold water
3 tablespoons plus 1 teaspoon passion fruit pulp (with seeds)
2 tablespoons sugar

Preparation

Base
1. Preheat the oven to 325 °F.
2. In a small bowl, stir the butter into the Graham cracker crumbs until well combined.
3. Spoon the loose crumb mixture into a small baking pan to toast; do not press the mixture.
4. Bake the loose crumbs for 10 minutes, until just toasted and light golden brown. Set aside to cool.
5. When the crumbs are cool, stir to loosen and divide the crumbs between 4 large red wine glasses. Set aside.

Mousse
1. In a medium bowl, combine the passion fruit pulp with condensed milk.
2. In a separate bowl, use an electric mixer to whip the heavy cream until it reaches medium to stiff peaks.
3. Fold the whipped cream into the passion fruit and condensed milk mixture.
4. Pour over the crumb base in the wine glasses and refrigerate overnight, or at least 4 hours.

Passion fruit Gelatin
1. In a small microwave-safe bowl, hydrate the gelatin in the 2 tablespoons cold water.

2. In a separate small bowl, combine 3 tablespoons plus 1 teaspoon of passion fruit pulp with 2 tablespoons sugar.
3. Microwave the gelatin for 20–30 seconds. (If not using a microwave, create a water bath by placing the bowl of gelatin in a slightly larger bowl partially filled with hot water.) Stir the gelatin until completely dissolved.
4. Add the passion fruit pulp and sugar mixture to the gelatin and stir well. Set aside and keep at room temperature.
5. To assemble, gently spoon some of the passion fruit gelatin on top of the mousse in each of the 4 wine glasses. Cover each glass with plastic wrap and return to the refrigerator for at least 1 hour.

Serving suggestion: Serve cold, with optional garnishes: mint sprigs, whipped cream, berries.

PISCO-AMARETTO AFFOGATO

Affogato de Pisco con Amaretto

SIGNATURE RECIPE

10'

2 SERVINGS

While this recipe isn't strictly Peruvian, I wanted to offer something easy, elegant, and delectable, and that would reflect my Italian and Peruvian heritage. So, we came up with this simple yet exquisite dessert, which brings back familiar flavors and happy memories for me.

The flavors and aromas of coffee and Amaretto are so familiar to me. They are stamped in my soul and in my heart, a taste of my childhood. I have a vivid memory of my Tata waking up from his 10 minutes after-lunch nap, and freshening up while my Mamama quickly made him an espresso before he returned to work. The fragrance of freshly-brewed strong coffee, and that moment—when he would kiss us goodbye... the look in his eyes, his walk... it all lives in my memory and in my spirit.

Amaretto would be a regular afternoon addition. When it was teatime, my Mamama used to make a pot of loose-leaf tea, and then, if it was winter, she would add either Amaretto or Pisco. I was allowed to taste it with a very tiny spoon, and I fell in love with it.

Ingredients

4 generous scoops best quality vanilla gelato or ice cream
Freshly brewed strong coffee or 2 shots of espresso
2 tablespoons Amaretto liqueur
1 tablespoon Pisco
Toasted slivered almonds (optional)

Preparation

1. Chill dessert glasses in the freezer.
2. When ready to serve, place 2 generous scoops of ice cream in each chilled glass.
3. Pour hot coffee over the ice cream and top with the Amaretto and Pisco.
4. Serve immediately, topped with a scattering of toasted, slivered almonds, if desired.

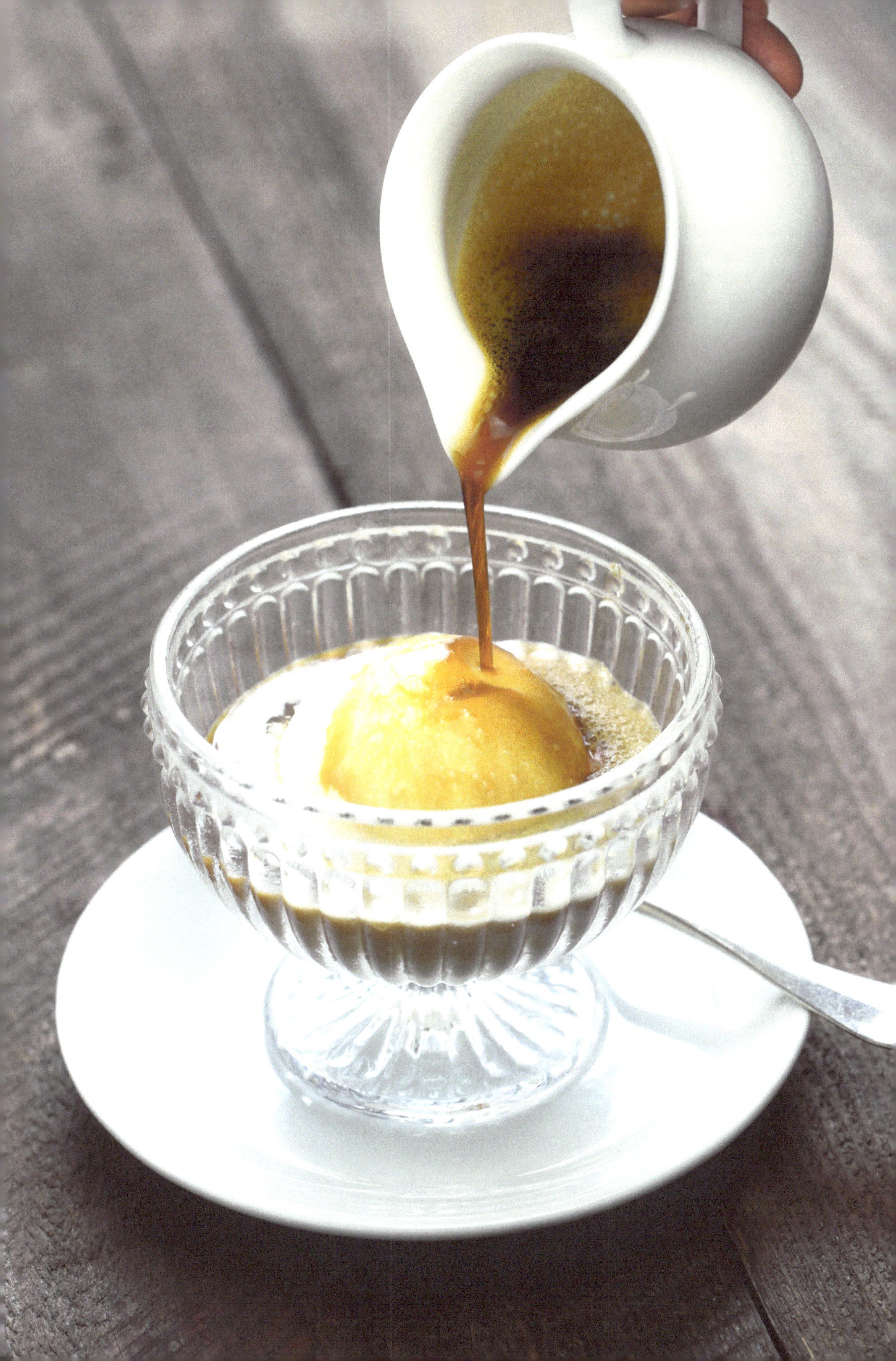

ROASTED MILK

Leche Asada

This is a dessert that heralds from colonial times. Considered in that era as the poor man's Crème Brûlée, it has conquered millions of taste buds. Leche Asada has no caramel and is characterized by its caramelized top. It's prepared with just few ingredients: fresh milk, eggs, sugar and vanilla, and baked in a water bath until set. This is Peruvian comfort dessert at its best!

GLUTEN FREE

90'

6 RAMEKINS

Ingredients

4 cups whole milk
2 cinnamon sticks
3 whole cloves
1 lemon, zest only, pared into a ½-inch-wide strip
6 large eggs
¾ cup granulated sugar
1 teaspoon vanilla extract
2 tablespoons Pisco, or Brandy

Preparation

1. In a saucepan, add the milk, cinnamon sticks, cloves and the strip of lemon zest. Bring to a simmer over medium-high heat, then reduce heat to low, and cook for 5 minutes. Remove from the heat and allow to cool to room temperature.
2. Meanwhile, set an oven rack at the middle position and preheat the oven to 375 °F.
3. In a bowl, beat the eggs and sugar together until the sugar has dissolved and the eggs are fully incorporated.
4. Remove the lemon strip, cinnamon, and cloves from the cooled milk. Add the milk to the egg mixture and whisk together. Add the vanilla and the Pisco and mix until well combined.
5. Pour the custard through a fine mesh sieve into a bowl, or large measuring cup with a spout. Pour or ladle the custard into individual ramekins set on a baking tray.
6. Place the ramekins in a large baking pan and create a water bath by pouring warm water into the pan to reach halfway up the outsides of the ramekins. Carefully transfer the baking pan to the oven and bake at 375 °F for about 30–35 minutes, until set, but still slightly jiggly in the centers.

7. Carefully remove the baking pan from the oven, take out the ramekins, and discard the water bath. Replace the ramekins in the pan and adjust the oven rack to the broil position. Set the temperature to broil and return the pan of custards to the oven. Allow to broil for 3 minutes or so, until the tops have developed spots of deep, dark brown.
8. Remove the custards from the oven and let them cool completely, then cover individually with plastic wrap and chill before serving.

SOURSOP MOUSSE

Mousse de Guanábana

GLUTEN FREE

90'

8-10 SERVINGS

Peru has an incredible variety of fruits and vegetables, but one of my favorites is Guanábana (Soursop). It has a velvety texture and it is a combination of sweet, tangy and sour.

The complexity of the soursop has always intrigued me... This sweet and sour fruit is native to parts of the Caribbean and South America. It is said to taste like a combination of strawberries and apple, with citrusy notes.

To make this dessert even more appealing, I top it with crumbled vanilla meringue cookies and the result is a beautiful, refreshing, sweet, exotic and elegant dessert.

Ingredients

2 packages (8 ounces each) cream cheese, softened
2 cups soursop pulp
2 cups heavy cream, well chilled
1 ½ cup sweetened condensed milk
Vanilla meringue cookies, crumbled; chocolate sauce, to garnish

Preparation

1. Using an electric mixer, whip the softened cream cheese in a large bowl, for about 5 minutes. Add the condensed milk and beat until well incorporated. Using a spatula, stir in the soursop pulp. Set aside.
2. In a separate, clean, cold bowl, whip the heavy cream until stiff peaks form.
3. Fold the whipped cream into the soursop mixture.
4. Pour the mousse into individual serving glasses; cover with plastic wrap and refrigerate for at least 1 hour.

Serving suggestion: When ready to serve, top with crumbled meringues and a drizzle of chocolate sauce.

Note: Soursop pulp is available in frozen food section in most Latin markets.

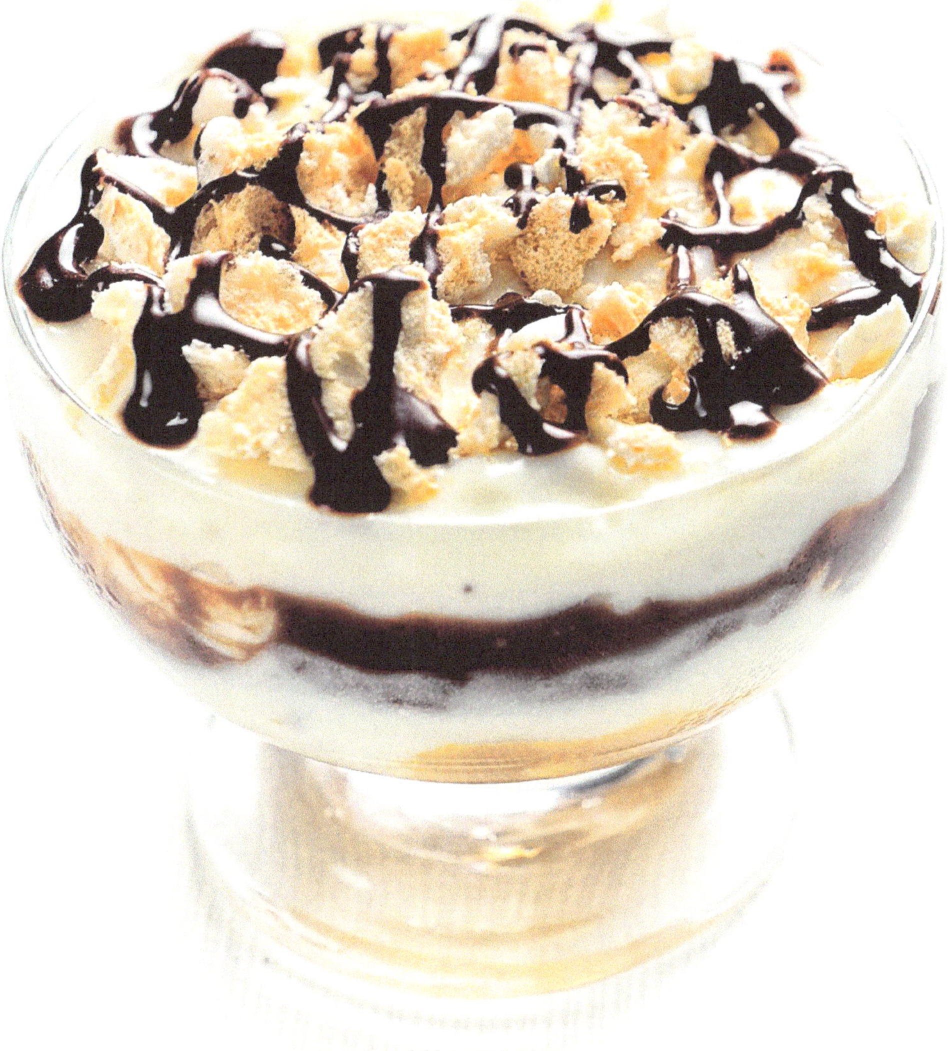

SWEET POTATO BARS

Camotillo

GLUTEN FREE

2h

12-15 BARS

You might be thinking, what on earth is Camotillo? Well, it's a Peruvian dessert or treat made with sweet potatoes and sugar. There's nothing that I can compare it with. It is unique and full of flavor and textures. Yes, because the inside is creamy and the outside is firm and a little bit crunchy.

This recipe is special to me because I can almost vividly remember seeing every Saturday my great-uncle Armando, showing up at my grandparents' house with Sweet Potato Bars and freshly baked bread from the bakery. The bread was still warm, and warm bread asked for butter, right? Then for dessert, we were having Sweet Potato Bars! It was a sweet tradition for him and a lovely treasure in my heart forever.

Ingredients

2 pounds sweet potatoes
2 pounds sugar
3 teaspoons of orange zest
¼ cup water
1 tablespoon cinnamon
Colored sprinkles (optional)

Preparation

1. Place the unpeeled sweet potatoes in a pot, cover with water and bring to boil until cooked and tender. Remove from pan, carefully peel it while warm, and pass through a ricer.
2. Place the mashed sweet potatoes, the sugar, orange zest and water in a heavy-bottomed pot. Bring to a boil over medium heat, stirring constantly until thickened.
3. Grease and flour a baking sheet pan. Once the sweet potato preparation is cool, use a piping bag, or two spoons, to form the elongated shape of 4 x 1.5-inches bars.
4. In a small bowl, mix 1 cup powdered sugar with ¼ cup of water. Mix well and brush evenly each Sweet Potato Bar with this sweet mixture.
5. Preheat oven to 300 °F.
6. Bake the Sweet Potato Bars for 90 minutes. They must be dry. Remove from oven and cool. They should be slightly sweet on the outside.
7. Peel off the Sweet Potato Bars from the baking sheet and store until ready to serve.

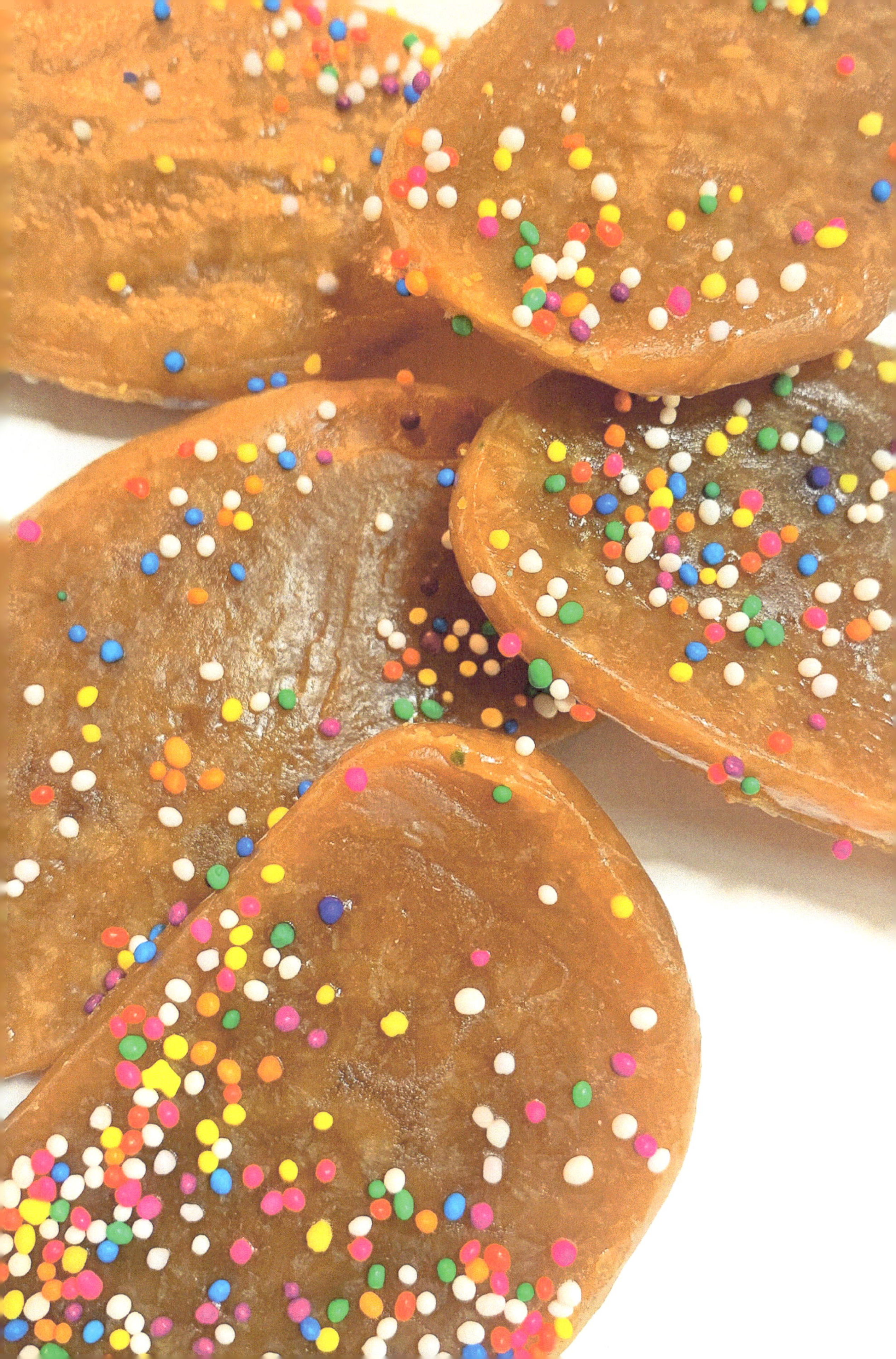

SWEET POTATO BREAD

Queque de Camote

One of the early lessons that I learned in my Mamama's kitchen was not to waste or discard food, when it's still edible, I should say. The key word she taught me was: REPURPOSE! With that principle in mind, I decided to get adventurous and use some roasted sweet potatoes that were in the refrigerator. It's very hard to tell there's sweet potato in this bread; some might think its pumpkin, or that it is actually a spice bread. You'll be the judge, but I'm sure you'll agree that it's definitely scrumptious!

DAIRY FREE

90'

1 LOAF

Ingredients

1 ¾ cups all-purpose flour, sifted
1 teaspoon baking soda
½ teaspoon ground cinnamon
½ teaspoon ground nutmeg
½ teaspoon ground ginger
¼ teaspoon salt
1 cup light brown sugar
½ cup vegetable oil
3 eggs, room temperature
1 cup cooked sweet potatoes, puréed and cooled
¼ cup raw sunflower seeds

Preparation

1. Preheat the oven to 350 °F. Grease and flour a 9 x 5-inch loaf pan. Set aside.
2. In a medium bowl, whisk together the flour, baking soda, spices and salt. Set aside.
3. In a large bowl, combine the sugar and the oil, and beat well with an electric mixer. Next, add the eggs, one at a time, and beat until well incorporated.
4. By hand, stir the dry flour mixture into the wet mixture.
5. Add the sweet potato purée and stir until just combined. Do not overwork the batter.
6. Pour the batter into the prepared pan and top with the raw sunflower seeds. Bake at 350 °F for about 1 hour, or until a cake tester inserted in the center comes out clean, or with just a few moist crumbs attached.
7. Transfer the pan to a wire rack and allow to cool for 10–20 minutes. Remove the bread from the pan and place on the rack until completely cool.

Note: If desired, sprinkle the loaf, while still warm, with flaky sea salt.

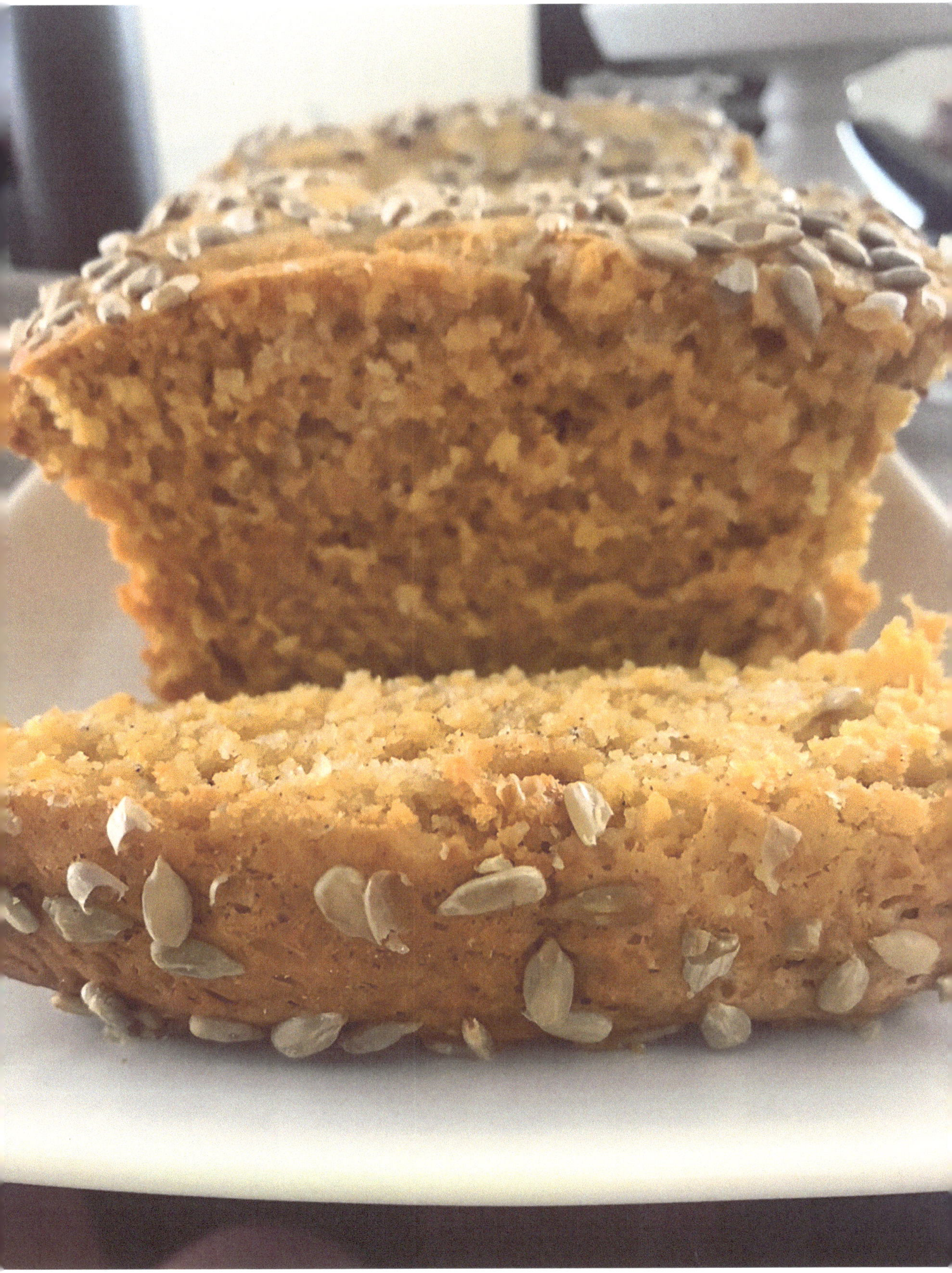

SWEET WALNUT BALLS

Bolitas de Nuez

As a child, I enjoyed helping my Mamama prepare delicious desserts for the whole family. Now that I'm a mom, I feel very lucky when I can share similar moments with my children, and these treats are fun and easy for kids to help make. But I must tell you something: I fell in love with these treats after trying them at the Tang family corner store near the home where I grew up. Oh, what a pleasure! Sweet, chewy, packed with roasted walnut flavor—ideal to have it with a cup of tea or coffee.

Ingredients

3 cups vanilla wafers, crushed
1 cup toasted walnuts, chopped
¾ cup sweetened condensed milk
1 cup Confectioners' sugar, sifted

Preparation

1. In a bowl, mix the crushed vanilla wafers, the walnuts and the condensed milk.
2. Shape the mixture into 1-inch diameter balls.
3. Roll the balls into the Confectioners' sugar, place on a platter and enjoy at room temperature.

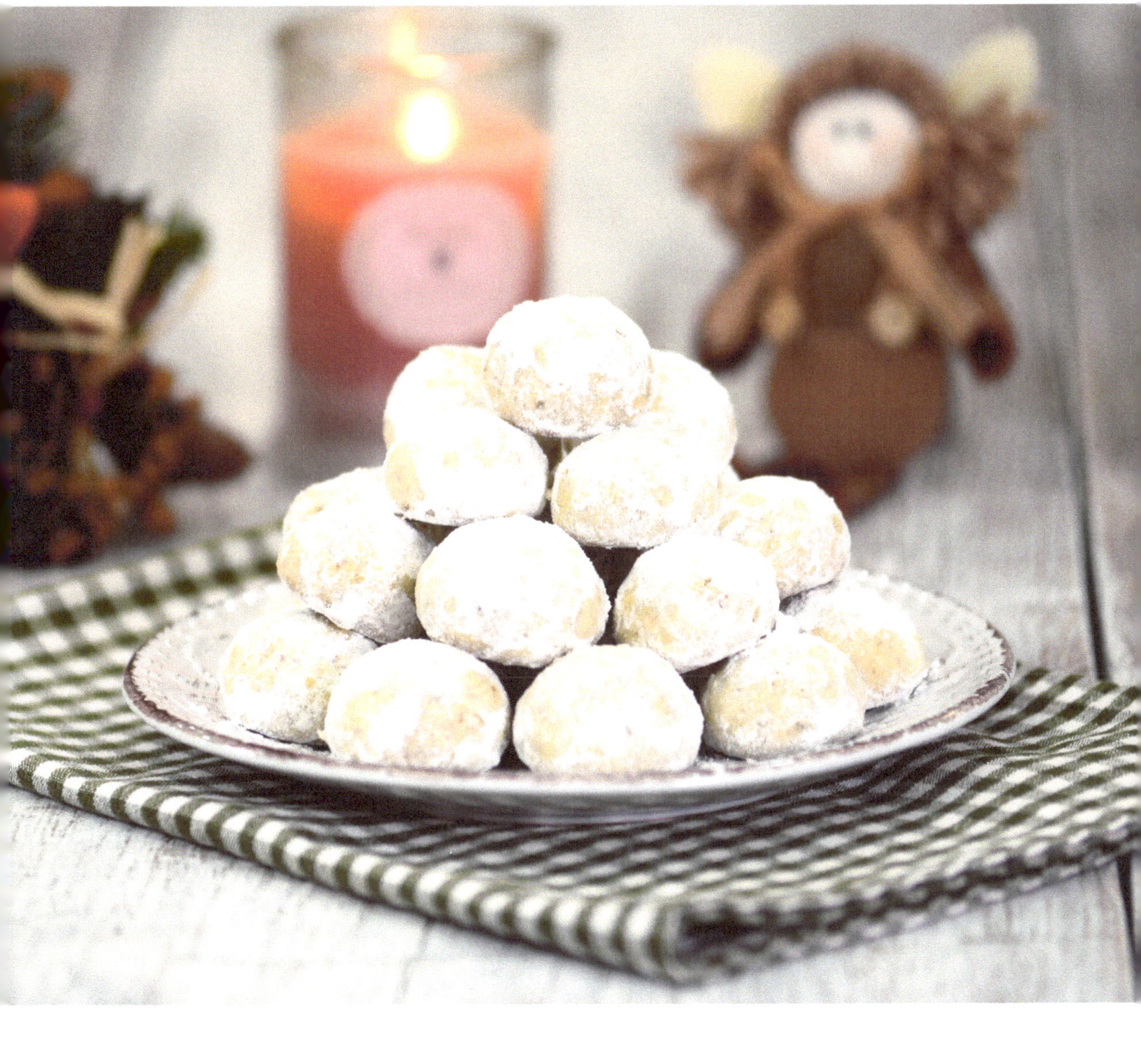

VOLADOR

Volador

DAIRY

2h

10 SERVINGS

Have you heard of a dessert called Volador? It has its origin in Lima and is said to have been invented by nuns. It bears that name because when you start baking, it looks like the layers are going to fly off like a flying saucer.

To prepare it you have to assemble many layers of very thin, light and crunchy dough, then you put them and intersperse with Manjarblanco or caramel, and apricot jam... The combination works excellent, and you have a rich and soft dessert!

I prepared a Volador for my husband's birthday and when Gramps saw the cake, he said to me: Olenka, *mamacita* (as he called me) and how do you plan to cut it without it falling apart? LOL... That's my secret, Gramps!

Ingredients

For the Dough
2 cups all-purpose flour
½ teaspoon baking powder
Pinch of salt
8 egg yolks
½ cup Pisco
1 tablespoon butter, melted and cooled to room temperature

For the Filling and Topping
1 cup Manjarblanco (see page 232)
1 cup apricot jam
Confectioners' sugar

Preparation

1. In a large bowl, whisk together the flour, baking powder and salt. Set aside.
2. In a separate bowl, whisk together the egg yolks, the Pisco and butter, until well combined. Then, add the dry ingredients set aside, and gently combine until a uniform dough is done.
3. Divide the dough in six equal pieces. Cover with a dry towel and let rest for 15 minutes.
4. When the dough finished resting, use a rolling pin to roll each piece of dough into a 10 inch diameter round.
5. Line one or more baking sheets with parchment paper, or a silicone baking mat and bake each disk for about 12–15 minutes, until golden.
6. As the rounds are baked, remove to wire racks, to cool.
7. To assemble, place a small amount of Manjarblanco, on the serving plate to hold the bottom disk in place. Spread the bottom disk with Manjarblanco. Place another disk on top and spread it with the jam. Top with another disk spread with the Manjarblanco and repeat,

alternating the fillings, ending with jam on the top layer. Follow with a dusting of Confectioners' sugar.

Note: You can make also 2 Voladores with 3 layers each.

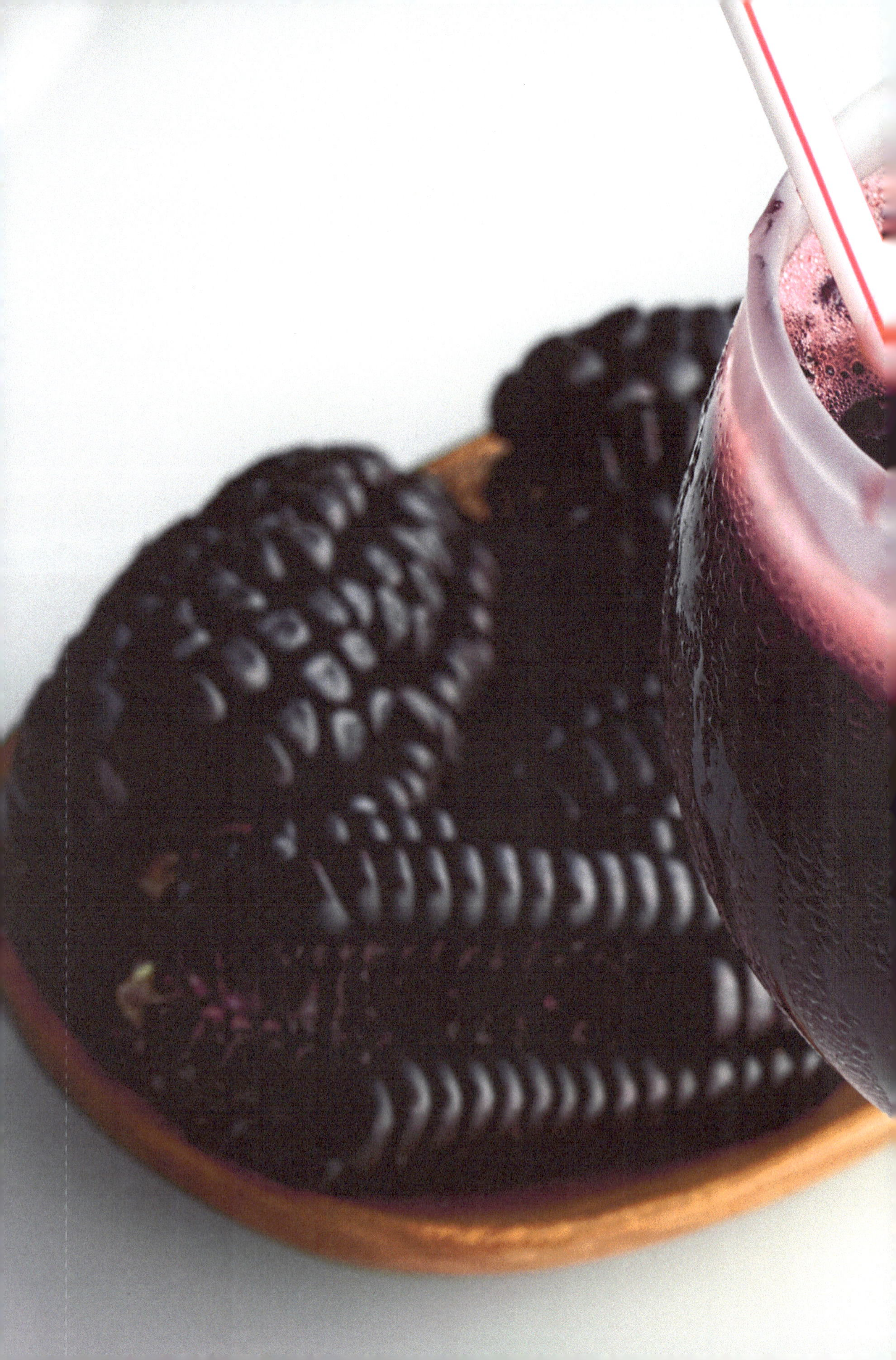

Cocktails & Drinks

CAROB SYRUP COCKTAIL
Cóctel de Algarrobina

At home in Peru during my younger years, family Sunday brunches were a wonderful tradition. The Cóctel de Algarrobina made by my beloved auntie Cucha, my Tata's younger sister, couldn't be missed. She would make a jug with Pisco for the adults and a virgin version for the children. It was a Sunday sensation!

Ingredients

5 ounces Pisco
3 ounces coffee liqueur
2 ½ ounces simple syrup
3 tablespoons carob syrup
¼ cup evaporated milk (unsweetened)
2 handfuls ice cubes
1 large egg
Ground cinnamon

Preparation

1. In a blender or a cocktail shaker, combine the Pisco, coffee liqueur, simple syrup, carob syrup, milk, ice cubes and the egg.
2. Blend for 30 seconds or shake for 2 minutes.
3. Strain into a chilled, stemmed glass with a round bowl (a brandy snifter or similar) and garnish with a dusting of cinnamon.

Note: If your blender doesn't have the power to crush ice, do it manually by placing ice cubes in a heavy-duty plastic bag. Seal the bag and cover with a kitchen towel, and carefully crush the ice using a hammer or other heavy solid object.

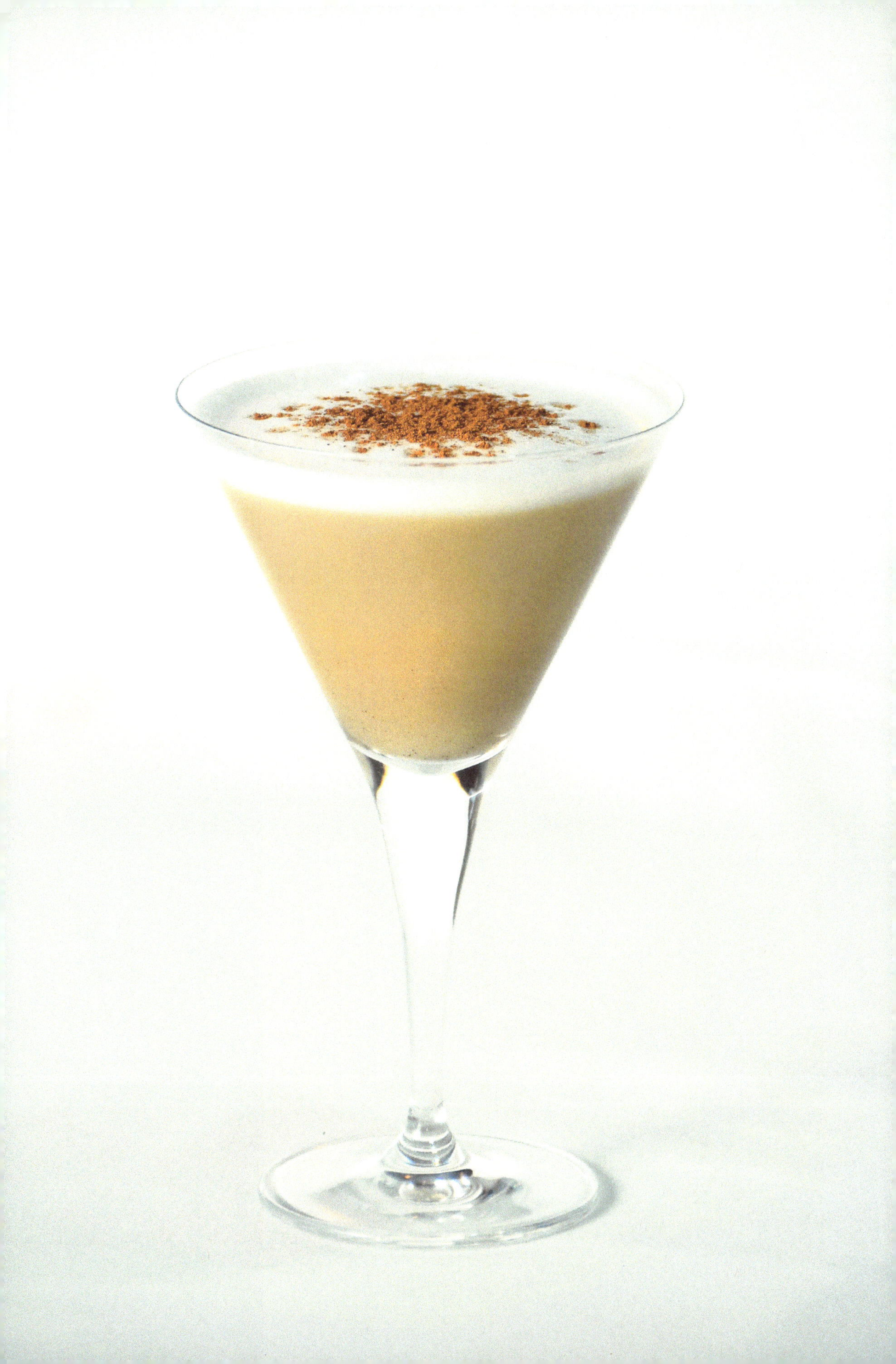

COCONUT SOUR

Pisco Sour de Coco

When my husband came to visit me in Peru while we were dating, I took him to get a cocktail at a well-known bar in Miraflores. We both ordered Coconut Sour, it was my first time trying it, and I got hooked for life. My mission, two years later, when I came to live in California was to make this cocktail, until I got the perfect version for us.

There's a unique marriage between limes and coconut, and if there's Pisco involved to bless the union, even better!

I absolutely love this tropical natural flavored cocktail, it's perfect for the summer, refreshing, tangy, and just with the perfect amount of sweetness. You can make a batch and let the pool party begin!

Ingredients

3 ounces coconut infused Pisco
1 ½ ounces lime juice
1 egg white
1 ½ ounce simple syrup
2 ounces coconut cream
Ice cubes
Angostura bitters

Preparation

1. Add all the ingredients but Angostura bitters to a cocktail shaker.
2. Fill with ice cubes and shake for 10 seconds.
3. Double strain into a chilled coupe or martini glass.
4. Drip a few drops of Angostura on top.

Note: Garnish with coconut flakes and a pineapple slice.

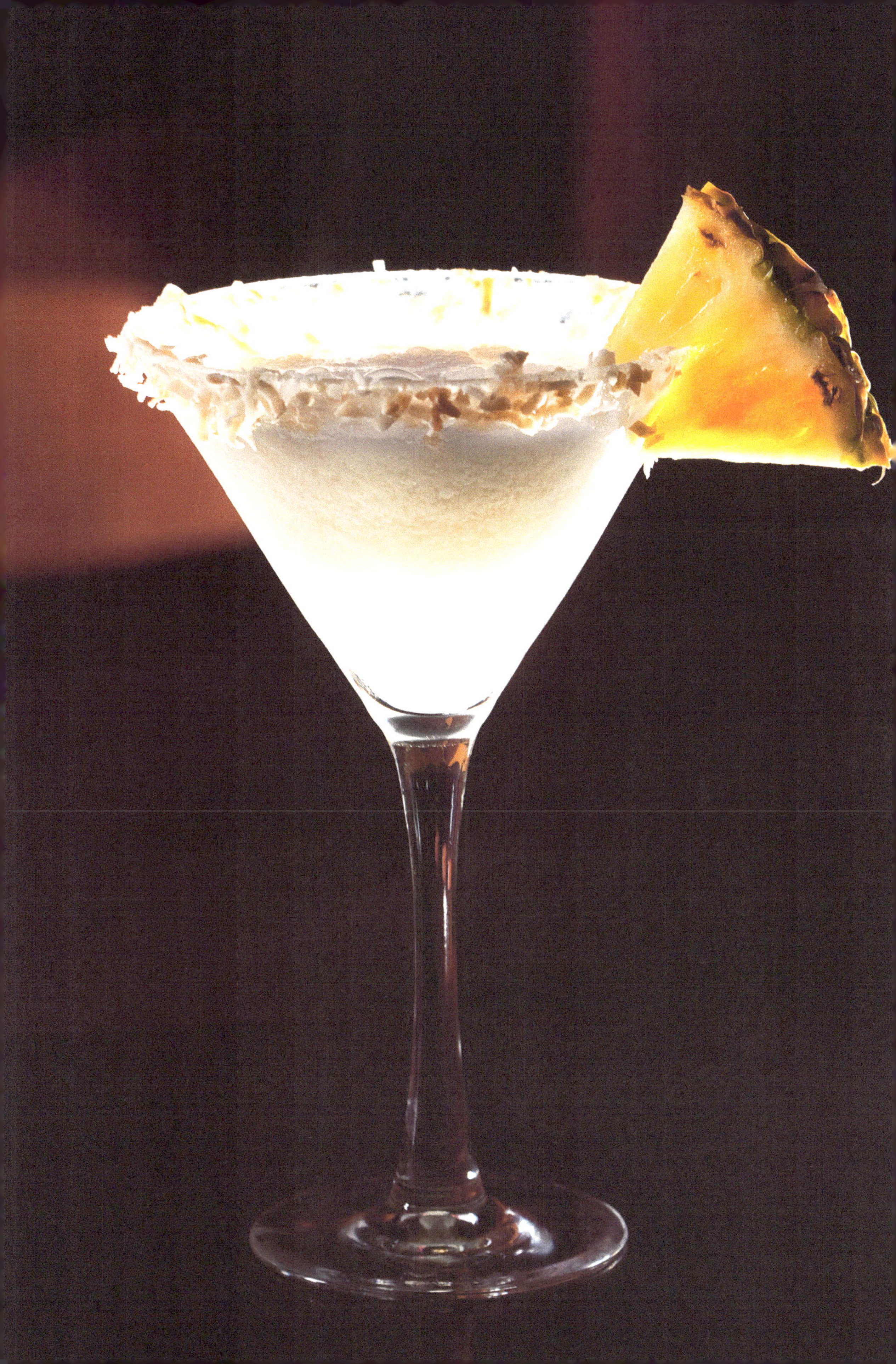

COFFEE PISCOTINI

Piscotini de Café

Are you a coffee lover? Good news! Then it's time to give it a Peruvian twist with Pisco, Oh, Yes! And let me tell you something, I love my coffee in the morning, it is a must to start my day, however, some evenings call for a spiked coffee indulgence… And Pisco does the trick.
This cocktail will refresh and wake you up, for sure! *Salud*!

Ingredients

1 shot of espresso coffee
2 ounces Pisco (Quebranta or Acholado varieties)
1 ounce coffee liqueur
¾ ounce Crème de cacao
1 cup ice cubes

Preparation

1. In a shaker filled with ice, add the espresso, Pisco, coffee liqueur, and Crème de cacao. Shake for about 10–20 seconds, until well-chilled.
2. Strain into a chilled martini glass.
3. Enjoy and relax!

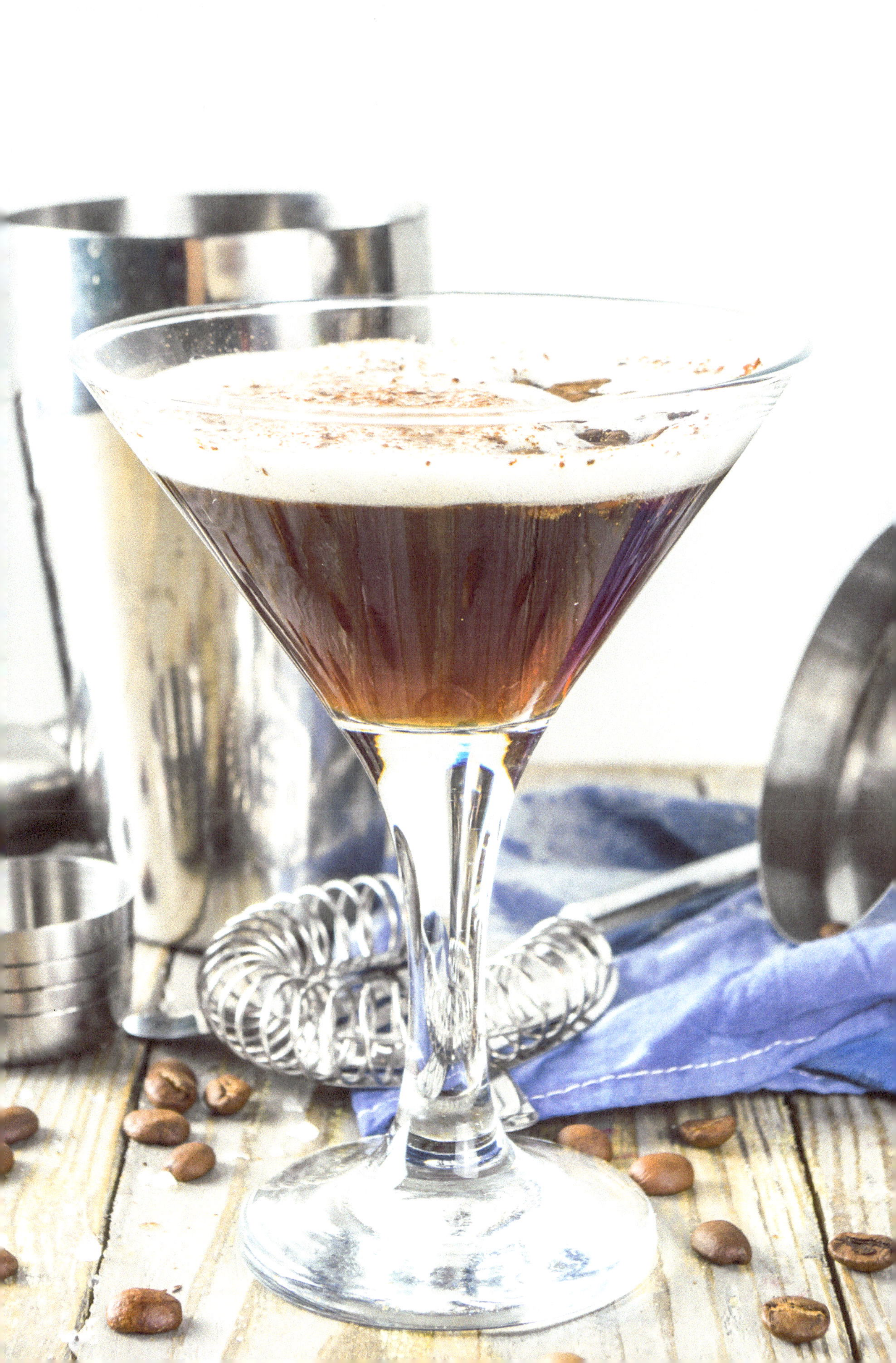

CHILCANO DE PISCO

Chilcano de Pisco

Chilcano de Pisco is a classic Peruvian cocktail that combines four elements to perfection: the zesty snap of fresh lime, the kick of a good Pisco, the fizz of ginger ale, and the austere elegance of Angostura bitters. Add ice, and this is one very refreshing cocktail to keep in your repertoire, especially for hot days. But don't let it trick you. It will reveal its power if you have too many, too quickly!

Ingredients

1 cup ice cubes
3 ounces Pisco
4 ounces ginger ale
½ ounce key lime juice
2 ounces ginger beer or ginger ale
3 drops Angostura bitters

Preparation

1. Fill a highball glass with ice cubes.
2. Pour the Pisco over the ice.
3. Add the key lime juice and the bitters.
4. Fill the glass with ginger ale or ginger beer, stir and garnish with a slice of lime.

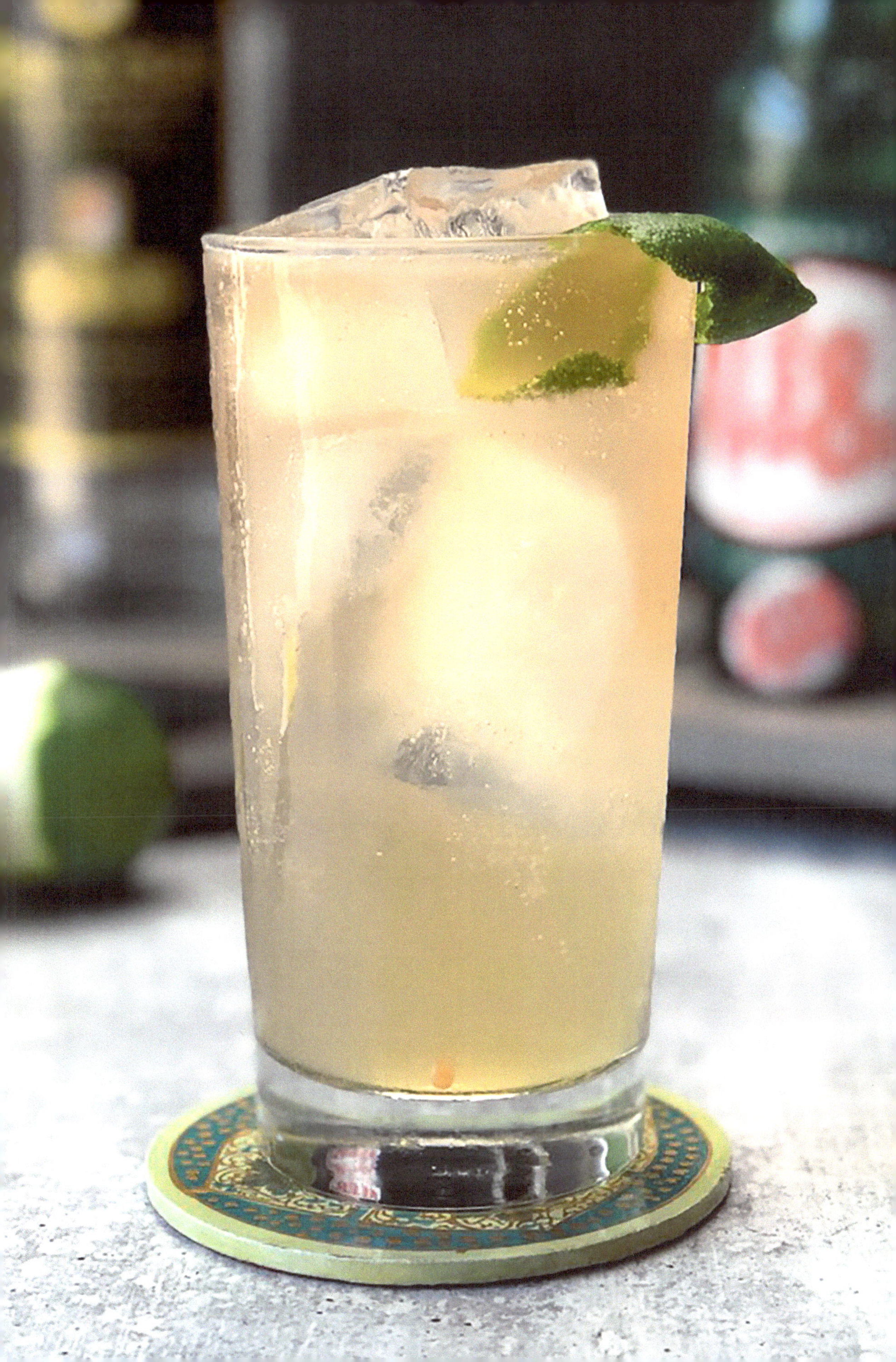

CHOLOPOLITAN

Cholopólitan

A Cholopolitan is the Peruvian version of the classic Cosmopolitan, with vodka replaced by Pisco. It's easily the newest of the Pisco cocktails. The typical pink hue in itself is an invitation to a pleasant experience. Try it! I'm certain you'll love it. *Salud*!

Ingredients

2 ½ ounces Pisco (Acholado variety)
3 ounces cranberry juice
¼ ounce freshly squeezed lime juice
¼ ounce Cointreau
¼ ounce passion fruit juice
½ cup ice cubes
Cape gooseberry, maraschino, or lemon twist or slice, to garnish

Preparation

1. Place all ingredients into a shaker with ice.
2. Stir for 30 seconds and strain into a large, chilled martini glass.
3. Garnish and enjoy!

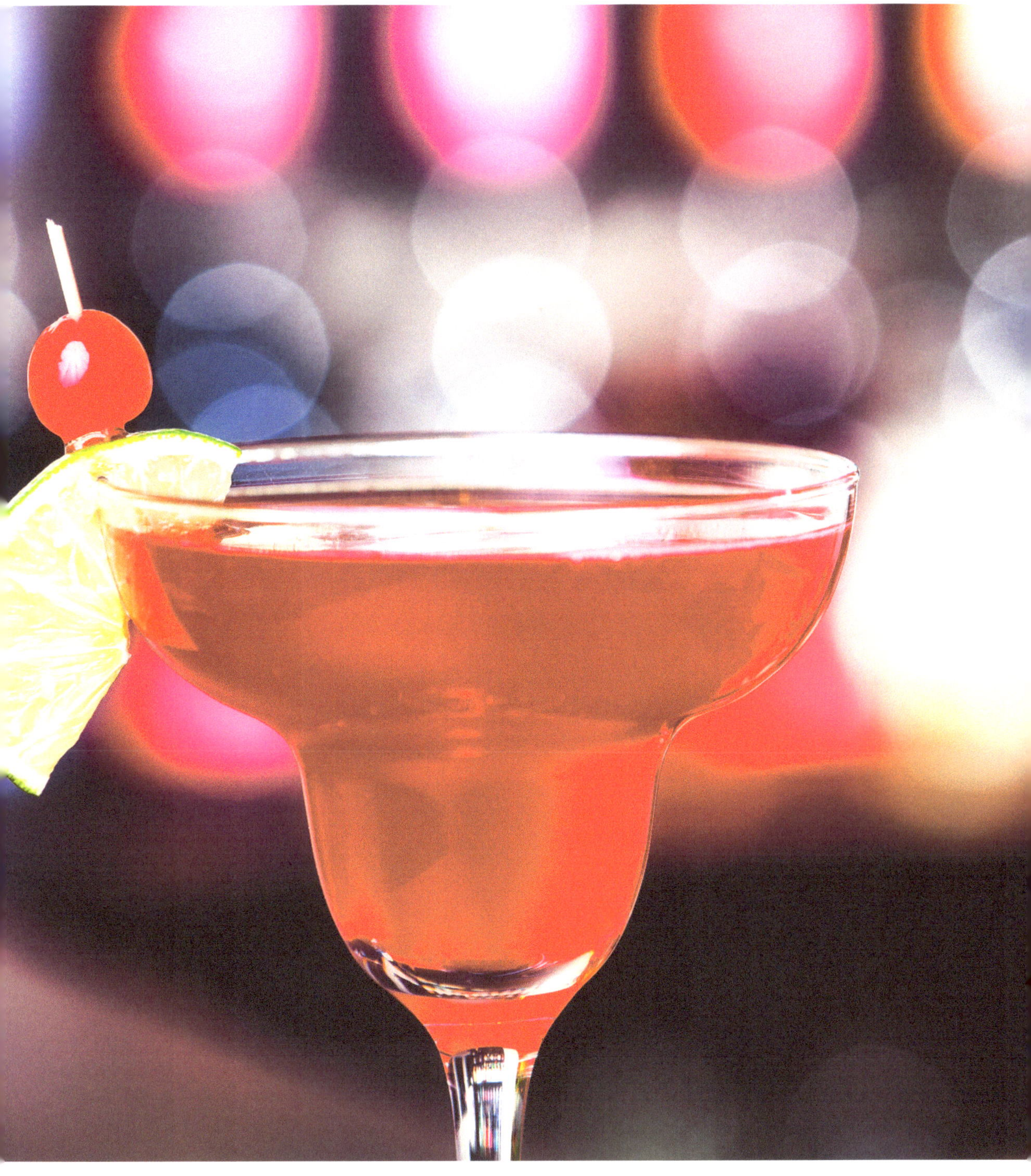

CINNAMON SOUR

Pisco Sour de Canela

WINE | 20' | 1 SERVING

I am a cinnamon lover, and if you are on my team; this is the perfect warming, yet refreshing cocktail, delicious and inviting. The citrus notes, combined with the aromatic cinnamon infused Pisco, with that gorgeous color, frothy foam on top, and a touch of simple syrup, is simply divine!

Once you get your Pisco, add some cinnamon sticks, let it rest for a few days, and the first step toward enjoying this out of this world cocktail will be closer to you.

Ingredients

3 ounces cinnamon infused Pisco (15–20 days)
1 ounces lime juice
1 ounces simple syrup
1 heaping teaspoon powder sugar
1 egg white
8 cubes of ice

Preparation

1. In a cocktail shaker place the ice, followed by Pisco, lime juice, simple syrup, and egg white. Cover and shave vigorously for about 30 seconds.
2. Single strain into a chill cocktail glass. Garnish with a cinnamon stick.

Note: To make cinnamon infused Pisco, in its own bottle, place 5 or 6 cinnamon sticks (3 to 4 inches each). Let it rest between 15–20 days. The longer you let it sit the hotter it will get!

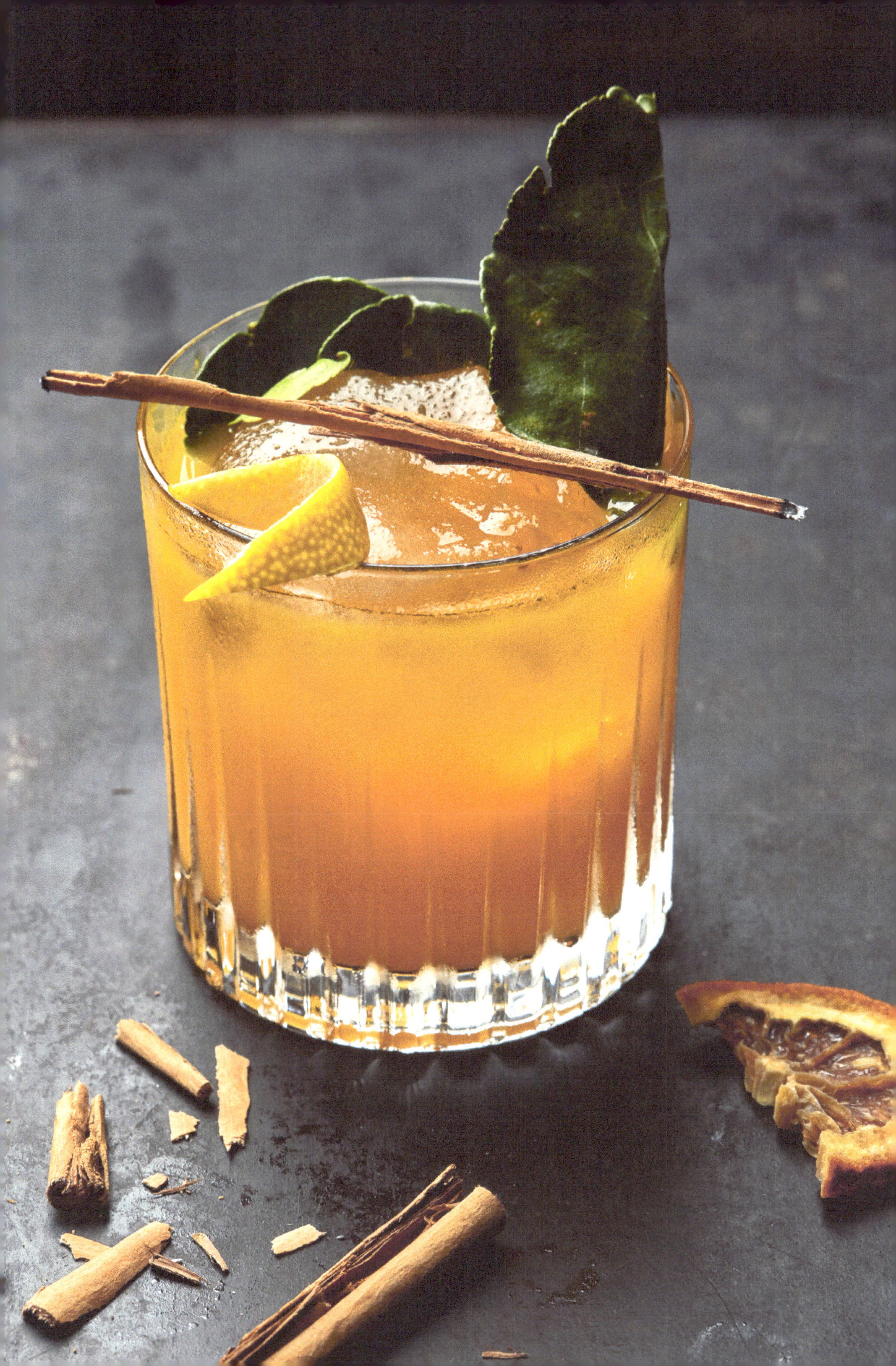

HOT CHOCOLATE
Chocolate Caliente

Hot Chocolate is a cold-weather and Christmas tradition almost worldwide. In Peru there are gatherings called Chocolatadas, where this delicious drink is served paired with slices of Panettone. Doesn't that make you wish for a blizzard right now? This chocolate is super easy to prepare, and warms and soothes both, the palate and the soul. At my grandparents' home in Peru, the tradition was to have dinner on Christmas Eve and, at midnight, celebrate the birth of baby Jesus. Then we opened the presents! The waiting between dinner and midnight gave us time to "leave room" for a delicious Hot Chocolate to toast Christmas day.

Ingredients

3 cups water
2 sticks cinnamon
4 cloves
¼ teaspoon nutmeg, grated
Orange peel
4 ounces semisweet chocolate, chopped
1 can (12 ounces) evaporated milk (unsweetened)
½ cup heavy cream
Sugar to taste
1 teaspoon vanilla
⅛ teaspoon salt

Preparation

1. In a heavy bottomed pot, place the water with the cinnamon, cloves, nutmeg, and orange peel. Bring to a boil for 20 minutes. Lower the temperature and add the chopped chocolate, stirring until melted.
2. Add the evaporated milk, the heavy cream, sugar, vanilla and salt.
3. Serve immediately while hot, or make it a day in advance for a deeper flavor.

Note: Enjoy with your favorite cookies or a good slice of Panettone!

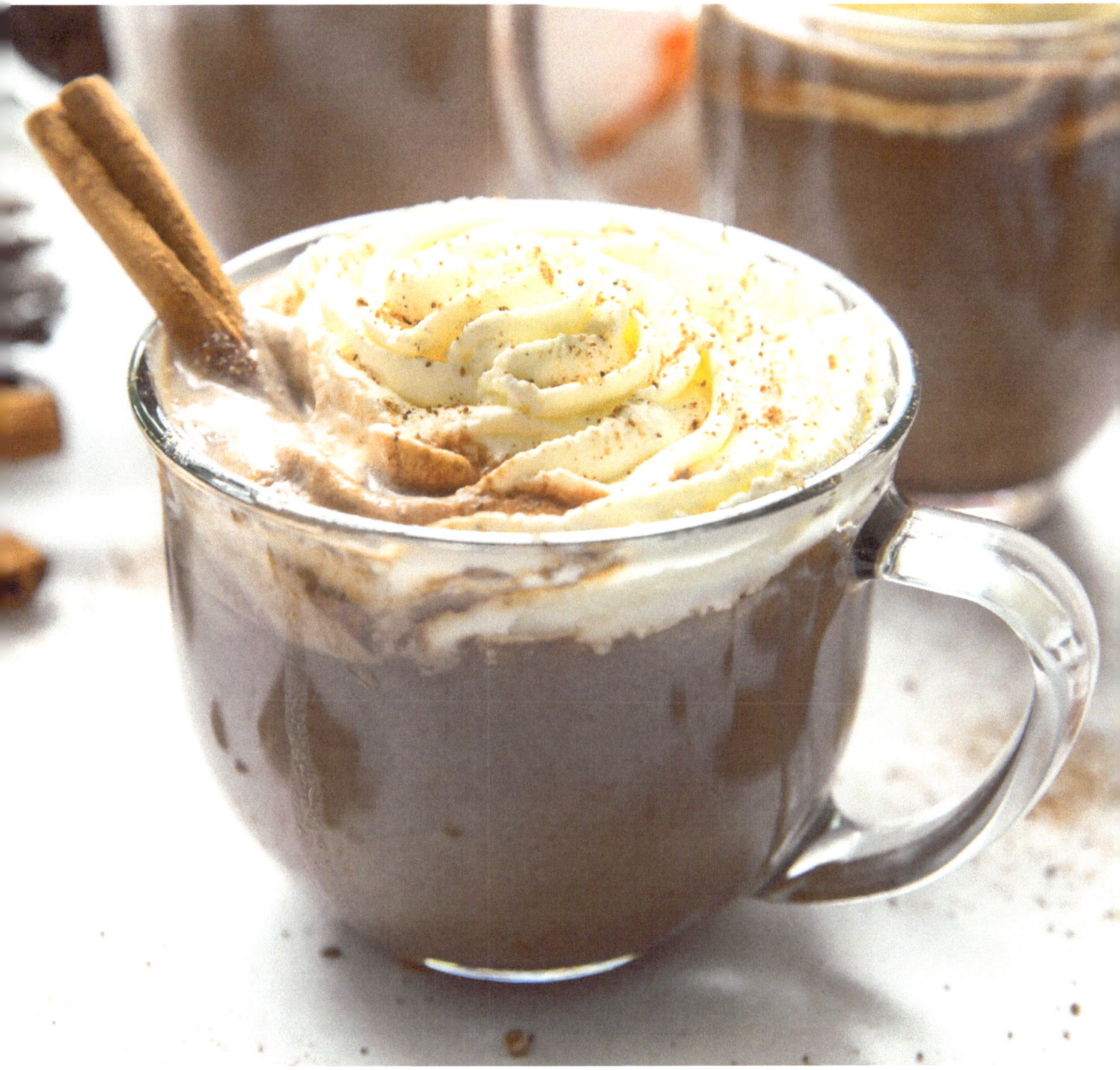

ORANGE PISCOTINI

Piscotini de Naranja

If you like the flavor and fragrance of oranges, this chic cocktail is for you. Served in a martini glass, you'll sip the flavors of Pisco and Grand Marnier, chilled to perfection over ice. Slip into this alluring, Pisco-orange embrace and you'll feel wrapped in a warm, silky hug.

Ingredients

2 ounces Pisco
1 ounce Grand Marnier
5 ice cubes
1 strip of orange peel or slice
1 maraschino cherry

Preparation

1. In a cocktail mixer add ice, the Pisco and Grand Marnier; stir with a spoon, do not shake.
2. Place the maraschino cherry in the bottom of a chilled martini glass; strain the cocktail over the cherry, and garnish the rim of the glass with a curl of orange peel or slice.

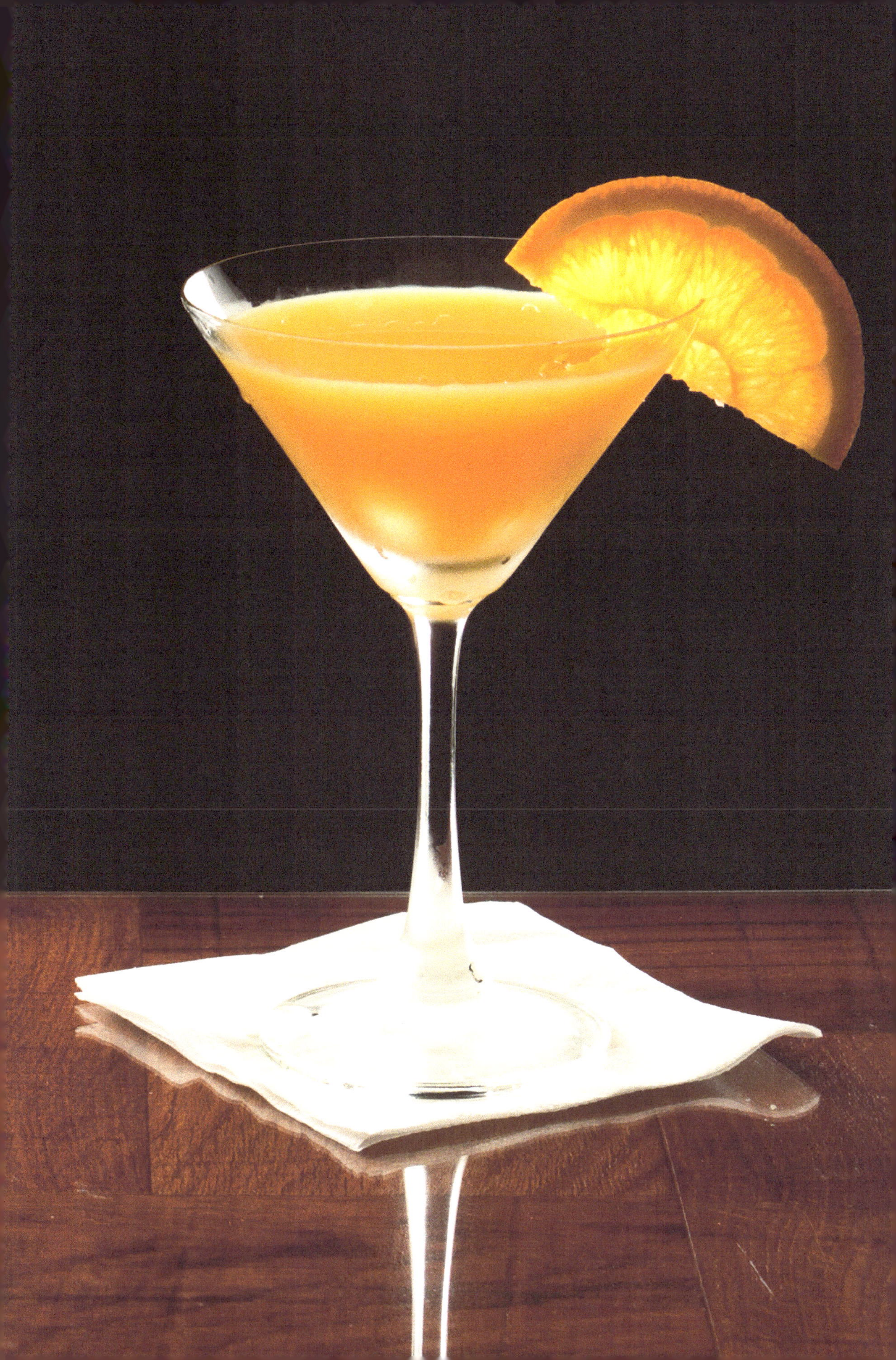

PASSION FRUIT SOUR

Maracuyá Sour

Have you heard of passion fruit? We know it as Maracuyá. It is an exotic tropical fruit with a very fragrant and alluring aroma.

Once, while visiting Peru, I was staying at some relatives' home, and I made a fruit ornament as a centerpiece for the table. Oh my—that passion fruit perfumed the entire apartment!

This fruit is used in many different ways, and one is in a drink known as Passion Fruit Sour, which is a version of the famous Pisco Sour. Only in this recipe, the passion fruit accompanies the traditional Pisco. Once you try it, I'm sure it will become a regular in your cocktail rotation. *Salud*!

Ingredients

4 ounces Pisco
2 ounces simple syrup
2 ounces passion fruit pulp
2 tablespoon lime juice
1 egg white
½ cup ice

Preparation

1. In a shaker or blender, place the ingredients in the following order: Pisco, simple syrup, passion fruit pulp, lime juice, ice and, finally, the egg white.
2. If using a shaker, shake the mixture for 10 seconds with a lot of passion! If using a blender, process for 30 seconds.
3. Strain into chilled, stemless martini glasses, and drink with delight!

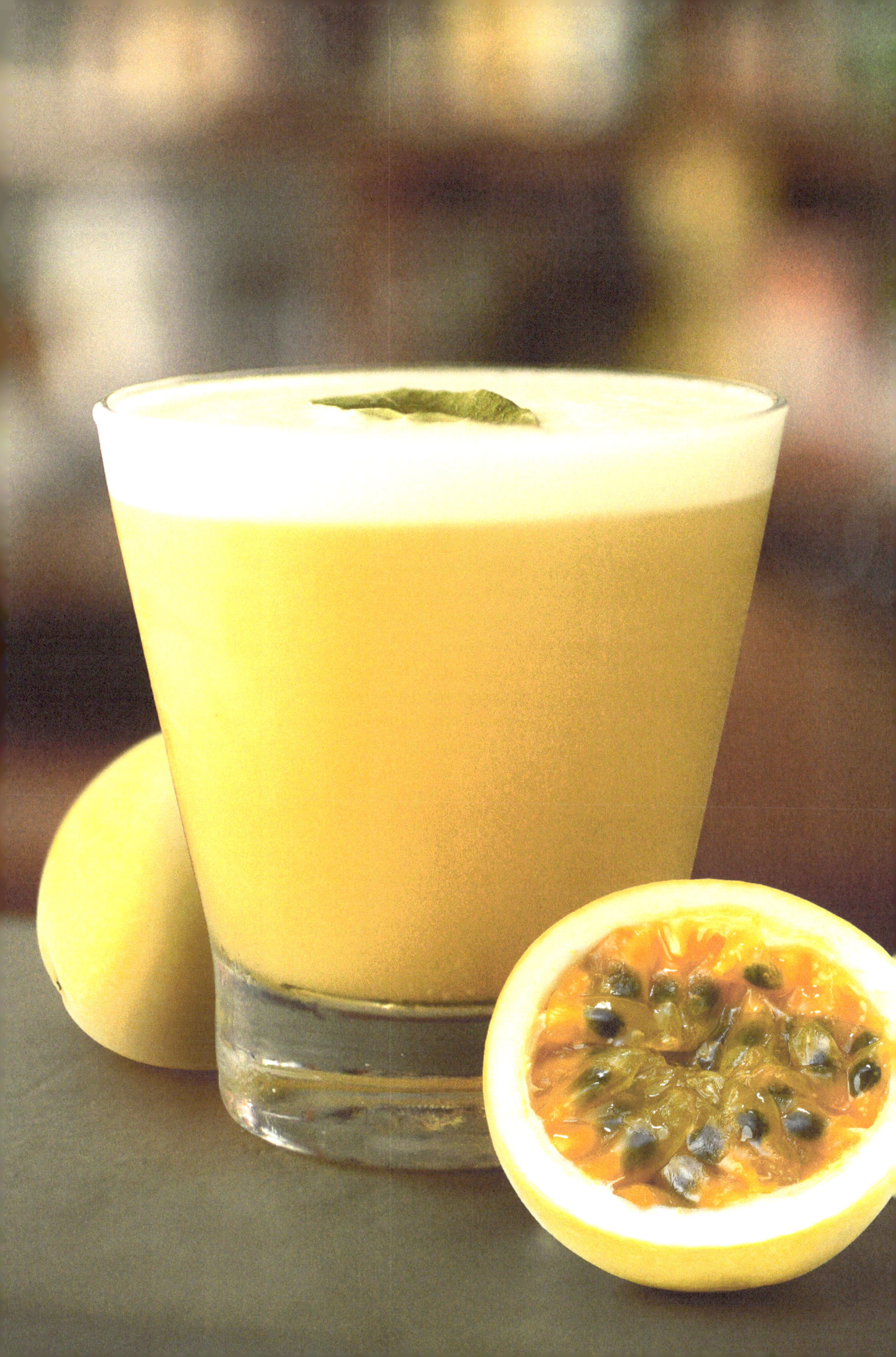

PISCNOG

Ponche de Huevo con Pisco

Eggnog is a traditional creamy holiday-season drink in the United States and Canada, and is served at most Christmas celebrations. I love it with a non-typical ingredient, but a treasure in Peru: Pisco! Try it and start a new holiday tradition of your own!

Ingredients

6 large eggs, separated
½ cup sugar
2 cups milk
1 cup heavy cream
¼ teaspoon ground ginger
½ teaspoon ground cinnamon
½ teaspoon ground, or freshly grated, nutmeg
⅛ teaspoon salt
2 ounces Pisco
Cinnamon sticks and freshly grated, to garnish

Preparation

1. Separate egg yolks in a large bowl, and set egg whites aside in other bowl until use.
2. Beat the egg yolks with the sugar until smooth. Add the milk, cream, ginger, cinnamon, nutmeg spices, and salt; beat together until well combined.
3. Beat the egg whites set aside, until they form stiff peaks.
4. Gently fold the whites into the egg yolks bowl, until the egg punch is light and frothy.

Serving suggestion: Pour the Pisco over ice, top with egg punch. Garnish with a dusting of fresh nutmeg and a festive cinnamon stir stick.

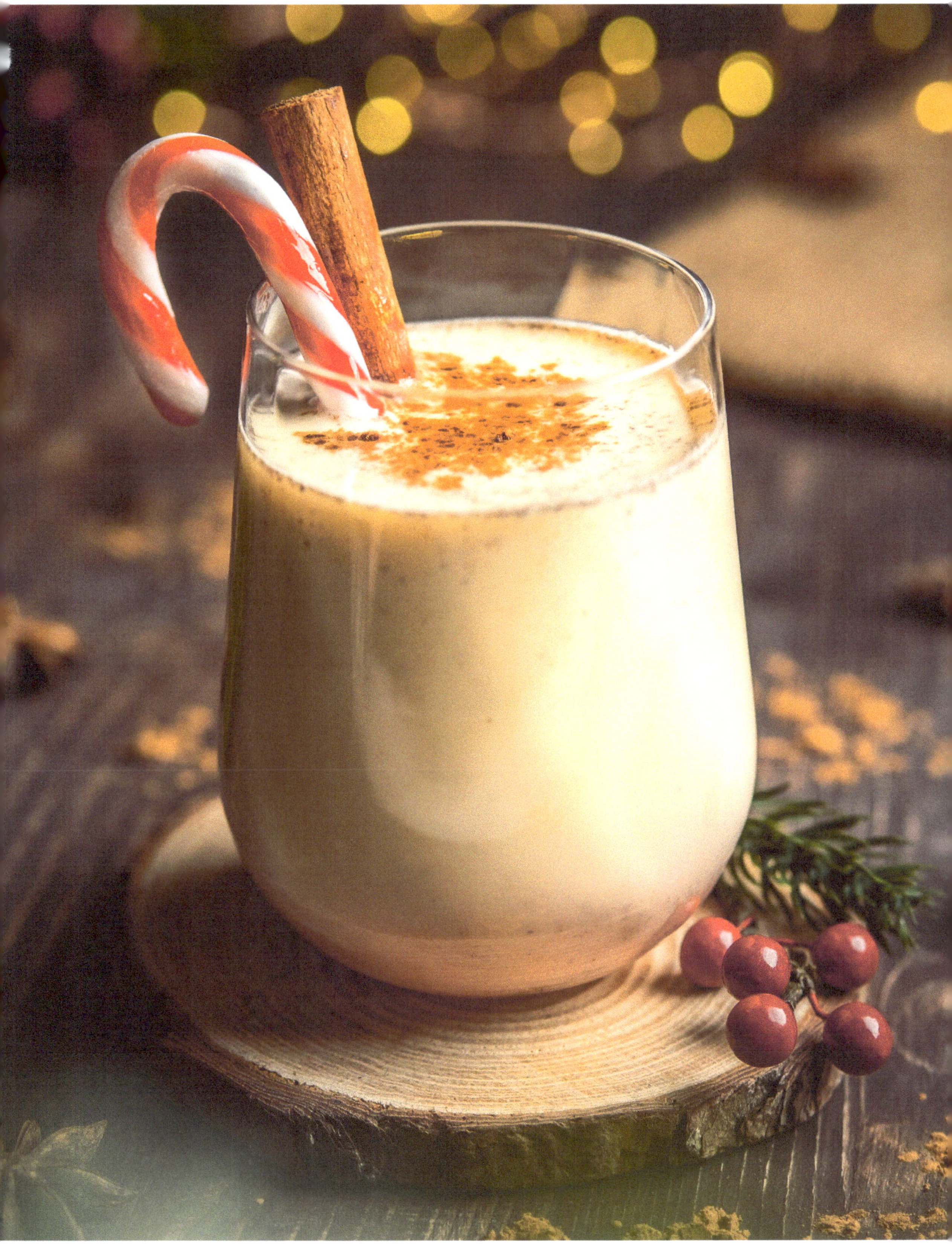

PISCO PUNCH

Pisco Punch

BASE LIQUOR

2h

6 SERVINGS

Did you know that San Francisco and Lima have a connection that dates back to the 19th century?

In the late 1800, at a fashionable San Francisco drinking establishment called the Bank Exchange, a deceptively smooth and fruity drink was concocted whose formula and ingredients were jealously guarded. The drink's popularity was only enhanced by the proprietor's limit of two drinks per customer, in light of its incapacitating properties.

The liquor used was none other than Pisco, which had been imported by merchants who brought it to San Francisco, during the California Gold Rush. Those in the know were aware that if you were looking to have a "high night" you had to order a Pisco Punch with the "secret ingredient." And what was it? Well, it is said to have been crushed coca leaf! The coca leaf is a natural stimulant that grows in the Andes, and is used for medicinal purposes as well. Ultimately, Prohibition brought an end to the Bank Exchange and its kicky cocktail, though it's now making a less lethal comeback.

Would you have dared to try a Pisco Punch? Here is the recipe for you to try, "secret ingredient" optional!

Ingredients

12 ounces Pisco (1 ½ cups)
4 ounces fresh lemon juice (about 3 lemons)
4 ounces water
4 ¼ ounces pineapple gum syrup, or simple syrup
1 ¼ cups fresh pineapple chunks
Large ice cubes
Thinly sliced pineapple, to garnish

Preparation

1. In a punch bowl or pitcher, combine the Pisco, lemon juice, water, gum syrup and pineapple chunks; refrigerate until well chilled, about 2 hours.
2. Add ice to the punch bowl or pitcher. Ladle or pour the punch into chilled coupes or wine glasses and garnish with pineapple slices.

Note: The pineapple gum syrup, a thickened pineapple simple syrup, and coca leaves can be found online.

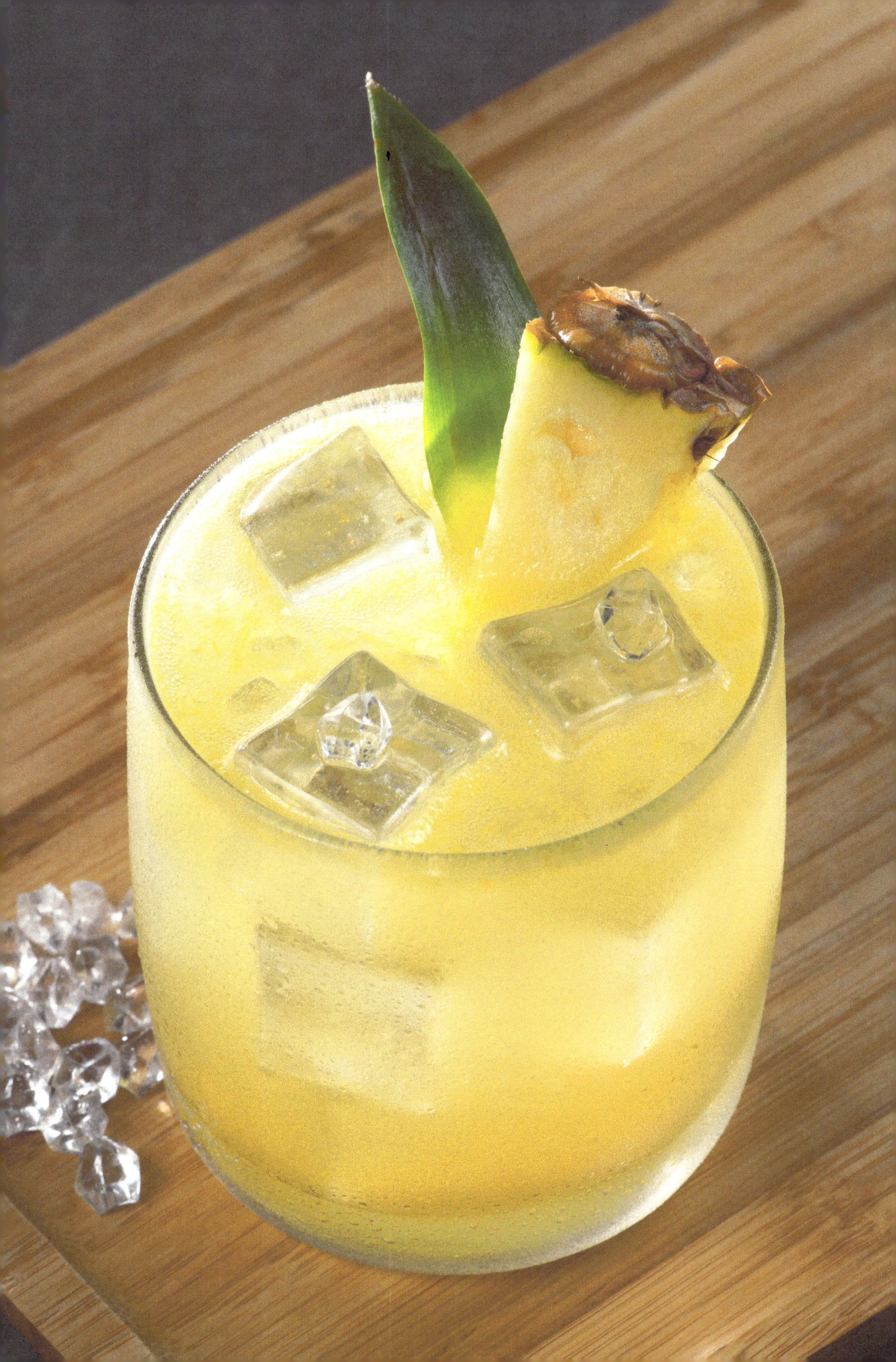

PISCO SOUR

Pisco Sour

How to describe the emblematic national Peruvian cocktail with accuracy? Well, let's begin by saying that Pisco brandy is to Pisco city in Ica, Peru, as Champagne is to France's Champagne region, and Tequila to the town of Tequila in Guadalajara, Mexico. It is an elegant, distilled pure brandy derived from grapes. But the ingredients that also make this cocktail special are its combination of freshly squeezed lime juice, simple syrup, and egg whites. It could almost be considered a protein shake, if you think about it... Anyway, this cocktail is easy-drinking and very likable, though it's deceptively powerful, with the hidden clout to impair judgement. So be sure to enjoy this refreshing drink on a full stomach, and you'll have a pleasurable experience!

Ingredients

6 ounces Pisco
2 ounces simple syrup
4 ounces key lime juice
12 ice cubes
1 egg white
4 drops of Angostura bitters

Preparation

1. In a shaker or blender, add all ingredients in the following order: Pisco, simple syrup, lime juice, ice, and, finally, egg white.
2. If using a shaker, shake the mixture for 30 seconds, *con fuerza*! If using a blender, process for 30 seconds.
3. Pour the cocktails into chilled, stemless martini glasses, and float 2 or 3 drops of Angostura in each glass. *Ay, qué rico*!

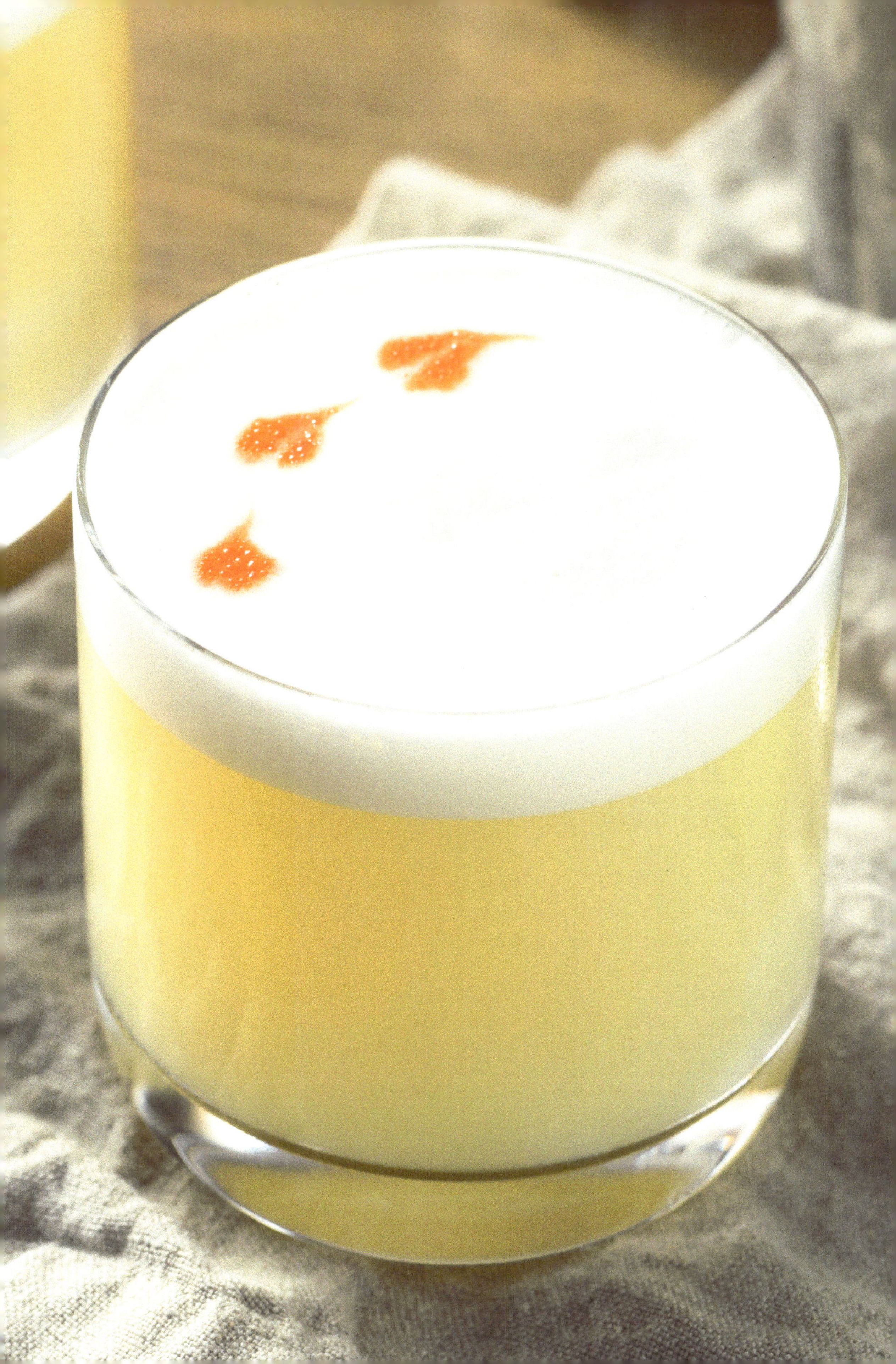

PURPLE CORN DRINK
Chicha Morada

NON ALCOHOL

3h

2 GALLONS

When I was little, not a single birthday that we'd attend lacked Chicha Morada. An indelible memory is being at my Mamama's house, when it smelled like Purple Corn Drink, because a party was coming! Oh, I just can't have enough of it...

Super refreshing, this drink has fruity, tangy and spicy notes from the addition of ingredients like pineapple, apple, lime, cinnamon, and cloves. Served cold, it makes a delicious non alcoholic punch. Or, spike it with Pisco for a boozy version!

Ingredients

2 gallons of water
2 (15 ounces) bags dried purple corn
Rind and core from one large ripe pineapple
2 tart Granny Smith apples, quartered
4 Cinnamon sticks, broken 6 cloves
Peel of 1 orange
Freshly squeezed lime juice
Sweetener of your choice: white sugar, palm sugar, raw sugar, simple syrup, agave nectar, honey, etc.
Slice of lime, or chopped apple and pineapple, to garnish (optional)

Preparation

1. Combine the purple corn, pineapple scraps, apples, cinnamon, cloves, orange peel and water in a large stockpot. Bring to a boil, cover the pot, and reduce to a simmer for 45 minutes. Uncover the pot and continue simmering for 30 more minutes until the liquid becomes concentrated and the corn kernels have cracked open.
2. Strain the concentrated liquid into a large open container and allow to cool at room temperature.
3. When cooled, store the punch in large covered containers, and keep refrigerated.
4. Just before serving, decant some of the punch into a carafe or pitcher. If desired, dilute the concentrate to taste with cold water. Stir in lime juice and sweetener and serve over ice.
5. Garnish with a slice of lime or chopped apple and pineapple, if desired.

Note: To avoid speeding up the fermentation process, do not add sweetener to the concentrate. Add sweetener only to the portion to be served immediately. The unsweetened concentrate will keep refrigerated for 2–3 days, maximum.

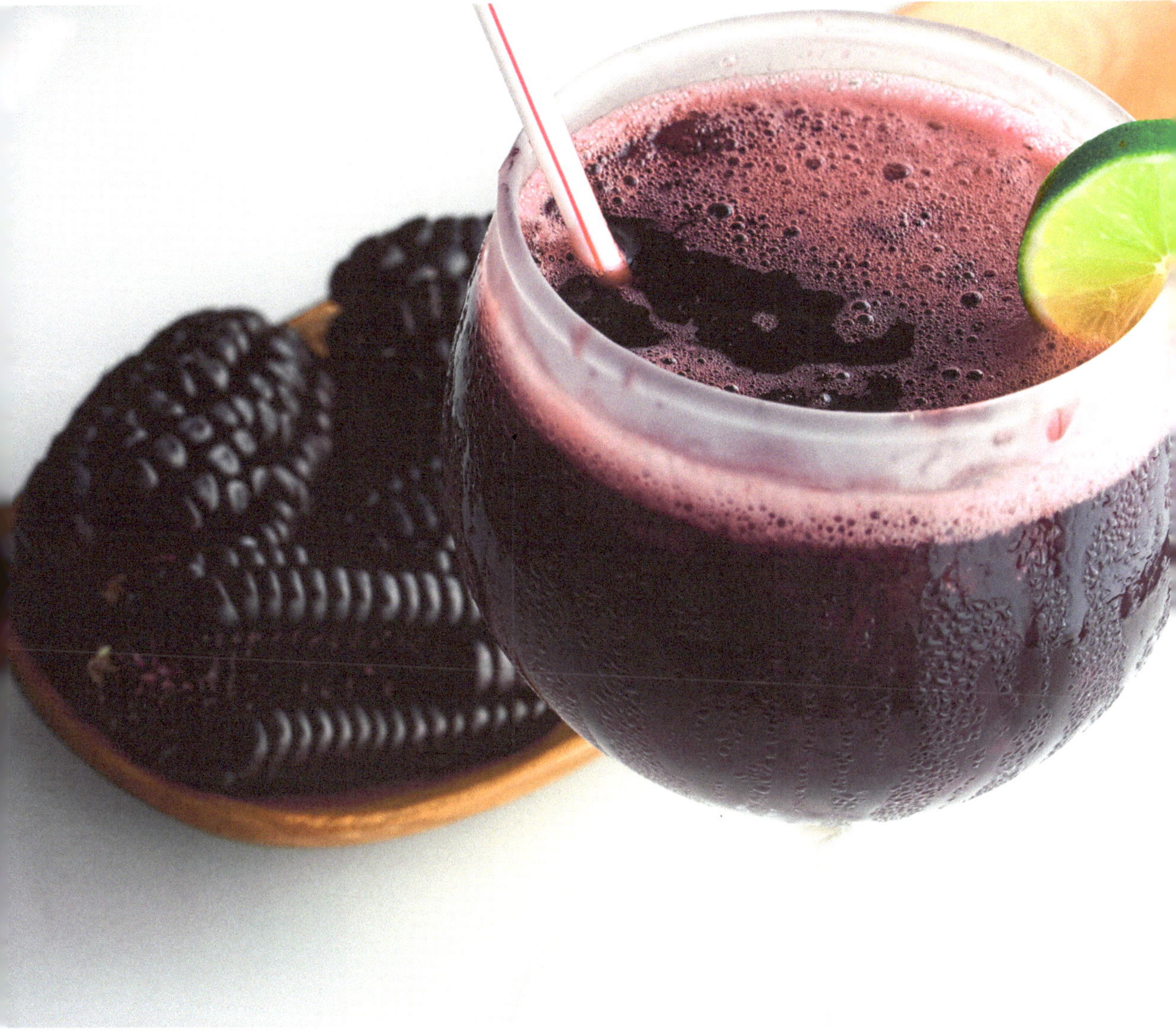

ROSÉ SANGRIA

Sangría de Vino Rosé

On a hot day one summer, my beloved cousin Claudia came to visit us in California from her home in Peru. When I was living in Peru, we used to get together at least once a month for our coffees after work, or at events, or in our homes, or her parents' home. We have a very special, deep bond and I love her. I know she likes Sangría, and I wanted to make a special one for her. So, I gathered some oranges, strawberries, and a good, well-chilled rosé wine, and I started combining all my ingredients in a large pitcher. My cousin was patiently observing what I was doing. She said, "That looks good, *primi*." Which comes from the word *prima* meaning cousin. After some mixing and tasting the sangria was done. And it was not only a lovely libation, but a moment that I'll cherish. *Salud primi*!

WINE
90'
1 PITCHER

Ingredients

1 orange
2 cups strawberries
2 tablespoons sugar
1 bottle dry rosé wine, chilled
⅓ cup Grand Marnier
3 ounces triple sec
½ lemon, sliced into rounds
ice cubes
Sparkling water, or Prosecco wine, for serving
Additional strawberry or orange slices, to garnish (optional)

Preparation

1. Cut the orange into chunks. Do not peel. Quarter the strawberries, and add the fruit to the pitcher, followed by the sugar. Stir to combine, and let the fruit and sugar macerate for half an hour at room temperature.
2. After 30 minutes, pour in the rosé wine, the Grand Marnier and the triple sec.
3. Add the lemon slices to the Sangria; stir and refrigerate until well chilled, but no longer than 4 hours, to avoid the fruit breaking down.
4. Place ice cubes in serving glasses and fill with the Sangria. Top with a splash of sparkling water, or Prosecco.

Serving suggestion: Garnish with additional strawberry or orange slices, if desired.

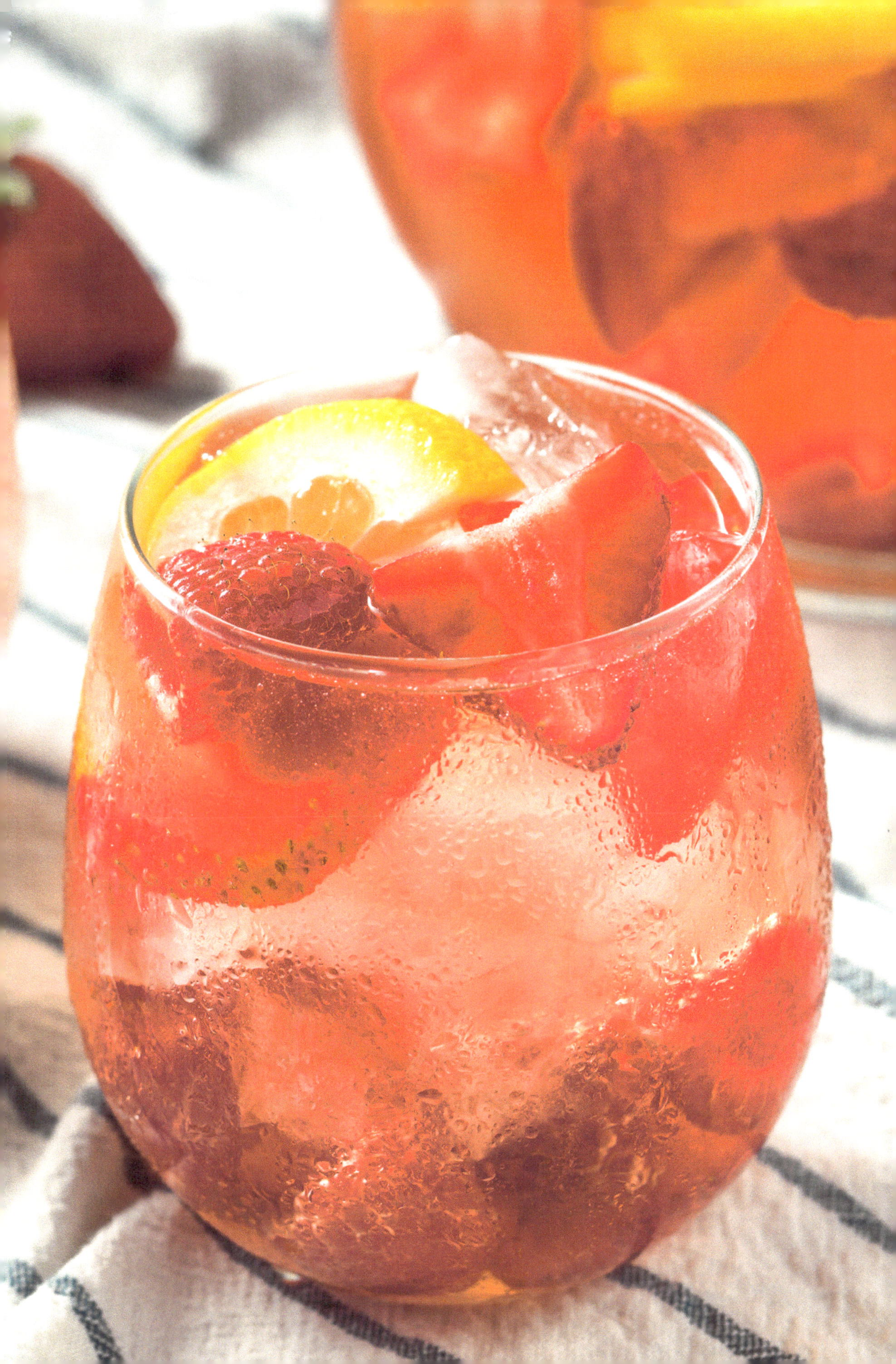

THE CAPTAIN

El Capitán

As its name suggest, this is a powerful and robust cocktail. Its compelling personality is ideal for a night of leisure. Delight your guests, your family or yourself, with this intense, aromatic cocktail made with Peru's famous Pisco. It will—definitely—help you relax. And overall let the "Captain" take command of your party!

Ingredients

2 ounces Pisco
1 ounce sweet Vermouth
1 ounce dry Vermouth
2 dashes Angostura bitters
Orange peel twist, to garnish

Preparation

1. In a mixing glass with ice, stir all the ingredients together for about 20 seconds.
2. Strain into a chilled coupe or martini glass.
3. Garnish with a twist of orange peel and/or a maraschino cherry. *Salud*!

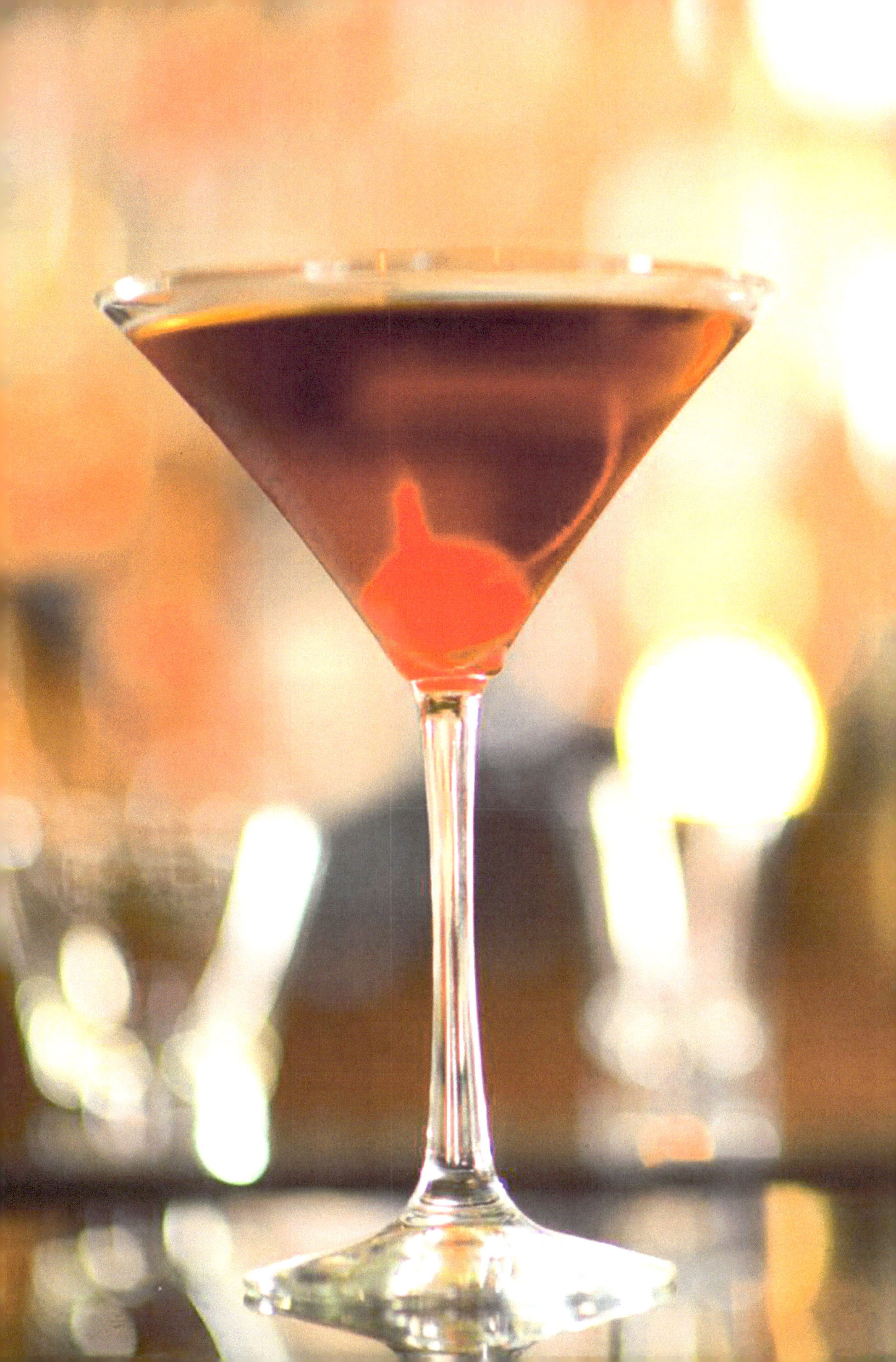

GLOSSARY

SPECIAL INGREDIENTS

Ají Amarillo: A mild yellow Peruvian hot pepper, also known as Ají Verde or Ají Escabeche. Can be found in stores specializing in Latin American foods, sometimes available frozen or in jars.

Ají Amarillo Paste: Mild yellow Peruvian hot pepper paste. Can be found in jars at some Latin Markets and online. (Or, see recipe in Sides & Sauces)

Ají Limo: A pungent and spicy yellow, red, green, or purple Peruvian hot pepper. Available frozen whole, and in jars, marinated, puréed or in paste form. Also available online.

Ají Mirasol: A mild, dried yellow Peruvian hot pepper; may be substituted by New Mexico bright medium heat chili powder. In a pinch, may be also be substituted with ground cayenne, but the flavor will be less bright.

Ají Panca or Ají Colorado: A dried Peruvian red hot pepper with medium-thick flesh and a smoky, earthy berry flavor. To substitute, use poblano or any other mild but flavorful ground chili. Available whole, dried and in powder form, and as a purée in jars.

Ají Panca or Ají Colorado Paste: Red Peruvian hot pepper paste. May be found in Latin American markets, or online.

Anticuchos: Thin beef heart fillets marinated in spices and vinegar, cooked on skewers of wood over a grill with charcoal, and then served with potatoes and hot pepper paste.

Botija Olives: A delicious Peruvian native Aceitunas de Botija with a unique, robust flavor and meaty texture, Botija olives are raw, brined and naturally fermented to maintain their many health benefits. (Kalamata olives are a good substitute.) Available at some Latin markets, or online.

Chancaca, Panela, Piloncillo: A sauce made of sugar cane. To obtain it, the juice of the sugar cane is cooked at high temperatures until it becomes brown sugar. In Peru, Chancaca is the basic ingredient of various traditional preparations.

Chicha de Jora: A pale, straw-colored fermented corn-based beverage with a slightly creamy or milky appearance, and a mildly sour aftertaste similar to hard apple cider. Available at some Latin markets, or online.

Chicha Morada: This deep purple, non-alcoholic, dry corn-based beverage is an iconic Peruvian refreshment. Mildly sweet and spicy, it is served everywhere in Peru, from casual food stalls to elegant restaurants and dining rooms. Available at some Latin markets or online.

Choclo: Peruvian corn. Can be found frozen as whole cobs or in kernels, and in cans. Available at some Latin markets and online.

Guanábana/Soursop: An exotic tropical fruit with a flavor described as a sweet combination of apple, pineapple and strawberries. The outside is green and spiky, while inside it has white flesh, black seeds and a texture similar to a banana. Available in the frozen foods section at some Latin markets, or online.

Huacatay/Black Mint: Its pungent flavor profile contains notes of basil, spearmint and citrus, with notes of tarragon. It can be found bottled in paste form, or in the frozen foods section of stores specializing in Latin American products.

Inka Kola Soda: Also known as "the Golden Kola", is a soft drink that was created in Peru in 1935 by British immigrant Joseph Robinson Lindley. The soda has a sweet, fruity flavor taste and a golden-yellow color. The main ingredient is the lemon verbena plant but the formula is a top secret.

Salchicha de Huacho/Huacho Sausage: Named after the small city of Huacho, located north of the Peruvian capital of Lima, this is a mild, flavorful raw sausage, full of garlic and spices. Don't be alarmed by its characteristic, almost fluorescent color, which comes from Achiote (annatto). Available in the frozen foods section at some Latin markets, and online.

Lúcuma and Lucuma Pulp: Native to the Andean valleys of South America, Lucuma is a round fruit high in fiber and antioxidants. It has a sweet smell and a very unique flavor that's a marriage of maple or caramel, combined with pumpkin and sweet potato. In Peru, it's popular in smoothies and in ice cream. Available in the frozen foods section in some Latin markets, or online.

Manjarblanco (Arequipe, Cajeta, Dulce de leche, Fanguito): An exquisite and sweet nourishment made from milk and sugar or milk and condensed milk.

Maracuyá/Passion Fruit: This sweet-tart, egg-shaped fruit is ready to prepare once the skin has begun to crease. Available at some markets and in grocery stores specializing in Latin foods; may be found fresh or in the frozen foods section, and online.

Mazamorra Morada: A typical sweet puddin of Peruvian gastronomy made from boiled purple corn, dried fruits and cornstarch. This dessert is specially prepared in October, called the Purple Month, when the Lord of Miracles is commemorated.

Palillo Molido/Turmeric: Available in powdered form in the spice section of most grocery stores.

Papa Seca: Small chunks of freeze-dried potatoes. Available at some Latin markets and online.

Peruvian Canary Beans/Mayocoba/Frejol Peruano: Meaty, creamy, tender beans, with a buttery consistency. Available at many grocery stores, Latin markets, or online.

Pisco: A Peruvian distilled brandy made from grapes. It has an herbaceous aroma with a touch of citrus. Its flavor is full, soft and creamy on the palate, with a long, clean finish. Available at liquor stores and online.

Rocoto Hot Pepper: One of the more intense Peruvian hot peppers. Available frozen whole or in jars at some Latin markets. Also available online.

Spicy: Flavorful.

Sublime Chocolate: Peruvian milk chocolate bars packed with plenty of peanuts. Available at many Latin markets, and online. (A suitable substitute would be a Mr. Goodbar.)

Yucca, Yuca or Cassava: A starchy root with a white or light cream color and a nutty flavor. Its texture is similar to potatoes.

SPECIALIZED WORDS

A lo Macho: Sauce made of a mixture of seafood based on tomato, garlic, onion where the star is a blend of hot peppers. The most important thing is to achieve an excellent consistency of the sauce to cover the main ingredient of the dish. Only for spicy lovers.

A lo Pobre: In Peru, A lo Pobre is an ironic name applied to a hearty dish that consists of a piece of meat accompanied by fried potatoes, bananas, and eggs.

Caserita(o): A person who buys from a market producer and this phrase would be used to ask you what you're going to buy and take away with you.

Cevichería: A restaurant that offers a menu based on seafood dishes and ceviche. These nautical-themed restaurants will make you feel like you're near the water.

Chocolatada: Social event that is a Christmas tradition on Peru, at which hot chocolate is served.

Graneado: Word used to describe that the grains of rice, after being cooked, stay apart.

Montado: It is said when a fried egg is placed on top of food, usually on main courses.

Picantería: These family restaurants are located especially in the Arequipa region, where traditional dishes are served with recipes passed down for generations. The word picantería refers to a place that serves picante, a dish of various stews.

Quequito: A sweet bread made with a mixture of flour, eggs, butter, and sugar. Usually it is a very simple recipe.

Sofrito: A basic preparation in Latin American cuisine. It typically consists of aromatic ingredients cut into small pieces such as garlic, onion and peppers, tomatoes and optional carrots, sautéed or braised in vegetable oil.

SPECIALIZED EQUIPMENT

Potato Ricer: A kitchen utensil with small holes through which cooked potatoes and similar soft foods are pressed to form a coarse mash.

Blender: Mixing machine used in food preparation for liquefying, chopping, or pureeing.

Ramekins: A small dish in which food can be baked and served without a lid.

FRIENDS & FAMILY

Mamama: An informal word for grandmother. By the way, she is the most important person in my life and the one who taught me to cook with lots of love.

Tata: My way to call my grandfather. He was my role model and the special person who taught me respect, honesty and whom I have admired since I was a little girl. In Quechua it's a sweet word that children use to call their father or grandfather.

OTHER PHRASES

¡Ay, que rico!: Yummy!
Con fuerza: Powerfully.
Resaca: Hangover
Salud: Cheers.

ACKNOWLEDGMENTS

Thanks!

This book is a great example of love, friendship, and collaboration. Although there are always challenges while creating a book, when you dig in together to figure things out, it becomes better. That's why, I want to sincerely thank "My Friends" who have joined forces in my life to make this book a reality.

To Teejay Lowe for opening the doors of the Ginger Grill Kitchen at G&G Supermarket in Santa Rosa CA, so I could teach my first cooking classes, marking the beginning of my journey… What an experience!

To Nancy and Peter Lang, from Safari West, for inviting me to retreat to their peaceful and inspiring guest house, so I could write uninterrupted.

To Pamela Hartnett, for helping me with the English edition in the United States, all during the pandemic.

To Myriam Vergara, from Editorial Planeta, for having had the patience to review multiple times photos, recipes, and all the details that publishing a book implies.

To my husband Percy, and children, Vincenzo, and Giacomo, for being patient when I told them at times, I was a "hologram" so I could focus on writing, and for tasting many of my recipes and being unfiltered critics. Now you have the book to help you cook your favorites and reminisce about our time together.

To my Mamama, who wherever in this universe she's at, sees me and guides me. Thank you for lovingly and patiently teaching me the basics and tricks of cooking with LOVE.

And to all my followers, family, friends, and people who, near or far, wish me well and success. Thank you!

Milton Keynes UK
Ingram Content Group UK Ltd.
UKHW051140300424
441968UK00003B/17